A Modest Homestead

Life in Small Adobe Homes in Salt Lake City, 1850–1897

Laurie J. Bryant

THE UNIVERSITY OF UTAH PRESS
Salt Lake City

UTAH STATE HISTORICAL SOCIETY
Salt Lake City

Copublished with the Utah State Historical Society.
Affiliated with the Utah Division of State History,
Utah Department of Heritage & Arts.

 The Defiance House Man colophon is a registered trademark of
the University of Utah Press. It is based on a four-foot-tall Ancient
Puebloan pictograph (late PIII) near Glen Canyon, Utah.

21 20 19 18 17   1 2 3 4 5

Library of Congress Cataloging-in-Publication Data

Names: Bryant, Laurie J., author.
Title: A modest homestead : life in small adobe homes in Salt Lake City
    1850-1897 / Laurie J. Bryant.
Description: Salt Lake City : The University of Utah Press, 2016. | Includes
    bibliographical references and index.
Identifiers: LCCN 2016025859| ISBN 9781607815259 (pbk. : alk. paper) |
    ISBN 9781607815266
Subjects: LCSH: Adobe houses—Utah—Salt Lake City. | Salt Lake City
    (Utah)—History. | Salt Lake City (Utah)--Biography. | Salt Lake City
    (Utah)—Buildings, structures, etc.
Classification: LCC F834.S26 A23 2016 | DDC 979.2/258—dc23 LC record
available at https://lccn.loc.gov/2016025859

All contemporary photographs of adobe houses are by the author, unless
otherwise noted.

Printed and bound by Edwards Brothers Malloy, Inc., Ann Arbor, Michigan.

A Modest Homestead

For Tom

Contents

Preface

When I moved to Salt Lake City in the fall of 2000, I had a demanding job that left me very little spare time. My energies were devoted entirely to family and my work as a paleontologist for the Bureau of Land Management. But within a few years I had retired. Retirement is a jolt after a lifetime of productive work, and I found myself needing another "job."

My usual route up and down the city's East Bench was and is 1300 South Street. By nature and training, I am an observer of everything around me—rocks, trees, birds, and houses, too. I've always found old houses interesting. The date escapes me, but one day my attention was caught by a tall, red brick house on a very large lot at 1205 East 1300 South, clearly older than the 1920s cottages around it. Behind it was an old barn. At the time, the barn made no sense in a suburban neighborhood. Its lower walls are made of fieldstone, carefully mortared; the upper walls are dark, weathered boards. A door high on the west wall opens into the hay mow. The current owners have taken great care to keep the property in fine condition. It was their barn that sparked my interest in historic buildings, and by extension, the people who built them.

I researched the barn's history and found, to my surprise, that it, along with the house, are on the National Register of Historic Places. Research, after all, is my stock in trade, so while I'm not a trained historian, my skills were readily transferrable.

That first discovery led to ever-expanding inquiries—not just into old homes, but schools, sheds, commercial buildings, streetcar lines, and canals. I studied Fuller's Hill, a vanished 1870s amusement park on Salt Lake City's East Bench, and John E. Forsgren, the first LDS missionary to Sweden who was ultimately excommunicated for preaching his own religion. The *Salt Lake Tribune* nicknamed him "The Bench Prophet."

The ultimate turning point came early in 2010 when I noticed an odd, two-story house at 1075 East Harvard Avenue. Its appearance was like nothing else in my experience. Facing the street, which ran incongruously close, was a full-width porch clad in shingles—clearly added to the original building. Behind the porch, the old walls looked to be about a foot thick. By that time, I knew how to use the Utah State Historical Society's historic photographs, books, manuscripts, and other treasures. I knew whom to ask about the curiously lumpy house: Alan Barnett, who had, it turned out, identified the house as an adobe years earlier when he was doing a survey of historic buildings.

We Californians are no strangers to adobe. Every schoolchild learns about the Spanish missions, still standing along the King's Highway, El Camino Real. We visited the missions and the old ranchos with school and scout groups, sometimes even enjoying the messy fun of making adobe bricks from mud and straw, pressing the stuff into molds and tipping them out to dry. The notion that there had been thousands of adobe buildings in Salt Lake City was a revelation, and seeing that first adobe house turned my casual observations into a study.

What is special about adobe buildings? What sets them apart as a group that might make them any more interesting or informative to a historian than, say, early brick houses of the same designs? They matter because adobe buildings are artifacts, things of the past, extinct. None have been built since Salt Lake City outlawed adobe construction in 1904. The thousands of adobe homes, stores, barns, schools, theaters, meeting houses, and walls that once made up the built environment are nearly gone—neglected, collapsed, demolished, thrown away. Many were stylish to the point of elegance, with beautiful woodwork, staircases, windows, hardware, and furnishings. Of those that remain, few are more than two- or three-room cottages.

Ironically, those buildings represent exactly the sort of history that has gone unrecorded. As I gathered and compiled information about the adobe houses, I realized that the buildings were not nearly as interesting to me as their builders and later owners, who seemed to have much in common with each other. I searched for their biographies and journals in all the usual places and found almost nothing. If they had left a written record, it was sketchy at best. It became obvious that many of Salt Lake City's early residents had been excluded from its history, and including them became my "job."

Acknowledgments

Not having been formally trained as either an architect or a historian, I am indebted to a great many people who mentored, helped, and encouraged me during the process of researching and writing this book. I owe a special debt to Thomas Carter, professor emeritus in the School of Architecture and Planning, University of Utah. Tom graciously welcomed me into the ranks of his colleagues and friends, shared his concepts of early Utah homes and landscapes, and offered ideas that helped focus my work. Tom also created most of the architectural drawings, and his former student James Gosney did the ink renditions, which are not only precise but works of art in their own right.

W. Randall Dixon, retired LDS Church archivist and historian, generously shared his extensive knowledge of individual buildings, historical photos, and pioneer history. Perhaps even more valuable, he shared an insider's knowledge of the LDS Church, for which this outsider will always be grateful. I knew I could count on Randy for thoughtful answers to every question.

Alan Barnett, Research Center manager at the Utah State Archives and an architectural historian, set me on the path to this book and kept me there. Alan introduced me to the fun of exploring hot and dusty attics and dim cellars, where old houses keep their secrets.

The Research Center at the Rio Grande Depot in Salt Lake City became my second home while I researched and wrote this book. The director and staff of the Utah Division of State History—Brad Westwood, Barbara Murphy, Holly George, Jed Rogers, Lisa Buckmiller, Cory Jensen, Chris Merritt, Don Hartley, Chris Hansen, Doug Misner, Michelle Elnicky, Nelson Knight, Melissa Coy, Greg Walz, and Heidi Orchard—not only offered their cheerful and expert assistance but also treated me like one of them.

No matter how obscure the records I wanted to examine, Ken Williams, Tony Castro, and Heidi Stringham of the Utah State Archives found them and brought them out—often the original documents. They gave me access to records of every kind, welcomed me to their offices and parties, and—best of all—let me watch while the elaborate system of "robots" located and retrieved boxes of documents from storage.

Rich Richmond, Salt Lake County Recorder's office, knows more about the origin and development of the Salt Lake County land record system than anyone alive. He likes to be known as the "Vault Ogre," clearly a misnomer because he welcomed me to the inner sanctum and taught me everything I know about researching nineteenth-century property titles.

Adobe home owners and realtors have been more than generous in allowing me and my colleagues to visit, measure, and draw some important houses. Rachel Bergvall and Matthew Christensen opened their home on Third Avenue and then joined in playing some old-time music. Other gracious hosts included Scott Christensen, J. P. Snyder and Katie Bailey, Leslie Smith, Lane Hughes, Jeff Walker, Carriene Silcox, Jolene Tanner, and Anne Rasmussen. Ronald L. Fox made available many important historical photographs, some of which illustrate this book.

The staff and missionaries at the LDS Church History Library and Archives helped me find information about pioneer families, and the LDS Family History Library gave me access to its millions of records, to say nothing of commercial databases like Ancestry.com. The Pioneer Memorial Museum staff, especially Cathy Tingey, not only welcomed me, but added information I had found to their trove of pioneer histories.

Friends at The King's English Bookshop, especially Jan Sloan, Anne Holman, Sue Fleming, and Paula Longhurst, have cheered me on as only authors and booksellers can.

My colleagues and friends in the field of vertebrate paleontology not only accepted my defection from their ranks but continue to be supportive and interested. For that I am most grateful to Sally Shelton, Tom Bown, Lucy Kuizon, George Callison, Suzanne Strait, Zhe-Xi Luo, Carrie Herbel, Ted Fremd, and many others. My editor, John R. Alley, encouraged me with quiet patience through every step of the process from manuscript to book. I will always be grateful for his guidance.

Throughout the process of writing this book, I have been inspired by my sons, Reid and Duncan Macdonald. Their courage reminds me on a daily basis that anything is possible, and that one can "push the reset button" at any age.

Thank you all.

Historic Street Names in Salt Lake City

Capitol Hill Area

Current Name	*Historic Name(s)*
200 North to Hillside Avenue	Curve Street
300 North between 200 West and State Street	Currant Street, Second North
400 North	Plum Street, Third North
500 North	Peach Street, Fourth North
600 North	Cane Street, Fifth North
Almond Street (part)	Crooked Street
Almond Street south of 300 North	Grape Street
Apricot Avenue at Quince Street	Cross Street
Clinton Avenue	Bird, Short, or Fir Street
Girard Avenue	Pear Street
Hillside Avenue	Grove Street
North Main Street	Beet or Oak Street
North West Temple Street	Apple, Melon, and Carrot Streets. The three together were called Crooked Street
Quince Street at Apricot Avenue	Locust Street
Quince Street north of Apricot Avenue	Citron Street
Wall Street	Back Street. North end was Narrow Street (1874)
West Capitol Street	Last Street (1874)

CEMETERY

11 AVE. · 10 AVE. · 9 AVE. · 8 AVE. · 7 AVE. · 6 AVE. · 5 AVE. · 4 AVE. · 3 AVE. · 2 AVE. · 1 AVE.

S. TEMPLE · 100 SOUTH · 200 SOUTH · 300 SOUTH · 400 SOUTH · 500 SOUTH · 600 SOUTH · 700 SOUTH · 800 SOUTH · 900 SOUTH

V ST. · U ST. · T ST. · S ST. · R ST. · Q ST. · P ST. · O ST. · N ST. · M ST. · L ST. · K ST. · J ST. · I ST. · H ST. · G ST. · F ST. · E ST. · D ST. · C ST. · B ST.

1300 EAST · 1200 EAST · 1100 EAST · 1000 EAST · 900 EAST · 800 EAST · 700 EAST · 600 EAST · 500 EAST · 400 EAST · 300 EAST · 200 EAST · STATE · MAIN · W. TEMPLE · 200 WEST · 300 WEST · 400 WEST · 500 WEST · 600 WEST · 700 WEST · 800 WEST · 900 WEST · 1000 WEST

900 NORTH · 800 NORTH · 700 NORTH · 600 NORTH · 500 NORTH · 400 NORTH · 300 NORTH · 200 NORTH · N. TEMPLE

21 WARD · 20 WARD · 18 WARD · 17 WARD · 19 WARD · 16 WARD · 15 WARD · 13 WARD · 14 WARD · 12 WARD · 11 WARD · 10 WARD · 9 WARD · 8 WARD · 7 WARD · 6 WARD · 5 WARD · 4 WARD · 3 WARD · 2 WARD · 1 WARD

PUB. SQ.

U. G. DEPOT · U. C. DEPOT · W. W. DEPOT

FAIR GROUNDS

The Avenues

Current Name	*Historic Name(s)*
First Avenue	Fruit Street
Second Avenue	Garden Street
Third Avenue	Bluff Street
Fourth Avenue	Wall Street
Fifth Avenue	Prospect Street
Sixth Avenue	High Street
Seventh Avenue	Mountain Street
Eighth Avenue	Summit Street
A Street	Walnut Street
B Street	Chestnut Street
C Street	Pine Street
D Street	Spruce Street
E Street	Fir Street
F Street	Oak Street
G Street	Elm Street
H Street	Maple Street
I Street	Locust Street
J Street	Ash Street
K Street	Beech Street
L Street	Cherry Street
M Street	Cedar Street
N Street	Birch Street
O Street	Hickory Street
P Street	Larch Street
Q Street	Box Elder Street

Map adapted from the historic S.W. Darke Map, 1887, page 14 this volume.

Introduction and Background

Brigham Young believed that the only way for followers of the Church of Jesus Christ of Latter-day Saints (LDS) to survive was to take everything they had and go west until they reached their Zion, not simply a place but a utopian association of the righteous. The Mormons would establish Zion on unclaimed land so distant from the United States of 1846 that they would be beyond the reach of the government and the tormentors who had driven them from their communities in Ohio, Missouri, and Illinois and killed their prophet, Joseph Smith. They would leave America and the evils it symbolized behind. As it turned out, for good or ill, they brought much of it with them.

People with money and influence generally write history, and they have almost always written about themselves, from their own viewpoints. That has become less true over time, but in late nineteenth-century Salt Lake City, it was the rule. Brigham Young, as president of the Church of Jesus Christ of Latter-day Saints and, for a time, Utah's territorial governor, had secretaries and clerks whose job it was to copy down his sermons, revelations, discourses, and decisions. All sorts of records tracked the activities of others in the church hierarchy—the Quorum of the Twelve Apostles, ward bishops, Seventies—because records had to be kept for official purposes.

It is true too that men's stories dominate history. Social custom everywhere in mid-nineteenth-century America confined women of all economic and social classes primarily to their homes, the care of their children, and the church. Much of their work was repetitive drudgery that has gone largely unnoticed and undocumented. A few Mormon women, literate and married to men with money or position, did speak for their sisters, and through the work of Claudia Bushman, Jessie Embry, Jill Mulvay Derr, and others like them, those stories have become public.

Home of Sarah Bracket Carter Foss, 44 South West Temple Street, date unknown. Sarah was a widow and pioneer of 1850. Her sister Phoebe married Wilford Woodruff, one of the Twelve Apostles of the LDS Church, and their home was directly north of this one. Sarah's three daughters also married prominent men: Mathias Cowley, Willard Richards, and David Sessions. This is now the location of Abravanel Hall. Utah State Historical Society photograph 7429, used by permission.

The great majority of women who lived in Salt Lake City's remaining adobe houses have so far been passed over as subjects of study. Some were illiterate, others could not afford a diary, a pen, or even a piece of paper. Their lives, like ordinary men's lives, were consumed with work. If they wrote, their stories are unavailable—perhaps in the hands of a family member, perhaps lost. Even the personal histories in the Daughters of Utah Pioneers Museum are most often the work of descendants—unsourced, softened, conflicting, brief, and almost always limited to recounting the journey west.

Businessmen naturally publicized their financial successes, and they advertised in newspapers, which preserve a record of what was made, bought, and sold. Their travels and their social lives made the news. Thanks to institutions like the LDS Church History Library and Archives, the Utah State Archives, the University of Utah's J. Willard Marriott Library, Brigham Young University's Harold B. Lee Library, and the Utah Division of State History, we have records of what these men, and to some extent their wives, thought and did. Other residents received, if any notice at all, only passing reference to their contributions, their struggles, and their accomplishments.

Leonard Arrington accurately summarized the way an early church policy had worked out in practice. He wrote, "Although the goal of equality seemed to become less important with advances in material well-being, the core of the policy was reflected in the system of immigration, the construction of public works, the allotment of land and water, and the many cooperative village stores and industries."[1] In almost every human society, however, "material well-being" is unequally distributed in daily life. Those who struggled to receive their share are generally missing from the chronicle of Salt Lake City, but they are the subjects of this study.

Ordinary people build ordinary houses made of basic materials. These builders may not have written and preserved their own histories, but there are other ways to identify and explore the events that shaped their lives and the lives of those around them. Those personal details that might have enriched our understanding of an ordinary man's or woman's life are seldom preserved, but their absence does not preclude drawing these people into the fold of written history.

We human beings, whether we perceive it or not, are profoundly affected by our surroundings, even though modern conveniences and our homes insulate us in many ways. Understanding the settlers in nineteenth-century Salt Lake City requires that we adjust our perceptions to appreciate what their experiences must have been. They were intimately connected to and affected by the landscape, the hours of light and darkness, heat and cold, the location of water sources, native plants and animals, and the Native Americans who preceded them to the Salt Lake Valley by thousands of years.

For the pioneers, the immediate physical environment determined the built environment. The kinds of building materials that were familiar to eastern and European immigrants—logs for cabins and frame houses, durable stone that could be cut and dressed—were too distant and too labor-intensive to prepare for use in ordinary homes. Improvisation was the key to survival, and here, mud bricks were the result. None of the pioneers, or even the later settlers, came from a culture that built with this material, but they realized almost immediately that having homes meant building with adobe. Then, having served their original purpose, adobe fell out of favor as more permanent and stylish building materials became available, at least to people who could afford them. The rich built larger and more fashionable homes with stone, brick, and lumber. Those who were unable to improve their economic status simply stayed put in their old adobes. The original large lots were subdivided, and on these small parcels, more and more ordinary adobe houses crowded in.

This book begins with an introduction to the local landscape, the arrival of the Mormons in the Salt Lake Valley, and the tribes of Native Americans who were here before them. Next, I summarize the early history of Salt Lake City, the design of its streets and large lots, the coming of the railroad, and the development of neighborhoods, both rich and poor. I explore local architecture and construction, the beginnings of adobe making in the Great Basin, and how quickly this simple material fell out of favor in Salt Lake City. Finally, I explain the methods and sources I used not only to identify and research adobe houses, but to learn about their builders and owners. The second part of the book, and its heart, tells the individual stories of the people who built 90 of the extant or recently demolished 201 adobe homes.

Ordinary Houses and Everyday Life

The Land Before

Any history of a place should start with some understanding of its landscape, the foundation that both supports and limits human activity. For its current residents and visitors, Salt Lake City's landscape may appear breathtaking or desolate, depending on whether the view is east toward the Wasatch Mountains or west toward the Great Salt Lake, the desert, and the salt flats. Neither is a static view.

The Great Salt Lake, the western hemisphere's largest inland body of salty water, is a tiny remnant of the freshwater Lake Bonneville that covered some 30,000 square miles in northern and central Utah. The ancient lake level was at times almost 1,000 feet higher than it is now. Following a catastrophic flood some 14,000 years ago, during which the lake level fell nearly 1,000 feet, the climate warmed and less rain fell. Lake Bonneville continued to shrink and the water became salty as more evaporated than fell or flowed in.

East of Salt Lake City, the Wasatch Mountains rise abruptly. The highest peaks rise to nearly 11,000 feet, far above modern lake level at about 4,100 feet. Ice-Age glaciers gouged out steep mountain valleys and dumped the resulting gravel at the canyon mouths. Forests of evergreens grow on the slopes.

Between the present lake shore and the Wasatch foothills there is a gently sloping alluvial plain where the original settlement, called Great Salt Lake City, was laid out. It is unlikely that anyone knew much about its suitability as a place to settle, or the resources settlers might need to establish a permanent home, but determined and resourceful people can succeed in almost any environment. As luck would have it, the rock and timber of the Wasatch Mountains, the cobbles and boulders that litter the slopes, and the lakebed sediments of the Salt Lake Valley provided much of what the pioneers needed to make and heat their first homes, build fences, and fashion useful tools. Level terrain could be plowed and farmed.

The "granite" (quartz monzonite) used to build the Salt Lake LDS Temple came from Little Cottonwood Canyon. It was cut first into huge blocks and hauled, initially by ox teams and later by rail, to the Temple Block. Closer to the settlement, clay and sand dug from the banks of creeks draining the Wasatch Mountains could be turned into adobe bricks.

In the desert a hundred miles west of Salt Lake City, less than five inches of rain falls in a year. Salt Lake City averages more than three times that, from both rain and snow, some of it generated by a "lake effect" that draws moisture from the lake and carries it east, dropping it on the city and the west-facing slopes of the Wasatch Mountains. For much of the year, the peaks are covered with snow, and as the snowpack melts in summer, the runoff, like an ice cube melting on the Fourth of July, provides water for drinking and irrigation—far in excess of what actually falls on the city. This fortunate combination of mountains and lake, mud and rock, forest and plain, snow and heat, kept the initial settlement going until the region's other attributes—mineral wealth and its position as a commercial crossroads—drew merchants and investors as well as the Mormon faithful.

The Mormons Come

In the 1840s, detailed information about the soil, climate, topography, and pretty much everything else west of the Missouri River was in short supply. Meriwether Lewis and William Clark brought back reports of their two-and-a-half-year journey of exploration in 1806. They described limitless game, forests and grazing lands, rivers and fish, and so much free land it could never be filled up.

Etienne Provost and Jim Bridger, both mountain men, had been to the Great Salt Lake. Benjamin Bonneville mapped its shoreline in 1837, but it would be John C. Fremont who most directly influenced Brigham Young's choice of a route west and the location of the new Zion. Assigned to find a way from the Missouri River to the Rocky Mountains, Fremont followed the Platte and North Platte Rivers across Nebraska and Wyoming. In 1844 he mapped the Great Salt Lake. His reports and maps made the West a reality. Mapmakers like S. Augustus Mitchell printed pocket-sized versions that showed the Great Salt Lake and perhaps helped Brigham Young to set his course.[2]

The first Euro-American settlers of Salt Lake City were members of the Church of Jesus Christ of Latter-day Saints, or Mormons.[3] Brigham Young, leading 143 people with 72 wagons, departed from "Winter Quarters," now a suburb of Omaha, Nebraska, in April 1847.[4] They followed the Platte River in the tracks of the previous year's Donner-Reed party. In that first year, several other wagon companies followed, made up almost entirely of church leaders and others who could afford to bring stockpiles of food, clothing, and tools, with herds of livestock, across some 1,300 miles of roadless plains, over the Rocky Mountains, and down to the Great Basin. The only way-station was the U.S. Army's Fort Laramie, 120 miles east of what is now Casper, Wyoming. When they reached the Salt Lake Valley late in July, they settled at what is now Pioneer Park and built a fort. It was made of logs and adobe bricks.

The pioneers of 1847 were well aware that their Zion did not actually belong to them, or to the United States. It was part of Mexico, but regardless, in August, 1847, surveyors began to lay out Great Salt Lake City. Brigham Young and his followers settled in as if they would be perfectly welcome.

Native Americans

No Native Americans were living in the Salt Lake Valley when the Mormons appeared, but both the Ute and Shoshone tribes claimed it as their own. Within days of the pioneers' arrival, members of both tribes had made their appearance. In his diary on July 27, 1847, William Clayton recorded that "two Utah Indians came to camp," trading animal skins for ammunition, and that "in the evening, other Indians came to 'Swop' buckskins &c."[5] Behind this innocent charade, the tribes were gauging the settlers' strengths.

Rather than take sides in potential hostilities, the Mormons remained neutral. Brigham Young advised against trading their limited supplies of ammunition for horses they neither wanted nor needed. As at Winter Quarters, where the Mormons had earlier camped between warring tribes, conflict avoidance became the norm in the Salt Lake Valley.[6] Gradually, as the settlement expanded and its residents became more secure, Native Americans might be taken into Mormon households as servants or adopted as children. Proselytizing efforts among the tribes yielded a few new church members, but far more came from the East, northern Europe, and later the Pacific Islands.

Making Shelter

From its founding in 1847 until the arrival of the railroad in 1870, unfired or adobe bricks were the most affordable and obtainable building material. Log cabins were impractical—there simply were not enough

City Wall, Wall Street near 700 North, date unknown. A wall surrounded much of the early city, in part for protection from local Native Americans but, more importantly, to keep grazing livestock out of the pioneers' gardens. Old St. Mark's Hospital in the background. Utah State Historical Society photograph 4438, used by permission.

nearby trees, and they were a waste of wood that was then the only source of fuel for cooking and heating.

Built in 1850, Abraham Coon's adobe farmhouse, at 1258 West Clark Avenue near the Jordan River, is the oldest continuously inhabited home in Utah. Only a very few of Salt Lake City's earliest homes survive—six log cabins and about fifty adobe structures built prior to 1860, including Brigham Young's Lion House and Beehive House near Temple Square. All the rest were built after that, some as late as about 1900. Individually undistinguished, these buildings nevertheless are important historical documents which, taken together, tell us about the people who built and lived in them. They represent the substance of what is ephemeral: a community history.

For more than twenty years after 1847, adobe bricks were the principal—almost the only—construction material in Salt Lake City. Not only was the raw material (clay) locally available, the techniques and the tools required to make bricks were simple. Adobes could be made in wooden molds, a few or many at a time, dried outdoors, and laid up by masons who brought their craft to the Salt Lake Valley. In the earliest days of settlement, virtually everyone lived in an adobe house—rich and poor, weak and powerful. A map drawn about 1856 by David H. Burr, the first territorial surveyor, shows "near 1250" dwellings, all "built of adobes or sundried bricks."[7]

The local adobe bricks are nothing like those used to build the southwestern pueblos and California missions. They are a pale dove gray, not the reddish brown seen in Arizona and New Mexico, and the houses were designed and built, not in the Spanish or Pueblo style, but to resemble those the people had left behind in the East. Some of the pioneers were sophisticated and well educated. By the early 1840s, missionaries from the Church of Jesus Christ of Latter-day Saints had traveled widely and seen the great cities of the East Coast and England before coming West. Yet in their new Zion, they built what was essentially a walled village of mud bricks, with its temple on high ground. It was a variant on Joseph Smith's City of Zion.[8]

Those who could afford them built impressively large adobe homes, but when the railroad reached Salt Lake City in 1870, bringing the machinery for efficient brick kilns and the coal to fire them, as well as logs and lumber from the north slopes of the Uinta Mountains, brick and frame homes became the norm. Adobe houses gradually became a statement about socioeconomic status. Owning, and especially building, an adobe home after 1870 was a hallmark of the ordinary, the "good enough."

Although some adobe houses—particularly in the Marmalade/Capitol Hill and Avenues districts—have been restored and are even sought after now for their historic values, most are in the city's less prosperous neighborhoods. Nearly all the great adobe homes built for people of means were either demolished to make way for commercial and public buildings downtown, or else were replaced by their original or later owners with homes of more fashionable materials that (not coincidentally) required less maintenance. The small, two- or three-room adobe homes that constitute Salt Lake City's legacy from this early period of construction suited the basic needs of owners, then and now, who lacked the means or the need to replace them.

Today only 194 adobe buildings remain of the thousands that once existed. These few offer an opportunity to examine how a primitive material was seized upon and then discarded by people of the Industrial Age, and how adobe, once hailed by George A. Smith as "the best way of building" came to represent the underclass.[9] The great majority of Salt Lake City's early residents were day laborers, housemaids, shoemakers, carpenters, farmers, and masons who left no obvious mark on written history. It is their adobe houses that provide a window into ordinary lives that have been for the most part unexamined. In this study, the view of early Salt Lake City is focused not on church leaders, prominent craftsmen, and influential merchants but on individual stories of ordinary people, connected through their adobe homes to the history of a city that is unique in American culture.

Great Salt Lake City

Brigham Young proposed the name "Great Salt Lake City" on August 21, 1847, and the name stuck until it was shortened by the Territorial Legislature in 1868.[10] For all its treeless isolation, this place on the western slope of the Wasatch Mountains at least meant an end to traveling. If the journey was over, the struggle to survive was not. While the Salt Lake Valley is not exactly a desert, its climate, soil, and water supply were nothing like the eastern fields and forests that pioneers had known. A great deal of time and energy had to be devoted, first to building shelter and growing food, and then to remaking the landscape to meet the pioneers' ideals.

The pioneers of 1847 planted crops in late July, dug irrigation ditches, and built a fort of logs and adobe bricks in what has become Pioneer Park. Many survived that first winter in their wagons. They dared not eat the few potatoes they had dug in the fall, or make flour from the few bushels of the wheat crop that their livestock had not destroyed. Everything was to be saved for next year's seed. For the most part, they ate what they had brought with them.

Tens of thousands of ordinary pioneers followed, in 1848 and for twenty years after that, hauling their goods in wagons and sometimes in handcarts. Most people—even children and the elderly—walked the entire distance. Nearly every one of the reminiscences on file in the Pioneer Memorial Museum in Salt Lake City includes some harrowing tale of the hardships, of "sickness, sorrow, parting, death,"[11] that occurred on the trail. The journey was a trial to be endured, the destination—a community, a home, land of their own—would be a promise kept.

Plats, Blocks, Lots, and Wards

When leaders and members of the LDS Church fled Nauvoo, Illinois, beginning in 1846, their intention was to escape not only what they saw as the tyranny of the federal government but also what was seen as "Babylon," the greedy and sinful world of American commerce for profit. Their Zion would be an essentially egalitarian society based on agriculture, in which all members contributed to the general good by producing food and fiber, or by practicing their trades and crafts. They would be religiously, socially, and economically separate from everything they had left behind.

On July 28, 1847, four days after President Young arrived in the valley, he declared, "No man should buy any land...but every man should [have] his land measured off to him for city and farming purposes, what he could till. He might till it as he pleased, but he should be industrious and take care of it."[12] Plat A, including the Temple Block, was the first area to be surveyed. The plat included 114 ten-acre blocks, each divided into eight lots, and each of them one and a quarter acres in area (165 by 330 feet). Lots were large enough to provide space for a house, a garden, domestic

Map of a portion of Plat A, Great Salt Lake City, c. 1856, showing four blocks between State and West Temple Streets and 300 and 500 South. Thomas Bullock map ("State Road" added by a different hand). Utah State Historical Society, used by permission.

Joseph F. Smith/Edna Lambson Smith home, 143 North 300 West, 1906. Each of the LDS Church president's five wives had her own house, and three were on this block. A parking lot now occupies the space. Shipler Commercial Photographers. Utah State Historical Society photograph 02432, used by permission.

animals, feed and food storage, and, as fruit trees were imported or domesticated, an orchard. The rule was: one house per lot, so that the city would have an open, consistent look and feel throughout. Unlike what Thomas Carter calls the "disheveled" look of some early cities in the East, an appearance of order would prevail.[13] There would be no place or need for an urban core or commercial district because the community would be self-sufficient.

The uniform street and lot grid, patterned after Joseph Smith's "Plat of the City of Zion," was meant to be a physical reflection of the egalitarian social and economic foundations of the church. As it was envisioned, every man would have exactly the same resources: a place to live, work,

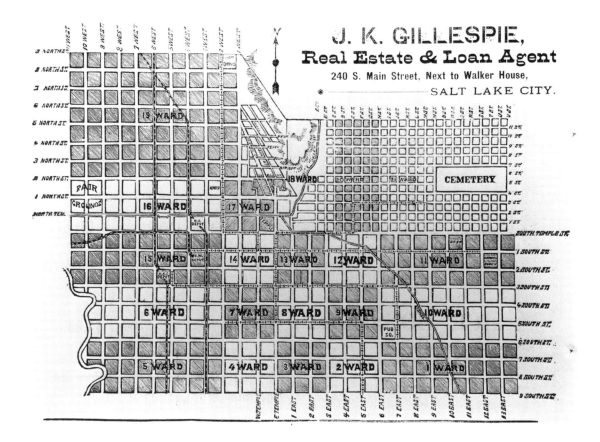

Salt Lake City Ward boundaries, from S. W. Darke, Salt Lake City, Illustrated, 1887. Utah State Historical Society photo 21482, used by permission.

raise a family, and participate in church life. Each would receive according to his need and produce according to his ability. Attractive as it sounds, the ideal did not materialize in quite that way. As land distribution in Great Salt Lake City actually played out, Brigham Young and members of the church Quorum of the Twelve Apostles chose their lots in 1847; they also chose lots for members of their adopted families.[14] No public announcement of the doctrine and practice of polygamy had yet been made, but many leaders already had multiple wives and large numbers of children; in some cases those families also received lots. People of influence and means therefore received land in the center of the settlement, not far from the Temple Block. Blocks and lots in Plat B, to the east, were surveyed in 1848 and distributed by a lottery system, and in later years, Plats C and D (and so on through the alphabet to Plat J) were surveyed.

Streets were named based on their distance from the southeast corner of the Temple Block (for example Third South, now 300 South, is three blocks south of the Temple Block). There were also North, South, East, and West Temple Streets (East Temple became Main Street). Some of this naming convention has survived unchanged, but there have been significant alterations in large parts of the city. This book uses the current street names.

Hilly areas north and east of Temple Square did not lend themselves to the four-square pattern of blocks and streets, and they were not formally allotted during the earliest period of settlement; squatters lived there nonetheless. When the slopes around what is now called Capitol Hill finally were platted, the lots were irregular, laid out to accommodate the terrain and to conform with the irregular paths and informal streets that had grown up without much reference to points of the compass.

The city was divided into nineteen ecclesiastical wards of various sizes in February 1849.[15] Each ward had a meetinghouse and was assigned a bishop, who answered to higher church authorities. The bishop was expected to minister to ward members and to get their cooperation in church assignments. Wards were not only religious entities, they had social significance as well. Members organized to assist each other, to perform common tasks such as construction of the city wall, and to meet for dances and other entertainments. Those who were better off than most were instructed to hire the poor of their own wards when there was occasional work to do. Organization and obedience—highly valued qualities—were carried over from the experience of overland travel right into the period of settlement. Original ward boundaries changed somewhat as the population grew; south of the city, the Sugar House Ward was added in 1854, and the Twentieth Ward was added in 1856. The eastern part of the Twentieth Ward was split off to form the Twenty-first Ward in 1877.

Rich and Poor

A home in, say, the Thirteenth, Fourteenth, or Eighteenth Ward implied high social status.[16] Church leaders who arrived in the 1840s had chosen their lots in these areas near the Temple Block. Years later, the Twentieth Ward acquired some of the same cachet, as important figures among the later immigrants, or those who moved out of the increasingly commercial areas of Plat A, moved in. On the other hand, the Nineteenth Ward was home to a few prosperous pioneers where there was level ground but soon lost its luster as poor people bought the oddly shaped

lots on the rocky hillsides. Wards around the outer fringes of town, in Plats B, C, and eventually E through I, tended to be socially and economically isolated until street improvement—and later the trolley system— made them accessible.

Beginning in 1848, lots were assigned to men who requested land; single men did not receive land, and only a few widows did. Tradesmen worked at their homes or in small neighborhood shops; there was no central business district. South of 900 South in what was called the Big Field, five- and, by 1850, ten-acre lots were available to men who had the draft animals and equipment to work these larger farms. Latecomers took whatever they could get, often buying from earlier immigrants or church leaders lots that had initially been free. South of the Temple Block, East Temple Street gradually became the commercial district and was renamed Main Street in 1906, as it would have been in any other city in America. Men who owned property there either built businesses or sold their lots to eager buyers, in spite of the original plan to make the new Zion a communal society that eschewed buying and selling. The communal society became a hierarchical society.

At the time of the 1850 territorial census (which was taken in February 1851), 503 individuals, including children, were enumerated in Great Salt Lake City. Many church leaders were absent, gathering the faithful in the East or on overseas missions. None of the men enumerated gave his occupation as "merchant," although there were tailors, carpenters, masons, painters, and saddlers who were certainly in business. By 1860, in the nine-block area of the Thirteenth Ward, where there were 141 households, twenty men gave their occupation as "merchant," and the value of

Opposite : The Gardo House, built in the American Second Empire style between 1873 and 1883, was initially the LDS Church's official reception hall. It was a wood-frame structure, but between the four-by-six studs, adobe bricks provided stability as well as insulation against cold and heat. Demolished in 1921, it was replaced by a Federal Reserve Bank. A towering office building now occupies the site at 70 East South Temple Street. Utah State Historical Society photograph 7445, used by permission.

their individual real and personal property was often in the thousands of dollars. Dozens of tradesmen were living, and presumably doing business, in what had become "downtown." Presiding Bishop Edward Hunter tacitly acknowledged in 1861 that the city's wards differed in status when he suggested that each ward's support of church-organized wagon trains should be based on its economic capabilities.[17]

Two years after the first pioneers made their entry into the Salt Lake Valley, the LDS Church established the Perpetual Emigrating Fund Company in 1849. The PEF, sometimes known as the Perpetual Emigration Fund, extended loans to church members who could not afford to reach the new Zion on their own. Long-time members, who may have waited years to emigrate, those who had particularly desirable skills, and those whose family or friends had contributed to the fund were favored in the selection process. The effect of the PEF was to bring an estimated thirty thousand poor people into the region before the fund was dissolved in 1887 under the Edmunds-Tucker Act, which disincorporated the LDS Church, criminalized the practice of polygamy, and sought to stamp out the flow of those who might engage in the practice.[18] In effect, the PEF delivered potential builders of small adobe homes to Utah Territory for almost forty years. Because the slow pace of travel meant that planning the immigration had to be done years in advance, long before anyone could forecast future harvests, it also brought thousands of hungry mouths when there was widespread famine during both the late 1840s and the mid-1850s.

Much of the economy, in money and in kind, went to provide labor and materials for church projects—a paper mill, a pottery, a sugar factory (in what is now the Sugar House business district), a canal from the Cottonwood Canyons to the Temple Block, iron production near Cedar City, and a complex system of stations along the immigrant trail, all of which were intended to reduce the need for imported goods. Every one of these projects failed after the investment of huge amounts of labor and money, although they did provide work and at least some income, in the form of goods, to the craftsmen and laborers who worked on them. In some ways, they were not unlike projects of the Works Progress Administration (WPA) during Franklin D. Roosevelt's presidency some eighty years later.

Leonard Arrington pointed out that gold-seekers and would-be merchants on their way to California in the late 1840s very likely provided the economic salvation of Great Salt Lake City.[19] By the time they had crossed the plains and Rocky Mountains, their equipment and their teams were wearing out. Many had brought too much with them and found they could haul it no farther. For the Mormons, this was a windfall of food, clothes, tools, heavy wagons, and livestock that they could buy very cheaply. Better still, goods that had been discarded along the trail were free to anyone who could ride or drive back and pick them up. Where the Mormons had grown enough food to spare, they could get very high prices from the gold-seekers.

Church determination to avoid participation in the national economy had long-lasting effects in Utah Territory as late as the 1890s. Zion's Cooperative Mercantile Institution (ZCMI), a cooperative venture that opened in 1869, was intended not only to give cash-poor settlers the means to obtain goods in trade for what they grew or made, but also to limit Mormons' purchases of imported goods. Church sanctions on non-LDS merchants drove many of them out of business, but eventually ZCMI suffered from a lack of cash business and ran into trouble with the U.S. Collector of Internal Revenue. The financial Panic of 1873 put thousands of miners (working in non-Mormon–owned mines) out of work and closed most of the banks in Utah Territory.

America Comes to Zion

At the time Salt Lake City was founded, Mormons believed that they would soon experience the end of the world. If any one event marked the end of the early millenarian concept of Zion, it was completion of the Transcontinental Railroad in 1869, followed by the arrival of the Utah Central Railroad line at Salt Lake City in January 1870. Both events were desired and anticipated with a mix of eagerness and anxiety. Groups of Latter-day Saints had met publicly as early as 1854 to petition the federal government to bring the railroad through Salt Lake City.[20] Church leaders including Brigham Young were among the directors of the Utah Central and the line was built by Mormon labor. Clearly, new converts could cross the continent much more cheaply, safely, and quickly via railroad to swell the numbers of the faithful. The advantages of a renewed connection to Babylon would be tempered by challenges, but the predicted apocalypse seemed not to be at hand, so Mormons would "settle in for the long haul."[21]

Bird's-eye map, 1875, showing the route of the first railroad tracks to reach Salt Lake City, on Fourth (now 500) West, and the Union Pacific depot at Fourth West and South Temple Streets. Utah State Historical Society map 588, used by permission.

Try to visualize Salt Lake City without the interstate highways, the railroad tracks and depots, and their cousins, the TRAX and FrontRunner lines. Notice that many of these lie between about 200 West and 900 West, a corridor nearly a mile wide. Now devoted to transportation, this space once looked much like the rest of town. Even the first line of track swiftly and profoundly changed the face of Salt Lake City. What had been a small city with widely spaced homes and shops was transformed within a few years into the most important commercial hub between the Missouri River and the West Coast. Rail transportation brought not only much-needed goods and materials—food, stoves, clothing, seeds, lumber, coal—but also the kinds of heavy machinery that had been impossible to haul across the country on wagons. Agricultural and mining

George Tall home, 71 North 700 West, date unknown. Tall was a blacksmith who began building this house about 1864. City Creek often flooded the property. The house was still standing in 1950, but now Interstate 15 passes directly through the site. Utah State Historical Society photograph 8919, used by permission.

William J. Lloyd home, 544 West 100 South, c. 1898. Lloyd was a Welsh shoemaker whose home expanded to accommodate his large family and later included a shop on its west side. Demolished sometime before 1950, it stood between today's Gateway Mall and Interstate 15. Utah State Historical Society photograph 17237, used by permission.

equipment, furnaces, saw blades, and mill parts allowed residents to farm more efficiently, extract valuable minerals, and make bricks, lumber, and flour quickly and cheaply from what they grew or harvested locally. Add to that the rapid influx of all sorts of people—not just converts but merchants, territorial bureaucrats, mining entrepreneurs, opportunists of all kinds, and even members of the religious faiths who had been the Mormons' enemies in the States—and Salt Lake City became an outpost of the same Babylon Mormons had tried to escape. The railroad not only blended Salt Lake into American society, but in an unforeseen consequence, it created a dramatic division within the once homogeneous city which lasts to this day.

Creating the "Westside"

John McCormick neatly summarized an often-neglected effect of the railroad's entry into Salt Lake City.[22] The first rail line entered the city from the north along a right-of-way on 500 West, continuing on to a depot at 400 West and South Temple Streets, about where the much later Union Pacific depot stands today. Later rail lines led south, east, and west, and other depots were built between South Temple and 400 South, creating a commercial and industrial district that extended east and west. What had been a neighborhood of farmers' homes on large lots, craftsmen's workshops, and small stores gradually became an area of warehouses, industry, and rooming houses along the tracks.

The railroad's advantages—cheap, abundant goods, ease of travel—were offset by a host of undesirable effects, among them saloons. In 1869, the city directory listed only three saloons (one of them named the Railroad Saloon, as a portent of things to come).[23] By 1874, there were thirty-eight saloons in the Salt Lake business directory, a twelve-fold increase in those five years.[24] Coal yards, lumber mills, and stables displaced or crowded between the adobe homes, adding their smells, dust, and commotion to an area that rapidly became blighted and overlooked by city officials. The church located its soap factory directly adjacent to the tracks at 500 North; two tanneries and a brewery were within a couple of blocks by 1889.[25] The first gas company placed its plant directly east of Hannah Newman's adobe home on 600 West, so that "the gas seeped through the soil and ruined all the wells."[26] By that time, several lines of track had been laid between 500 West and 800 West, forming a physical barrier hundreds of feet wide. Even though rail travel and transport lost some of their dominance when highways, cars, and trucks took over many of their functions in the mid-twentieth century, railroads had long since separated the east and west sides of Salt Lake City in a way that was permanent and irreversible. Today, Interstate 15 (with all its ramps and connectors), light rail, and high-speed rail lines are crowded into the same rights-of-way.

When the first settlers arrived in 1847, the marshes of Parley's Creek, which extended north from today's 1700 South Street before flowing into the Jordan River, formed a de facto city limit near 700 West; for several blocks east, the ground was typically wet, and flooding was common in the spring as snowmelt filled the creeks. Most of the early west-side residents were small farmers or craftsmen; before 1870 nothing prevented them from walking or riding a few blocks east into the center of town, to work, to meetinghouses, or to schools. For them, railroad tracks and trains posed a new series of obstacles and hazards, as well as to travelers and goods headed west. Dirt, noise and smoke were not the only dangers; established crossings were few and the risks were many—trains moved at unaccustomed speed and could not turn aside or stop, sometimes colliding with slower, horse-drawn vehicles trying to cross the tracks. The carnage continues even now as the daring and the unwary step or drive into harm's way.

Occupations and Social Status

For the first time, occupations such as locomotive engineer, railroad hand, railroad clerk, conductor, and even railroad newsboy appeared in the 1870 census records among households in the Sixteenth Ward. Store clerks and bookkeepers were numerous, indicating that commerce was thriving; farmers, who in 1860 had been a mainstay of the Sixteenth Ward (17 percent of households) by 1870 made up less than 10 percent, or 15 of 158 households.[27] Railroad workers became increasingly specialized in their tasks; the 1880 census lists occupations such as coal heaver, depot timekeeper, watchman, and engine wiper.[28] Women found a few opportunities to help support their families, but nearly all were married, had many children, and were "keeping house," a term that included every sort of home manufacture, cleaning, cooking, raising a large garden, and caring for small livestock. In 1870, there were a dressmaker, two weavers, and a dozen domestic servants, six of whom lived adjacent to

Devereaux House, the mansion of merchant William Jennings, and no doubt worked there.[29] (One prostitute, who was in a small hospital with a "bad cold," was enumerated in 1880.)[30]

Arsenal Hill

If the west side of the city was low and wet, north and west of the Temple Block the land was hilly and dry, too steep for teams and wagons, and unsuitable for the large garden plots and outbuildings found in other parts of town. The Territorial Arsenal was just south of today's State Capitol grounds. Squatters settled on the hill before land records were kept and when Plat E was surveyed, about 1855, the lots were irregularly shaped and the streets, or paths, followed the topography, not the compass.[31] This is today's Capitol Hill. It includes what is called the Marmalade District, where the earliest street names were descriptive, such as Crooked and Short. Later the streets were renamed for fruits—not just today's Quince, Apricot, and Almond, but Pear, Grape, Currant, Melon, Apple, Strawberry, and Peach, because orchards thrived on the west-facing slopes.[32] Parts of the neighborhood today have an appeal that is much more recent than the neighborhood's early attraction as a cheap (but undesirable) place to live. The city's greatest concentration of extant adobe buildings is in the original Nineteenth Ward, which stretched from the hilltop and across the tracks to the Jordan River.

The Avenues

Another neighborhood with a concentration of adobe houses is called the Avenues, north and east of Temple Square in the Twentieth (and later the Twenty-first) Ward. Initially the streets there were named for shade trees (the north-south streets now have letter designations; the east-west streets are numbered). Some of the largest homes in The Avenues represent a resurgence of adobe use in the 1870s and 1880s, but the earliest belonged to herders, Temple craftsmen, and small farmers who eked out a living on the "Dry Bench." The Avenues has a reputation for having been a neighborhood of widows and plural wives during the 1880s and later, but few of the remaining adobes were built by or for them.

Those three general areas—the Westside, Capitol Hill, and The Avenues—most of the adobe buildings in this study, about 70 percent. The

Home of Brigham Young, 1848. Utah State Historical Society photo 9033, used by permission.

rest are widely scattered all over town, a few in cohesive groups but most with their original context completely lost.

Houses

Brigham Young's first home outside the 1847 adobe fort was a two-room adobe house built in 1848. The first church office, about twelve-by-eighteen feet, was built in 1848 as well, south of the Council House.[33] Patty Bartlett Sessions, a prominent midwife whose son Perrigrine captained a wagon company in 1847, was thrilled to have a similar home completed in 1850.[34] Both the church president and the midwife had been able to bring with them supplies of food, warm clothing, furniture, and the great luxury of cookstoves, but their houses were exactly like those of the poorest settlers.

In the first few years of settlement, the need to survive was the great

Adobe home (lower right) of merchant John Kimball at 400 South and Main Street, before it was demolished to make way for the New Grand Hotel, c. 1908. Utah State Historical Society photo 20599, used by permission.

equalizer. But as people's basic needs were met and the settlement became a city, the stratification of society began to be reflected in, among other things, architecture. For those who had the resources, adobe houses could be substantial and even stylish. There were any number of two-story Neo-classical-style houses built for church apostles and wealthy non-Mormon merchants like John Kimball, all made of adobe. Size, ornamentation, and, of course, furnishings distinguished these from the adobe homes of ordinary people. Later still, the grand adobes were replaced by commercial buildings or by brick and stone mansions. Yet small adobes, few of them on desirable real estate, seem to have had staying power. Even some of the earliest—one built in 1850, others built in 1854 and 1855—are still in use, along with dozens of others that were built as late as 1897.

Alfred and Melissa Bigler Lambson at their home, 75 North 200 West, on the southwest corner of North Temple Street. Lambson was a blacksmith who came to Utah in 1847 with his wife and baby daughter. Photograph taken sometime before Melissa died in October 1899. Utah State Historical Society photograph 7632, used by permission.

Architectural Type, Style, and Fashion

All the adobe buildings in this book were designed and built by skilled tradesmen. The term for these folk buildings is "vernacular," but the finished product is anything but crude or clumsy. While mud bricks may be an unsophisticated material, that should not suggest that the builders who used them simply drew a rough floor plan on the ground and then laid up bricks to make walls. Bricklayers and masons, highly sought after during the settlement period, had a very clear understanding of both form and function—how houses should look and how they should work for the people who would live there.

A later view of the Lambson home, showing the porch along its south side. On the north side, City Creek, now confined to a culvert under North Temple Street, ran west toward the Great Salt Lake. A large parking lot now occupies this space, one block west of Temple Square. Shipler Commercial Photographers, 1910. Utah State Historical Society photograph 11207, used by permission.

Even these common buildings for ordinary people were designed.[35] They embodied proportions that were well known and generally accepted during the second half of the nineteenth century. The most basic dwelling, perhaps a two-room house with a centrally placed front door flanked by small windows, still had to please the eye of the builder, the owner, and his neighbors, regardless of their social and economic class. Its proportions were based on houses familiar to pioneers who came from the eastern United States and from Western Europe. It had to meet their expectations for what architectural historian Thomas Carter called "the geometry of civilization" so that human society could feel separate, both

This must have been a substantial home when it was new. The two-story adobe was dwarfed by its brick neighbor by the time this photograph was taken between 1905 and 1910. It stood at 358 West 300 South, where Caputo's Deli now faces Pioneer Park. Two older women wait in the shade of the porch while the young dandies seem to mug for the camera, date unknown. Courtesy Alan Barnett, all rights reserved.

visually and emotionally, from the threatening wilderness just outside the village. Proportion—the result of a specific design—was as well known to the local mason as it was to the pioneer architect. The length and width of rooms, the height of walls and gable ends, the pitch of roofs, all were planned before construction began, and all conformed to familiar (and therefore comforting) rules.[36]

Without some knowledge of architecture and an eye for detail, virtually all the adobe buildings in Salt Lake City would be unrecognizable as such. They have been covered with stucco, faux brick, shiplap, or aluminum siding—whatever was available to provide protection from the elements, or when their owners had enough money to "modernize" them. Added rooms, partial demolitions, and upper floors distort their original footprints; updated window treatments hide their early simplicity. Recognizing these houses requires mentally stripping off the additions and decorations and focusing on their unique features. Recognizing the common types, the basic "bones," is the first step.

By far the most common house type was the hall-parlor, as at 844 East 100 South, two simple rooms with a front door that opened into the larger room, the hall, which was both living room and kitchen. The parlor, or formal room, stood to one side and was usually a bedroom. Most family activities, from cooking to sleeping, took place in the hall. No architect was needed (or available) to design these little buildings—immigrants from the eastern United States and England had built houses like this for hundreds of years, from logs, lumber, brick, and stone, employing proportions and measurements that were familiar and pleasing.

An even simpler house plan was the single-cell, which is just what it sounds like: one room with the door offset to one side. Very few single-cell houses survive. Several central-passage and side-passage houses remain, built primarily for prominent and wealthy citizens like Ebenezer Beesley who could afford a more elaborate home (80 West 300 North). A few saltbox and temple-form houses were built, but after about 1870 the predominant plan was the cross-wing, usually an L-shaped one- or two-story house (442 North Quince Street).

The style of a house refers to the appearance of its overall composition, and fashion refers to its decorative and structural features. Most adobe houses conformed to one of the classical styles—Georgian, Greek Revival, and Federal. Carter and Goss succinctly describe and illustrate these styles and the buildings displaying them, and their volume is an invaluable reference for Utah architecture.[37] As with house types and proportions, style and fashion were not inventions of the pioneers but rather familiar forms they brought from their place of origin.

Where and When

Of the 201 remaining adobe buildings in Salt Lake City that are the subject of this study, 29 are west of the railroad tracks (seven others were demolished between 2011 and 2016), and 61 are on the south and west slopes of Capitol Hill. All were in the original Fifteenth, Sixteenth, and Nineteenth Wards where a majority of Salt Lake City's ordinary people lived. There are still a few large, early adobe homes in both areas, but the great majority are small (two or three rooms) and were built after 1870. It seems unlikely that so many remain in these areas through pure chance, or that chance was entirely responsible for their being built in those locations.

Of the 146 small adobe houses, 64 (44 percent) were built and first occupied by men and women who were indebted to the Perpetual Emigrating Fund Company (PEF), or whose parents had been. In some cases, subsequent owners were also PEF travelers. By contrast, only seven of the 39 remaining larger adobes in Salt Lake City (which include Beehive House, Lion House, and the Isaac Chase home in Liberty Park) were built by men who emigrated with help from the PEF, about 17 percent. Success in escaping poverty, while possible, must have been as elusive then as it is now.

Thirty-eight small adobe houses, built before 1869 by pioneers who came in wagon trains or handcart companies, are still standing. Age alone—the combined effects of weather, gravity, and human use—probably accounts for most losses of the earliest homes. Those in areas of commercial, industrial, or railroad development were simply wiped off the map when they became obstacles to progress.

Later in the city's history, adobe homes were built by or for small farmers, shop clerks, laborers, craftsmen and tradesmen, teamsters, widows, and plural wives. A few were built as rentals. The women residents were seldom members of the Relief Society, but much more often recipients of its assistance.[38] Most of these households paid their tithing, if they could, in labor for the church Public Works Department rather than in goods or money.[39] Their property taxes might be abated (cancelled or reduced) when they could not pay even the few dollars they owed.

"Two Rooms Unplastered"

Crop failures in 1847 and 1848, the grasshopper plague of 1855 followed by an extremely cold winter that caused food shortages in 1856, and the Utah War in 1857–1858 meant that agricultural expansion fell far behind the needs of a growing population. Beginning in 1856, impoverished handcart pioneers, who brought almost nothing with them, made the shortages of food and goods even worse. In the midst of widespread suffering, wheat, flour, and livestock were welcomed by the church as tithing and distributed to the needy. It was enough to prevent starvation, but malnutrition must have been widespread. Coupled with constant work and inadequate housing, this deprivation had devastating effects on the lives and the recollections of common people. In February 1848, between diary entries telling of dining at friends' homes, Patty Bartlett Sessions reported the death of a young man who was poisoned by roots he must have hoped were edible.[40]

About 1855, John P. Squires bought the lot where his adobe house still stands at 78 North E Street. When Brigham Young called for city residents to abandon their homes and flee south in 1858 ahead of Johnston's army, the family left behind everything they could not carry. They returned to find their furnishings gone and another family living in their house. Still, they reclaimed the place and started over. Squires's son recalled that the family had withstood years of eating "roots, segos, weeds or anything chewable" and living in "two rooms unplastered."[41] Half of Catherine Squires's eight children died before her death from tuberculosis in 1865.[42]

A Material Change

The coming of the transcontinental railroad predictably swept away the pioneers' early expectations of self-sufficiency and isolation. That vision was simply allowed to expire. Consumer goods, whether they were luxury fabrics, china dishes, glass for windows, fine food, or mechanics' tools, were either too tempting or just indispensable. The railroad, and some of its freight, also brought about profound changes in that most basic consumer item, shelter. Once the Utah Central Railway (and its successors) reached Salt Lake City, locomotives and railcars could follow. Spur lines were built in all directions. Trains could bring in coal to fire the brick kilns. Huge quantities of timber and building stone, hauled from distant sources and up steep grades with only a small fraction of the effort and expense that were needed before, made those materials readily available for buildings.

Machinery for sawmills and the steam engines to run them meant that the cost of frame houses fell dramatically, and many more people could afford them. The plodding ox teams hauling stone from Little Cottonwood Canyon to the Temple Block were replaced by trains on a rail line, and eventually the Salt Lake & Fort Douglas Railway reached the stone quarries in Red Butte Canyon, bringing the handsome red sandstone down to Salt Lake City where it was cut into foundations and facades. Brigham Young never abandoned his adobe homes, but other church leaders, like the merchant class and the mining barons, made the switch to brick, frame, and stone.

The adobe houses built before 1870 and still standing, while not a random sample, belonged to a cross-section of society, from LDS Church president Brigham Young (the Chase Mill in Liberty Park), his clerk George D. Watt, businessman Richard Vaughan Morris, and wagon company leader Peter Nebeker, to the Welsh miner Edward Jones and his wife, Kate, or James and Elizabeth Smith, English immigrants who worked at every sort of odd job.

The nineteen larger adobe houses built in 1870 or later belonged to people with names like Romney, Young, Arnold, and Snow, whose families were prominent in the LDS Church. For whatever reason, these owners stuck to a traditional material, even though their homes were stylish and in the best neighborhoods. None of that was true for the rest.

A History of Adobe

Mud brick construction has a long history on almost every continent, not just in the Americas. Adobe bricks were used in Mesopotamia and in the Roman Empire, and by a variety of routes the technique made its way to such places as Denmark and the East Anglia region of Norfolkshire, England, where they might have been familiar to at least some of the European converts.[43]

But there were more immediate influences on the choice of adobe for construction. William Clayton wrote, as he entered the Salt Lake Valley with the pioneer company in 1847, "There is no prospect for building log houses without spending a vast amount of time and labor, but we can make Spanish brick and dry them in the sun."[44] Samuel Brannan, a Mormon convert, had sailed from New York to California on the ship *Brooklyn* in 1846. Visiting Salt Lake City in August 1847, he spoke highly of his adobe house in a council meeting. Even before that, two articles in the *Nauvoo Neighbor* explained not only the techniques of making adobe bricks, but how to build with them as well.[45]

Veterans of the Mormon Battalion almost certainly put the concept into practice. The Mormon Battalion was a group of five hundred men recruited from among the pioneers in 1847 to fight in the war with Mexico (1846–1848). Some got only as far as Colorado and returned via Pueblo and other adobe settlements, joining the pioneers in Wyoming. Most of the battalion reached California, where they built brick forts and saw adobe buildings in the Spanish style. These men almost certainly helped build the log and adobe fort in the autumn of 1847 at what is now Pioneer Park. Settled as they were along the wide marshes of Parley's Creek where it meandered north to join the Jordan River, the pioneers found the basic ingredient of adobe—mud—all around them. The first adobe pits were just northwest of the site of the Old Fort.

The pioneers of 1847 lived in the fort, or in their wagons and in dugouts, until they could build permanent housing. Building with wood, essential for cooking and heating, making household furniture and tools, roof timbers and floorboards, or constructing water mills and other equipment, was limited. Instead, the pioneers began to build with adobe bricks. Early adobe makers mixed mud with straw and pressed it into molds with their hands and feet. Much later, the height of technology was a pug mill, "drawn round and round by horses," which at least saved the physical labor of mixing.[46]

The pioneers' first attempts at construction may not have been very skillful as they experimented with different brick dimensions and varying combinations of clay and sand. Hiram Clawson's house collapsed in 1852. Thomas Bullock went to "visit the ruins" and saw that "his house is a perfect wreck."[47] Lorenzo Brown wrote that "Hiram Clawsons house but just finished fell in consequence of water running into the cellar being poor foundation There was no one injured His house cost 4000."[48] Some builders were more successful; the oldest continuously occupied home in Utah was built by Abraham Coon in 1850 and is standing today. Inside its attic walls, the adobes are so smooth and solid, they might just have been tapped out of the mold.

If the first company of pioneers hoped to build their Zion in an environment something like the one they left in the East, or in England, the Salt Lake Valley was a cruel disappointment. Small trees bordered the few stream courses that crossed the slopes east of the Great Salt Lake, but otherwise the landscape was essentially an unbroken sea of grass. (The sagebrush that seems natural today is an invader; it moved

LDS Church Tithing Office, on the northeast corner of Main and South Temple Streets, about 1869. At two and a half stories, this was the tallest adobe building in pioneer Salt Lake City. Utah State Historical Society photograph 06757, used by permission.

in after livestock herds grazed the native grasses to the roots.) A salty lake spread out almost to the western horizon, and the mountains they had crossed on the way were thousands of feet higher than anything they had seen before.

Richard F. Burton, the English explorer, described the city of 1860 as "somewhat Oriental.... None of the buildings, except the Prophet's house, were whitewashed. The material, the thick, sun-dried adobe, common to all parts of the Eastern world, was of a dull leaden blue, deepened by the atmosphere to a gray, like the shingles of the roofs. The number of gardens and compounds...how lovely they appeared after the baldness of the prairies!"[49]

Burton had seen the Beehive House and Lion House, which dwarfed every other home in the city, but he was particularly enchanted by the small gray houses and their gardens.

Brigham Young, who might have been speaking more from hope than knowledge, promoted the use of adobe as the perfect building material. In a sermon at the fall conference of the LDS Church in October 1852, he told his listeners,

> Being a chemist in theory, I should say according to my mind…you will find that temple which is built of adobes [rather than sandstone or other rock] still remains, and in better condition than it was the first day it was built. It will petrify into rock, and will become solid stone in 500 years, so as to be fit to cut into mill stones to grind flour…. Rock is either growing or decomposing all the time, and the moment it becomes as hard as is ever going to be, that moment it begins to decompose.[50]

A geologist, even in 1852, would have said otherwise, but adobe has proved to be a very durable building material. Then too, because adobes could be made almost in the middle of town, production became a vital home industry, as well as a function of the church Public Works department.

Aroet Lucious Hale reached the Salt Lake Valley in 1848. In his journal he recorded:

> We arrived in the valley of Great Salt Lake in the fall of 1848. We camped around the Old Fort that the pioneers of 1847 had built. In the fall of 1848 all the Saints had liberty to scatter out and farm nearby settlements, and settle on their city lots. President Kimball, my good advisor, sent for me to come and see him. Said he, 'Aroet, you are naturally ingenious. Go to the adobe yard and make you 7 or 8 hundred large Spanish adobes. While they are drying, enclose one of your wagons. Go to the canyon and get a load of logs. Take them to the saw pit. Have them sawed for your doors, frames and window frames, and by that time I will show you your city lot.' I did as my advisor counseled me to do. I took one of the end gates out of the wagon and went to the carpenter shop. I found there

Brother [Charles] Shumway [a] Carpenter, an old Nauvoo acquaintance. He was glad to see me and soon had a pair of adobe molds made. The adobes that were first made for our small houses was 18 x 9 x 4, what were called Spanish adobe. The first week I had my seven hundred adobes laid out to dry. I unloaded one wagon and went to the North Canyon [the first major canyon north of Salt Lake City] in company with other teams, got a small load of logs, and took them to the saw pit which was run by Blazard. For my share, I got lumber enough to make us one door frame, two window 6 liter [light] frames and two plates for the wall.[51]

These large adobe bricks were typical of the earliest made in Great Salt Lake City, but they may not have been practical.[52] For whatever reason, perhaps so that buyers could expect all to be the same size, Great Salt Lake City regulated the size of adobe bricks beginning in 1854. They were to be twelve inches long, six inches wide, and four inches thick.[53] Of course there was some variation during drying, but most of those I have measured are about eleven-by-five-by-three, so the spirit if not quite the letter of the ordinance was followed.

In 1847, the topography of Salt Lake City had not yet been disturbed by human intervention, and streams had not been diverted for irrigation, drainage, and drinking water. Lake level was higher than it is now, and the marshes of creeks flowing into the Great Salt Lake came as far east as 600 West between 200 and 400 South. As suitable and accessible clay in the original adobe yard was worked out, diggings expanded northwestward. Adobe manufacturing continued there at least through 1879, when the mayor was authorized to sell twelve lots from the "old adobe yard" at public auction.[54] Two adobe makers still lived in the area in 1884.[55] Today the Rio Grande railroad depot, home to the Utah State Historical Society and the Division of State History, stands about a block southeast of the original yard. The nearest marsh is miles to the west.

Clay from the adobe yard made durable bricks and was used for the first fort, the wall around the Temple Block, for many public works projects, and for thousands of homes. Brigham Young arranged for 250,000 adobes to be made from clay found "on the [Twentieth Ward] bench" for construction of the Salt Lake Theater, completed in 1862.[56] Assuming these were the smaller adobe bricks then in use, that would mean

The Pioneer Planing Mill produced finished wood products that were an improvement over simple sawn lumber. It stood on the southwest corner of 300 West and South Temple Streets, now the site of Salt Lake City's basketball arena. Photo by C. R. Savage, date unknown. Utah State Historical Society photograph 7869, used by permission.

excavation of at least 1,543 cubic yards of earth. Other sources of adobe came into use as the city spread out—one near 803 South 300 East where the home of adobe maker Joseph Buckley still stands. James Leach, who reached the valley in October 1847, recalled years later that in 1848, he had "made adobies for brothers kimbel [Heber C. Kimball] some in the adobie yard and ten thousand under the old oak tree that stands to this day right south west of his large house," which would have been near the course of City Creek at Main and North Temple Streets. Leach also made adobes somewhere in the Second Ward.[57]

There was no need for builders to invent entirely new construction techniques. They used traditional masonry bonds (patterns) that, like traditional house plans, reflected the bricklayer's experience in his home country. The English bond, for instance, used alternating courses of headers and stretchers (see drawing page 114) and made a very strong wall using the minimum number of bricks. But the physical properties of adobe bricks did mean making some important concessions. First, adobe has little resistance to crushing or tensile stresses. The mortar, made of mud that did not necessarily come from the adobe yard, might not always bond well to the brick. Lime from kilns in Emigration Canyon could be added to improve these qualities.[58]

Room size was limited by the length, breadth, and number of joists, rafters, and ties, which served to hold the whole structure together. Foundations—first made from local fieldstone, later of sandstone from Red Butte Canyon, and then from fired brick—kept the adobe bricks off the wet or snowy ground, where moisture would soon disintegrate them.

Openings for windows were narrow (although they might be stylishly tall), because without the support of a very strong header, the weight of the masonry above might collapse into the opening or force the window casing to twist, causing structural failure. Since the narrow windows admitted little light into a room, window openings customarily widened towards the interior of the house. A unique feature of adobe buildings, and instantly recognizable, is the depth of window and door openings—usually twelve to fifteen inches—that reflects the thickness of the solid walls.

Adobe construction had a subtle but crucial advantage over building with wood: very few iron fasteners—nails, screws, bolts and other hardware—were needed. Early efforts at iron mining and smelting in Utah were essentially failures, meaning that these heavy and expensive manufactured items had to be imported from the East if they were to be used.

No framing was needed in the walls, so that if the owners settled for a dirt floor, the only essential wooden elements were door and window frames and roof timbers. Even the roof might not be shingled but instead covered with brush and dirt, another saving on nails and on the work of making shingles. At least until it rained.

The very earliest adobe buildings, including the Abraham Coon house and the Anders Winberg house, are distinguished by their use of whole tree trunks as roof joists and ridge poles. Sawmill capacity would have been very limited, and production of sawn lumber was most likely reserved for uses where no other material would do the job. It must have made sense for most pioneers to cut, trim, and skid entire trees to their lots, peel them, and then work with their neighbors to lift them into place.

Adobe buildings were reasonably cool in summer. Their pale gray color, or a coat of whitewash, reflected heat, and their great thermal mass meant that it took a very long time to heat the walls all the way through. If they had gable-end windows, these could be opened to let out heat trapped under the roof—if not, the attic could be an oven in summer. Heating an adobe house was more difficult than keeping one cool. As for any other kind of house, cutting and hauling firewood was hard work and time-consuming; coal, which was not readily available until the 1870s, had to be bought. Doors and windows that didn't fit tightly let in the cold. Thin, uninsulated ceilings allowed warm air to escape into the attic and out through the roof. Fireplaces were the most common form of heat production in the early settlement, but most of a fire's heat goes up the chimney. An imported sheet metal or cast-iron stove, if the homeowner could afford to buy one, threw a great deal more of its heat into the room. Even after fired bricks were widely available, the use of adobe bricks as an insulating material continued into the late nineteenth century, even in the grandest homes.[59] Adobe's fireproof qualities—especially when frame buildings might burn to the ground before the neighbors arrived to help or a fire company could harness and hitch up its horses and arrive at the scene—were no less important.[60]

Maintenance and repairs to adobe buildings were time-consuming, but materials were cheap and available. Mice, ants, and other small pests found it easy to make themselves at home in convenient cracks, but that was no less true in log houses, and a coat of plaster or calcimine helped to minimize the annoyance of walls that were always shedding dirt.

In this 1911 photograph, Brigham Young's "White House," begun in 1849, has fallen into disrepair and the adobe bricks are visible. Young and his first wife, Mary Ann Angell, lived here after it was completed about 1854. It was demolished in 1922 and has been replaced by the Brigham Apartments at 119 East South Temple Street. Harry Shipler, photographer. Utah State Historical Society photograph 11794, used by permission.

The Salt Lake Theater was built of stone and adobe and measured 80 by 144 feet. Designed by architect William H. Folsom under the direction of Brigham Young, it stood on the northwest corner of State Street and 100 South from 1862 until it was demolished in 1928—over the heated objections of the Daughters of Utah Pioneers and many others. Photo by Andrew J. Russell, c. 1869. Utah State Historical Society, used by permission.

As Salt Lake City prospered in the late nineteenth century, the old adobe homes became objects of derision. They were called "unsightly piles," or "bed-bug infested," and the end of adobe construction was predicted with delight. Even the iconic Salt Lake Theater and Brigham Young's residence, the "White House," begun in 1849 on South Temple Street, were demolished during the 1920s. Not until many of the old landmarks were gone did residents express some regret at their loss.[61]

Yet for nearly thirty years after the railroad reached Salt Lake City, even though a wide variety of building materials was readily available, the advantages of building with adobe sometimes outweighed the drawbacks.

A steadily diminishing number of builders continued to produce, for themselves and others, these traditional homes until, without offering a reason, the Salt Lake City Council outlawed the use of adobe bricks "not faced with hard burned brick" in construction.[62]

Domestic Life

Few pioneers bore any resemblance to the pretty, smiling girls in clean pastel dresses, the stalwart men in white shirts and broad-brimmed hats, depicted in murals or riding on floats in Utah's annual Pioneer Day parades. Those clean and cheerful images somehow cheapen and diminish the sacrifices made by thousands of men and women who overcame great obstacles to reach and build their Zion. They were often tired and hungry, sometimes sick or injured, dirty and cold. Photographs of pioneers taken in the latter nineteenth century show faces that were lined by stress, hard work, and too much time in the weather. It may not have been the custom to smile for the photographer, but if they had had any pleasure in life, very little of it shows in their portraits.

Adobe homes were, for the most part, built by men, but they were the domain of women. Women spent their lives in and around their homes, caring for their many children, doing every chore imaginable, creating virtually everything, from cloth and clothing to rag rugs that were made of the tattered remnants, planting and tending big gardens and orchards, raising chickens, milking the cow (if they had one), and caring for the sick.[63] Men did the exhausting and often risky manual labor in fields, quarries, shops, and industries, walking wherever they needed to go if they had neither horse nor wagon.

Even if these ordinary people had the ability or the materials to record what mattered to them, there would hardly be time in the day. At first, paper was a rare commodity; tiny slips less than four inches square, some with one side already used, had to suffice even for important documents like deeds. Poor people, if they could write, would have no access to such luxury. What little was written by or about them, even after paper became common and cheap, was written well after the fact and through the filter of elapsed time.

Five years of research has yielded only a single account—rich in detail, names, places, and dates—that reveals its author as an intelligent, thinking, feeling, and outspoken person in spite of grinding poverty.

The writer was Elizabeth Fovargue Smith.[64] She came here with her husband James and his parents in 1853, when all of Great Salt Lake City was built of adobe. Her vivid account of the family's life—births and deaths of children, of her husband James, and her children's rise into the middle class—was written between 1884 and 1891 in an 1883 daybook, beginning with reminiscences of life in England and on the journey west. Her adobe home, built in 1855 at 727 West 400 North, is still standing.

Elizabeth Fovargue was born in 1828, one of several children of a farmer in the village of Doddington, Cambridgeshire, England. She went to school until she was thirteen (unusual for a girl at the time) and then worked as a domestic servant. When she heard about the LDS Church and listened to missionaries preach, she defied her father and was baptized. She married another convert, James Smith, in January 1853, and within a month departed with him and his parents for the United States. Elizabeth wrote of leaving her family, whom she never saw again, at the railroad station:

> Richard and Isaac and James went to the station with us. They gave me some small presents. Father gave me a sovereign. Poor little brother James did cry. He said, O Sister Bessy I shall never see you any more. I told him when he got an opportunity, to obey the Gospel and then he could come here. I felt very soryful at parting with my relations and couldn't help shedding a few tears. I thought James very unkind. He said what are you crying for? If you think more of your relations than you do of me and my relations, I will send you to them if you say so. I didn't feel any better for such talk as that. If my mind had not been set on coming to Zion I might have gone back but my religion was not so easy turned.

The four Smiths arrived in Great Salt Lake City on September 29, 1853, after a relatively uneventful trip across the Atlantic, up the Mississippi, and over the plains and Rocky Mountains. They seem to have arrived with nothing but some basic clothing, a few cooking utensils, and James's stonecutting tools.

Finding Adobe Buildings

What this study required was a comprehensive list of adobes in Salt

Margaret Sharp home, 509 East South Temple Street. The Sharp family organized their own wagon train and arrived in Salt Lake City in 1850. Margaret, the widow of Joseph Sharp, lived here between his brothers John and James. John was the first LDS bishop of the Twentieth Ward, and later, a director of the Union Pacific Railroad. After raising her children, Margaret studied medicine and became one of the first female doctors in the territory. The home was demolished in 1900. Utah State Historical Society photograph 8810, used by permission.

Lake City, but none existed. Fortunately there is a way to find them—the Sanborn Fire Insurance maps. Created for Salt Lake City on an irregular basis between 1884 and 1969, the Sanborn maps were made for many cities and towns in the United States. Their purpose was to show every building, shed, street, sewer, water line, and alley perfectly to scale—and sometimes, doors and windows, porches, and chimneys—so that insurance companies could rate the fire risk and determine the premium for insuring any structure. Each building was color-coded to show what it was made of—pink for brick, yellow for wood frame, blue for stone, gray for concrete, and, best of all, brown for adobe.

These elegant maps greatly simplified the task of finding a large number of the remaining adobe buildings in Salt Lake City. I created a database of addresses from the 1961 edition of the Sanborn maps, checked each address online with the County Assessor's office to see if it still existed, and finally, used Google Maps street view to decide which buildings would require an on-site visit. Eventually, I saw them all. At least, I think I did, because Sanborn's mapmakers occasionally mistook adobe for stone or some other material, or missed it altogether. Even now, after almost six years on this project, I occasionally spot another when it's being restored and the stucco, wood siding, or asbestos shingles have been removed.

My initial objective was simple: to create a comprehensive list of the remaining adobe buildings in Salt Lake City. Early on, it even seemed possible to extend my study to surrounding pioneer settlements like Holladay, Murray, and Bountiful, but that was before I'd found 192 just in Salt Lake City.

Finding the Builders

Adobe buildings are fascinating in themselves, but more so because they are a life-sized link to the owners and builders. Details like floor plans, fasteners and hardware, the positions of doors and windows, saw marks on the lumber, chimneys and stairs, even the position of the house on its lot, are clues to the tools and techniques used by nineteenth-century craftsmen. And what of their owners, few of whom even mentioned their home's location? What did they need and want from a home, and what sorts of lives did they have? Finding out became the focus of my study.

Every one of the 201 extant or recently demolished adobe buildings in Salt Lake City has a human story, but the challenge is to find it. Each has something to tell about family life, the westward migration, tradition, construction techniques, the LDS Church, trade and commerce on the frontier, or the influence of the railroad. Here the focus is on 91 homes, most with only two or three original rooms, selected because they offer a unique view into the connection between their builders and everyday nineteenth-century life in Salt Lake City. A few larger homes are included because they illustrate how even mud bricks could be used to satisfy the pioneers' desire for the fashion and gentility that were so highly valued. All the buildings are grouped by their position in the original nineteen wards, and the later Twentieth and Twenty-first wards, reflecting the way their builders would have associated, economically, socially and religiously, in the Mormons' city of Zion.

As a group, the builders of these individual houses literally built Salt Lake City. History may ignore them, but they were the ditch diggers, farm laborers, bricklayers, masons, loggers, road graders, and teamsters. They made shoes and boots, rag rugs, clothing, horseshoes, and baskets; they slaughtered animals, plowed fields, and harvested crops. Their children drove the livestock out to pasture and brought them home at night. Boys chopped firewood, and girls heated wash water over an open fire. Almost none of this was considered noteworthy unless someone was injured or killed in the process.

Family histories written by descendants are valuable, especially for the personal details that exist nowhere else. Some of them are remarkably candid, but too often they present only the most flattering view and omit the frailties common to us all. Public records can be mined for the hard facts.

Where records exist to document the lives of ordinary people, they may be difficult to find. Women's names are especially elusive, their essential but unpaid and repetitive tasks not considered noteworthy. A woman's newspaper obituary, her last chance at earthly recognition, typically just listed her children's names.

Men's lives were lived for the most part outside the home. Some might be chronicled in church records, a few in court or police records. Some were able to parlay an unusual skill or talent into an escape from anonymity. Their small businesses ran newspaper advertisements and listed the names of their partners. A few had the time and education to

Three generations pose for a photograph near their adobe and log house. As a family grew, an original log cabin might be enlarged with adobe rooms and, eventually, dwarfed or enveloped by wood-frame and brick construction. Date unknown. Photo courtesy Ronald L. Fox.

act as ward teachers or hold other church positions.

Most of the personal histories in this book have been pieced together from historic newspapers, property records, tax rolls, city directories, censuses, death and burial records, and well-documented online databases. A few include information from diaries or family histories held by the Daughters of Utah Pioneers Museum, the LDS Church History Library, or the Utah State Historical Society.

All Salt Lake County property records are held by the County Recorder. These document every purchase or sale of land, along with mortgages, liens, tax forfeitures, and more. In most cases, these documents provide a fairly clear picture of when a house was first built and later enlarged, or when a man's business expanded and he borrowed to finance this. City and county tax assessment rolls may confirm purchase and sale dates, especially if a property's value rose sharply coincident with, say, a new

446 East 700 South, date unknown. When Salt Lake City's Plat B was laid out in 1848, this lot was assigned to Horace Drake, a pioneer of 1847. Either he or the next owner, Charles Woodard, built the center room of this house before 1856 when it appeared on a map drawn by surveyor David H. Burr. Woodward sold the house to gunsmith Jacob Heusser in 1871. Part of the original room may still exist, enveloped by the existing brick house. Photo courtesy Ronald L. Fox.

mortgage. City directories can place a person's residence (before there were house numbers) at an approximate location, and at an exact address by 1884. Historic newspapers may also report real estate transfers or a family's move to a new home. The University of Utah's historic newspaper project has made over 1.3 million pages available online, where those revealing details that family historians forgot, or might prefer to omit, can be found.[65]

Census records are an unparalleled resource, commonly including people's occupations and the value of their property, tracking upward (and downward) economic mobility. Women were nearly always described as "at home," or "keeping house," but occasionally as "seamstress" or "domestic." But census enumerators commonly misspelled surnames, turning "Baddley" into "Manley" or Raleigh into "Ilriah." Sometimes an entire ward's census records must be searched online before a mangled name is recognizable from its context.

Death records indicated a person's residence, birthplace, and parents' names. The Church of Jesus Christ of Latter-day Saints and Brigham Young University maintain excellent websites with information on immigration data, family connections, and the travels of pioneers. The information found in sources like these is what makes history whole.

Small adobe houses can embody human stories of the darkest tragedy; others reveal astonishing courage, transcendent faith, and eventual triumph. When William Robinson's home on B Street was built in 1867, the city wall extended the length of Fourth Avenue, shading the family's lot. Robinson's son recalled seeing bears and Indians in City Creek, but never mentioned that his mother burned to death while being held at the city Insane Asylum in 1878. George Edward Anderson, the pioneer photographer, likewise wrote nothing about his childhood on Third Avenue, where his father beat his mother and threw their children out in the snow. Still, John Picknell, who lost most of his family between England and Utah, survived to build his home and a successful butcher shop at the top of First Avenue about 1866. Soren Peter Jensen, a handcart pioneer, and his wife, Matilda, built their tiny home on 500 East in a neighborhood of fellow Scandinavians about 1873, enlarging it when Soren found work on the new railroad.

When the original benches in the Salt Lake Tabernacle were removed and replaced during a seismic upgrade in 2006, the *New York Times* printed a story that included this:

> For Robert Charles Mitchell, a retired newspaper editor from Salt Lake City who lives in Logan, the fate of the pews and the [1919 First Security] bank tower hit the 'same vein.' 'It's an issue of values,' he said. 'We glorify our pioneers. We talk about their travails and bless their devilishly hard work. We laud them on the one hand and run roughshod over them on the other. We're dishing up ersatz history and throwing away the real thing.'[66]

This study attempts to present "the real thing."

Houses by Ward

First Ward

The First Ward was far from the center of the young city. Its two remaining adobe houses were both built in the 1880s, long after the pioneer homes that once dotted the area. Most early residents were farmers or tradesmen. A few, like Hugh Moon, were distillers at a time when drinking alcoholic beverages, in moderation, was quite acceptable for Mormons, and selling whiskey in the downtown saloons brought needed cash into the economy.[1]

852 South 700 East—August and Freidericke Arndt Dittman, 1888(?)

In 1898, there were only three other houses on this block, all of them wood frame. The narrow-gauge tracks of the defunct Salt Lake & Fort Douglas Railway, by then part of the Utah Central/Denver & Rio Grande Western, lay in the center of 700 East.[2]

August Dittman (1850–1926) was a German immigrant from Berlin who came to Utah about 1885, accompanied by his wife, Freidericke (1849–1912), and their large family. August, a carpenter, first appeared in the city directory in 1889; his son Adolph, also a carpenter, was living with the family in 1892.[3]

What made this property attractive to the Dittmans? It was not especially cheap for its size, perhaps because it already had some sort of dwelling on it. The present house seems to have been built as a hall-parlor type that faced south. A rear wing, now almost invisible, might be a remnant of a much earlier building that faced east, and subsequent alterations have given the whole structure an English-cottage look. If Dittman did build the house in 1888, a notice should have appeared in the *Salt Lake Tribune*'s January 1, 1889, issue, where the past year's construction projects were listed, but it did not. He did build a "barn and improvements" in 1890.[4]

Land records leave no doubt that Alexander Finley (Findlay) and William Wood received Lot 8, Block 4, Plat B as its "original occupants," meaning their names were drawn in an early land lottery. J(ames) Houston bought it from Findlay for $35 in 1856. His name appears on an early map of Plat B that dates to about the same time. By 1888 the block as a whole had passed through several hands, and August Dittman had paid $400 for this small portion of an original one-and-one-quarter-acre lot.[5]

August Dittman mortgaged the property several times before 1895, apparently getting new mortgages to pay off old ones, or perhaps investing in mining concerns. He lost the property in a tax sale in 1893 but regained it soon after.[6]

By 1896, Dittman had become "Pres[ident,] Harmon Mining & Milling Co." in Big Cottonwood Canyon. Another German immigrant, Otto Hanisch, was the company secretary. Hanisch later moved to Chicago, changed his name to Otoman Zar-Adusht Ha'nisht, and founded the short-lived religious movement known as Mazdaznan. August Dittman's son Adolph was the mining company treasurer but then took up a completely different line of work. He gave his occupation as "magician" in 1898. With his wife, he remained one of Hanisch's followers for years.[7]

The mining venture seems to have been less than successful. In 1899, August registered a brand at Butlerville (now Cottonwood Heights, about 2700 East and 7000 South) and presumably turned to raising livestock. The 1900 census placed August in Butlerville with Freidericke (Friedericka) and five children, working again as a carpenter, but by 1910 he was back in Salt Lake City, near the old house at 662 Ely Avenue (between 600 and 700 South, off 700 East).[8] The family apparently lived quietly, and little other information about them is available.

August died in 1926 of stomach cancer. Freidericke had died of a stroke in 1912. Both are buried in the nondenominational Mount Olivet Cemetery, indicating that they had left the LDS Church.[9]

1004 East 800 South—Thomas and Ann Sarah Dearns Johnson, 1883

Edmund Ellsworth was the first owner of the land where this adobe stands. A pioneer of 1847, he was married to Brigham Young's oldest child, Elizabeth. Ellsworth served a mission to England and became the captain of the first handcart company on his return in 1856. He built two houses (demolished) on this ten-acre block, one for Elizabeth and one for his fourth wife, Mary Ann Bates, and their children. In 1860 Edmund gave his occupation as "farmer" and was also cutting timber for the early settlement. The 1867 city directory lists "Ellsworth, H [*sic*], farmer, 1st wd., on the beach [bench] outside city wall, bet 8th and 9th S."[10] 1000 East Street did not yet exist.

Edmund moved to Weber County and in 1867 sold this entire ten-acre block to Francis Daniel Clift for $4,000. Clift was a non-Mormon merchant whose commercial empire came to include a hotel, stores and shops, mines, and other real estate. His widow financed the Clift Building which still stands at the corner of 300 South and Main Streets. Clift finalized his claim to this lot in 1873 with a land title certificate issued by Mayor Daniel Wells, and then sold it in 1878 to another real estate investor, George Goddard. Thomas Johnson (1832–1912), a farmer or laborer whose home was one block east, bought the lot where this house stands from George Goddard in 1884.[11]

The 1884 city directory lists a gardener named William D. Powell living at the southeast corner of 1000 East and 800 South.[12] Although the house may have been built somewhat before that, there is no record of a resident here in earlier city directories. Initially a hall-parlor type that faced north, the house has been modified by the addition of porches and a south wing but remains largely intact.

The Jordan and Salt Lake City Canal, completed in 1882, is just east of the house. It carried irrigation water in an open ditch from the north end of Utah Lake all the way to Temple Square. Today it is underground but still carries storm runoff, and high-tension power lines mark its path. Thomas Johnson sold a right-of-way on the west dike of the canal to Brigham Young's son John W. Young, who laid the narrow-gauge Salt Lake & Fort Douglas Railway tracks there in the late 1880s.[13] For about two years, the railroad hauled freight from the city to the fort and sandstone down from the quarries in Red Butte Canyon. The noise, smoke, and dust so close to the house must have been terrible.

By 1890 the railroad line was defunct, and someone had scavenged ties from the roadbed to hold up the cellar walls of an addition to the south side of this house.[14] William Powell was living elsewhere; Thomas Johnson, a laborer, and his large family had either built the house or moved in. Their arrival in Utah is undocumented, but their seven-year-old daughter, Maggie, was born here about 1873.[15] After Johnson's wife, Sarah (1838–1891), died, Thomas remained here until 1903. At his death in 1912, he was living in Idaho with one of his sons, but he was buried next to Sarah in the Salt Lake City Cemetery.[16]

Johnson sold the house to Albert C. Spears in 1905, probably after renting it to him for a year or so. Albert was a candy manufacturer from Indiana who evidently had larger ambitions. He joined the city police force and by 1910 had risen to the rank of sergeant, becoming the "best liked 'man on the desk'" before he died unexpectedly in 1914. His funeral was held in this house, attended by so many friends that groups of mourners spilled out into the garden and then boarded two special streetcars and a police automobile for the trip to the Salt Lake City Cemetery.[17]

Albert's widow, Annie, remained in the house. She married again in about 1920, to Nels Lindfors, a Swedish immigrant like herself, and when he died in 1934 she simply stayed put. Annie died in this house in 1952 and was buried beside Albert and some of their children in the Salt Lake City Cemetery.[18] In Annie's old age, her widowed daughter, Alberta Spears Reasoner, lived with her.

Second Ward

All of the eight remaining adobe houses in what was the Second Ward lie within a one-and-a-half-block radius. Most were built during the 1870s by Scandinavian immigrants. Their builders accurately represented the social makeup of the area at that time, when, like the First Ward, it was far from the city's center. Artesian wells like the one at 500 East and 800 South were common and probably were one of the most attractive features of the neighborhood.

For the most part, the homes began as simple vernacular structures just large enough to shelter a family and a few possessions. The oldest remaining homes, which may include remnants of early 1850s construction, and the newest, built about 1887, are almost unrecognizable as adobe buildings. None has escaped the remodeler's hand.

803 South 300 East—Joseph and Jane Ann Kipling Buckley, c. 1869

By the time Joseph Buckley (1846–1917) was seventeen, he was mining coal with his father in Lancashire, England. The family, including three younger siblings, sailed from Liverpool to New York City and came west with the W. S. Warren Company in 1864. Like others in the company, Joseph's father died, probably from dysentery, along the Sweetwater River in Wyoming. His mother, Ann, lived only eleven days after arriving in Salt Lake City.[1] Joseph was left to support his brother and sisters.

Jane Ann Kipling (1849–1925) was born in Yorkshire. She sailed from Liverpool to New York on the ship *Underwriter* in 1860, accompanying her widowed mother, Dorothea. The ship's roster identified the pair as "hand cart" passengers in "lower steerage." They reached Genoa,

Nebraska Territory, by June, where Dorothy (Dorothea), a "washerwoman," and Jane were recorded in the 1860 federal census. Within days, mother and daughter joined the Daniel Robison handcart company for the long haul to Salt Lake City, arriving in late August. (Another census enumerator recorded them a second time in August—almost certainly an error—living adjacent to a pimp and four harlots in Omaha.)[2] Jane's story, like Joseph's, explains some of the appeal of the LDS Church in the English Midlands: the poor and uneducated understood that a new faith in a new country might offer not only salvation but their only hope to escape a life of grinding poverty in rigidly stratified English society.

Joseph Buckley found work in a trade no less physically demanding than mining coal—he became an adobe maker at the city adobe yard. He and Jane Ann married in 1867. Jane's mother also found a husband, another English convert named Abraham Duffin, who owned this lot. Abraham was a factory worker who left his wife, Eliza, in England in 1859 and arrived late that year with the George Rowley handcart company.[3]

The Buckleys were living here at 800 South and 300 East by 1869. They had two children at the time of the 1870 census, and those were followed by eight more. Even in 1875, the house was at the far south edge of town.[4]

Although Buckley was living here by 1869, his father-in-law remained the owner until January 1875, when Joseph paid $300 for a large lot—six by ten rods. Later the Buckleys moved to 338 East 600 South, near

Jane's mother, and in 1889 they sold this property to Daniel Turngren for $3,000.[5]

The original adobe portion of the house faces west and was a simple hall-parlor type with gable-end chimneys. Its low roof and small size are a testament to the builder's limited means. A brick addition forms a cross wing on the north side. Buckley was assessed city taxes in the Second Ward beginning in 1872, and by 1877 was assessed on part of this lot.[6]

Abraham Duffin died in 1892. Dorothy was run over by a streetcar and died in 1895. Joseph Buckley died of cancer in 1917, just after his fiftieth wedding anniversary, and Jane lived until 1925.[7]

768 South 500 East—Soren Peter and Matilda Andreasen Jensen (or Hansen), c. 1875

One block east of the James Petersen home at 768 South 400 East is another adobe house, this one built by Soren Peter Jensen (1850–1925). The Jensen, Petersen, and Christensen families would have been well acquainted. All were from Denmark, and all reached Philadelphia on the *Westmoreland* in 1857. From there the pioneers went by train to Iowa City and bought the supplies and handcarts they would haul for the next thousand miles. The Perpetual Emigrating Fund had no money to loan that year, so the Jensens—Soren Peter, his parents Hans and Sidsie Marie, two brothers, and two sisters—had to pool their slim resources with some

EAST ELEVATION

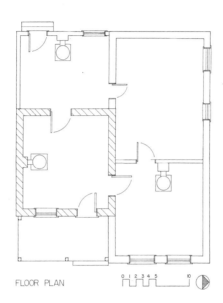

FLOOR PLAN

0 1 2 3 4 5   10

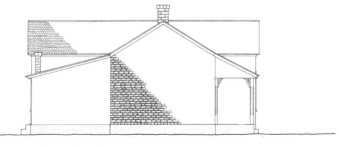

SOUTH ELEVATION

768 South 500 East. Architectural drawings by the author and James Gosney. Used by permission, Western Regional Architecture Program Collection, J. Willard Marriott Library, University of Utah, all rights reserved.

325 other members of the Christian Christiansen Handcart Company. Along with a blind woman and a girl with a wooden leg, the company was able to buy only sixty-eight handcarts, three wagons, ten mules, and a cow (which soon died). Sophia, the baby of the Jensen family, died in Nebraska and was buried with a sieve to cover her face. Even the soldiers in Johnston's Army, heading west to quell the "Mormon Rebellion," took pity on the starving immigrants and offered them a lame ox to slaughter.[8]

Matilda Andreasen (1856–1935) came with her widowed mother from Flensburg, Schleswig-Holstein, in 1865, perhaps to escape ongoing military conflict in the region. She was nine when they crossed the plains with the Miner G. Atwood Company. She and Soren Peter married in 1873 and bought this lot, then one and a quarter acres, from Frederick Dungard. Soren Peter and Matilda ultimately had thirteen children, three of whom died in childhood. Matilda sang in the Second Ward choir, and in the Tabernacle Choir while George Careless (see 323 East Second Avenue in the Twentieth Ward) was the director (1869–1880).[9]

The 1879 city directory shows that the Jensens lived on this block, and almost certainly in this house. Soren Peter found work with the Utah Central Railroad as a section hand, and by 1889 he had been promoted to foreman.[10]

In 1890, the family moved to the Big Cottonwood area where Soren Peter took up farming. Sometime before 1910, they moved to a brick house at 460 East 800 South, adjacent to Stephen Tucker's adobe home at 450 East (below), where they lived for the rest of their lives.[11]

The earliest part of this house may have been a single-cell or hall-parlor type that faced east. A large adobe cross-wing, which would have been quite stylish in the 1880s, was added to the north side of the house before 1898, reflecting the family's growing size and prosperity. Its veneer of soft orange brick is probably original. By 1911, the west room of the original house had been demolished and replaced with newer brick.[12]

804 South 600 East—John Alexander and Georgianna Thompson Cuthbert, and Eleanor Jane Blair, c. 1870

In 1870, this house stood alone on the block bounded by 800 and 900 South, 500 and 600 East, north of what was then a large farm owned

by Brigham Young and Isaac Chase. That farm is now Liberty Park, and the 1853 Chase adobe home is near its center.

The block's original occupants were the brothers Archibald, Robert, and William Gardner. All were Scots who reached Salt Lake City with the Edward Hunter–Joseph Horne Company in 1847 with their large extended family. The Gardners did not stay long, Robert and Archie moving on to build grist and lumber mills on Mill Creek and in West Jordan. The block then reverted to Brigham Young as trustee-in-trust for the LDS Church in 1855. Young bought it as his personal property in 1859 and sold it to John Cuthbert in 1869 for $1,000.[13]

John Cuthbert (1847–1908) was born at Winter Quarters, Nebraska, in 1847. His parents, Edward and Margaret, and two young brothers traveled to Utah in the Willard Richards Company in 1848.[14]

The Cuthbert family, at least in later years, seems not to have been a happy one. John's father, Edward, was fined for drunkenly striking another man with a saber. Margaret was in the process of divorcing Edward, citing his "intemperate habits," when he died in 1868. John's brother William committed suicide, and his brother Joseph had his ear bitten off in a street fight.[15]

In spite of the turmoil, John Cuthbert appears to have lived an ordinary life. When he married Georgianna Thompson in January 1869, he built this simple hall-parlor house, which was later modified by the addition of a rear lean-to or shed extension and a full-width porch, as their home. The entire surrounding block of twenty acres was their farm. (Both house

EAST ELEVATION

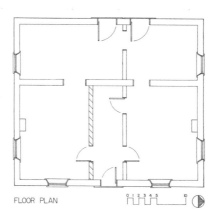

FLOOR PLAN

NORTH ELEVATION

804 South 600 East, John Alexander and Georgianna Thompson Cuthbert. Architectural drawings by Thomas Carter and students, and James Gosney. Used by permission, Western Regional Architecture Program Collection, J. Willard Marriott Library, University of Utah, all rights reserved.

and farm appear on a detailed 1875 map of Salt Lake City.) The Cuthberts had three sons, and a daughter who died at birth, before Georgianna died in 1875. Their youngest son, Edward, died in 1876. John married again in 1877 to Eleanor Jane Blair, and fathered five more children.[16]

In 1881, John Cuthbert sold the block to Samuel H. B. Smith for $3,300 and moved to Idaho, where he died in 1908 and was buried in the Pioneer Cemetery in Rigby. Smith in turn sold the block to Louis R. Erich for $12,000 in 1887, and it became Erich's Park Avenue Subdivision.[17] Now surrounded by later houses, apartments, and a small brick store, the farmhouse remains after almost 150 years. Park Avenue (now Park Street) is a continuation of the tree-lined promenade that runs north out of Liberty Park.

450 East 800 South—Stephen and Eliza Ann Mercer Tucker, c. 1867

The original owner of this lot was George Washington Hill, an interpreter and missionary to Native American tribes (see 270 West Reed Avenue, Nineteenth Ward). Hill seems not to have lived here, and sold the land to Lucian Nobles in 1850. A stone foundation east of the present house may have been the remains of early building efforts, but it no longer exists.

Stephen Tucker bought the west half of the lot in 1871 and received the Mayor's Deed in 1873.[18]

Stephen Tucker (1831–1901) came from England, traveling overland to Utah with the Ansil Harmon company in 1862 and a loan from the Perpetual Emigrating Fund Company. With him were his wife, Eliza Ann Mercer (1830–1918), their son, Henry, and a baby daughter who died on the trail. The Tuckers were living on this block in 1867.[19]

What was once an east-facing hall-parlor house, with a full-length porch and added shed, has undergone many alterations and additions. Much of the house has been faced with brick. An English cottage–style entry now faces 800 South, and the original east entry door has been made into a window.

Over the years, Stephen Tucker variously gave his occupation as laborer, farmer, gardener, and section hand on the Utah Central Railroad, indicating an improvement in his economic status. He had been repairing the front steps when his wife called him to dinner, but he collapsed and died as he entered the house. Eliza lived on here until 1917 and died in Murray in 1918.[20]

Right: The Chase Mill was built in 1852 and is still standing in the northeast corner of Liberty Park. Liberty Park was the Brigham Young/Isaac Chase farm until the city bought it in 1881. Water from Red Butte and Emigration Creeks turned the machinery to grind wheat. Utah State Historical Society photograph 5914, used by permission.

Third and Fourth Wards

No adobe buildings remain in the original Third and Fourth Wards. Never a fashionable address, in 1869 it was home to laborers, small farmers, craftsmen, and at least one matchmaker.[1] The area has become part of Salt Lake City's commercial district.

Fifth Ward

In the 1870s, railroad tracks began to cut the original Fifth Ward into pieces. Tracks ran down the center of 400 West, and between 600 and 700 West. What had been a neighborhood of laborers' and tradesmen's adobe homes rapidly industrialized to serve transportation-related needs. Today it is a landscape of warehouses and empty lots, and only a single adobe house (now a woodworking shop) remains.

455 West 700 South—Thomas and Ann Bennett Fitt; William and Anne Hansen Fitt, c. 1882

Thomas Fitt (1828–1890) was an English brick maker from Buxton, Norfolk. His wife, Ann Bennett, came from Yorkshire, where all of their eight children were born.[1] Their son William came ahead of the family,

NORTH ELEVATION

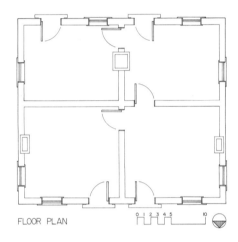

FLOOR PLAN

WEST ELEVATION

455 West 700 South, Thomas and Ann Bennett Fitt, William and Ann Hansen Fitt. Architectural drawings by Thomas Carter and students, and James Gosney. Used by permission, Western Regional Architecture Program Collection, J. Willard Marriott Library, University of Utah, all rights reserved.

reaching Utah in 1871. The others arrived in the United States in 1873, sailing from Liverpool to New York on the ship *Nevada* with hundreds of other Mormon converts.[2] All likely rode the newly completed transcontinental railroad to Utah, avoiding the tedious and dangerous journey that wagon trains and handcart companies once made.

The city directories for 1869 and 1874 show a Samuel J. Brown in approximately this location.[3] In 1880, Brown sold part of the current property to Edward Doman for $50. Doman, an English pioneer of 1868, never lived on the property, although he did mortgage it twice, along with an adjacent lot, before selling it to James W. Thomas in 1882. The purchase price, $130, suggests it was an empty lot at the time. Salt Lake County tax records and the city directory for 1874 show that the Doman family lived on Lot 7, at the west end of the block.[4]

Thomas Fitt bought the west two rods of this parcel in 1882 for $140; his son William bought the east seven rods of the adjacent lot soon after and sold a one-rod-wide parcel to Thomas, creating the current lot, which measures about 50 by 165 feet.[5] Thomas and William probably built this house soon after, perhaps making the bricks themselves or trading for them with their labor, because there is no indication of a mortgage.

The house is a duplex or double-cell type; the rear lean-to was an integral part of the house, probably used as a shop and still used as one today. One of the two original front doors has been made into a window. The relatively large windows have brick detailing on the exterior sills, and the window openings widen toward the interior to admit maximum light. Protruding window frames on the west side of the house suggest that, as on the north side, the protective stucco has disappeared and the weathered adobe can be seen. Interior chimney fittings show that the rooms were heated by stoves rather than fireplaces.

City directories and county tax records are not especially helpful in identifying the residents of this house after it was built. In 1884, William Fitt was living here; his father and brothers lived in the next block west on the north side of the street. Olson Harper, an adobe maker, lived at 464 West 700 South, just across the street. The LDS Fifth Ward Meetinghouse, also an adobe building, was on the southwest corner of 700 South and 400 West.

Very little is known about the Fitt family. Thomas was admitted to citizenship by the Third District Court in 1879. Only brief funeral notices were printed in the *Deseret News* for Thomas and Ann; they are buried together in the Salt Lake City Cemetery. Thomas apparently had a second wife, Elizabeth Farnsworth, who married him in 1888, and she too died before he did. William, a mason, and his family moved on to Sanpete County and eventually to Carbon County, where he died in 1920.[6]

Sixth Ward

Like the Fifth Ward, the Sixth Ward was disrupted early in its history by railroad tracks, and more recently by the mass and noise of Interstates 15 and 80. Salt Lake City's earliest settlement, the adobe fort at what is now Pioneer Park, was at the northeast corner of the Fifth Ward. A few blocks northwest of the fort was the adobe yard where, for decades, earth from the floodplain of Parley's Creek was excavated, molded, and air-dried to make adobe bricks. The one remaining adobe house in the Sixth Ward may have been home to a family or families of adobe makers.

877 West 300 South—builder unknown, before 1884

The ramps, sound barriers, and traffic lanes of interstate highways now hover above the block between 300 and 400 South and 800 and 900 West. Railroad tracks and the Rio Grande Depot extend another four blocks east. This was once the western edge of Salt Lake City, a low and wet area that had to be drained by canals and conduits to make it habitable. Mayor Jesse C. Little owned much of the block after 1860, and in 1881 it became [John W.] Pitt's Subdivision, but this lot at 877 West 300 South had no individual owner until 1887.[1]

This simple hall-parlor type house looks as though it were built in the 1870s or even earlier. It might have been home to an adobe maker who worked at the city adobe yard. The low roof pitch suggests either an early construction date or a builder with few resources and simple needs. The rear lean-to is a brick addition to the original two rooms.

Robert (1830–1891) and Mary Smith Lamont (1831–1904) were Scottish LDS converts who emigrated in 1881. They sailed from Liverpool to New York on the *Wyoming* and then probably traveled by train the rest of the way.[2]

In 1884, Robert was a coaler at the Utah Central Railroad depot and lived on 300 South, west of 700 West, probably in this house, although he did not buy it until 1887.[3] He and Mary may have been renting the house or another nearby. House numbers had not yet been assigned in what was then a farming or stock-raising area.

The Lamonts' property taxes were reduced in September 1891 due to Robert's infirmity, but the action had no effect until well after his death in May. Mary stayed on in the house through about 1893 and then moved to Nephi to live with her daughter and son-in-law, where she died in 1904.[4]

Seventh Ward

The Seventh Ward was a sought-after location in the earliest days of Salt Lake City. On level ground and not far from the Temple Block, residents had easy access to the center of town. After the pioneer period, the area remained a desirable address undisturbed by the railroad tracks. Only one adobe house remains, and it is of great architectural and historical importance.

442 South 200 West—John "Bookbinder" and Helena Quirk Kelly, by 1865

The John B. Kelly house, now vacant, overgrown, and dilapidated, is the last remaining adobe building in the original Seventh Ward. One of only two temple-form adobe houses in Salt Lake City today, its central one-and-a-half-story section is flanked by single-story side wings. Its exact construction date is uncertain, but it seems to be represented on an 1870 map. Tax rolls show that John Kelly was living in the Seventh Ward by 1860, and by 1872 his property was valued at $1,800, a substantial sum for the time.[1]

John Kelly, or Kelley (1824–1883), and his first wife, Helena Quirk (1827–1877), were born on the Isle of Man in the Irish Sea west of England. John converted to the LDS faith in 1841, and the couple married in 1844. Their first three children were born and died on the Isle of Man. John and Helena, with their surviving sons, George and Albert, sailed from Liverpool to New Orleans in 1853 on the *Camilla*. By October the family of four had reached Utah with the John Brown Company.[2]

Census enumerators found the Kellys in the Seventh Ward in 1860, perhaps in this house. Their family included four children (of twelve, only eight survived to adulthood) and John was working as a bookbinder, which became his nickname.[3] Kelly was a man of varied talents and interests. He acted in plays at the Salt Lake Theater and grew excellent pears in his yard.[4]

In 1866, John Kelly was married to a second wife, Emma Eliza (or Elizabeth) Sims (1831–1899). Her own house was just south of this one. Emma was an English immigrant also trained as a bookbinder. She worked at the *Deseret News*, probably where she met John Kelly. Emma and John had a son, John Sims Kelly, who lived only a year, and a daughter, Lillie.[5]

When Helena Kelly died of dropsy in 1877, Emma and Lillie moved into this house with John and his other children.[6] John B. Kelly died of cholera in 1883; his oldest son, Albert, built the large brick house that is still standing next door at 418 South 200 West in 1884.[7] Emma Kelly lived in this house until her death in 1899, and it has been owned by Lillie Kelly and other descendants ever since. Alterations to divide the original home into apartments, and even the addition of second-story rooms and staircases, did not seriously impair its exterior architectural integrity, but time, neglect, and the elements certainly will.

Right: Independence Hall, 27 West 300 South, was built in 1865 with donations from Congregationalists all over the West and as far away as New York City. It was the first non-LDS house of worship in Salt Lake City and was used by other denominations as well. By 1898, other churches had been established in the city and the old hall was transformed into a Dancing Academy and demolished in 1902. Utah State Historical Society photograph 05067, used by permission.

May 1st 1881

Eighth Ward

No adobe buildings remain in the Eighth Ward, now part of the commercial center of downtown Salt Lake City.

Ninth Ward

By 1860, Ninth Ward residents were primarily skilled tradesmen, among them many blacksmiths, shoemakers, and woodworkers of all kinds, as well as farmers and laborers, who probably worked in the Big Field, an area of small farms a few blocks to the south.

446 East 500 South—Carlos N. and Celestia Pendleton Gillett, c. 1867

Carlos Newton Gillett (1842–1880) was twelve years old when he came with his family from New York State to the Salt Lake Valley in 1854. His father, Horace, reportedly died of cholera on the journey, yet in 1860 the census enumerator reported that Horace Gillett was living with his wife, Sarah, and their children in the Ninth Ward. This may have been an error or perhaps a deliberate deception. "Gillett Mrs." had been the taxpayer there since at least 1856.[1]

In 1863 Carlos married Celestia Ann Pendleton (1843–1923), the daughter of Benjamin Franklin Pendleton. The Pendleton family were blacksmiths who owned and occupied much of the block where this house and one other adobe (at 407 East 600 South) still remain. Benjamin purchased this lot from Charles Smith, the original occupant, in 1867 and probably built the house for his daughter. It appears on a map published in 1870.[2]

Although later modifications have given the house an English cottage look, interior details provide a much different story. The original house was a hall-parlor type, two rooms separated by a wall which here has been replaced by an arch. Fireplaces in each room provided heat. After the initial period of settlement, cast-iron stoves were available if owners could afford to buy them, so the fireplaces suggest that this house was built quite early, before the railroad reached Salt Lake City. A floor beam visible in the cellar shows the marks of having been shaped and joined with hand tools and square nails. The rear porch was added prior to 1898, and the front windows have been enlarged.[3]

Carlos Gillett's name appeared in the 1867 Salt Lake City directory when he lived on the south side of 500 South between 400 and 500 East. It was Celestia, not Carlos, who received a Mayor's Deed for the lot, which was valued at $1,000 for tax purposes in 1872. The couple had six children, two of whom died as infants.[4]

Late in April 1880, Carlos had some business concerning land in Weber County. He had stayed the night at his mother's house, where he appeared agitated about someone trying to take the land from him, and then left to buy a pair of boots. His body was found in the Mill Creek area of Salt Lake County, where he was assumed to have committed suicide. The *Deseret News* reported that he killed himself in "a fit of derangement." Celestia lived in this house and then relocated to Fremont County, Idaho, where she joined two of her sons. She died there in 1923.[5]

541 South 300 East—Peter Hutz and Mary Jaquette Davis Reinsimar, c. 1867

The LDS Church has a long history in Philadelphia. Joseph Smith organized a branch there in 1839 and in 1840 spoke to a crowd of thousands at the First Independent Church of Christ.

Like the Pendletons, and other Ninth Ward men, Peter Reinsimar was a blacksmith. Born in Philadelphia, he attended the First Independent Church but formally withdrew from its membership in 1851—the word "Mormon" appears in membership records on the line after his name.[6]

Peter and Mary Reinsimars's journey to Utah is undocumented, but they must have arrived in 1859, because Peter's name appeared in the 1856 Philadelphia directory, and he addressed a group of Latter-day Saints there in August 1858. It would have been too late that year to join a wagon company bound for Utah Territory. Also, the Reinsimars had three children: Sarah, born about 1849, John, and Emmanuelle (Emma). John was born in Philadelphia in 1857; Emma was born in Utah about 1861. These dates, and the family's appearance in the Utah territorial census taken in July 1860, bracket their arrival date.[7]

Unlike the Pendletons, who remained in the LDS Church, Peter Reinsimar joined the Reorganized Church of Jesus Christ of Latter Day Saints (Josephites or RLDS, now the Community of Christ) sometime after his arrival in Salt Lake City. Josephites believe that Joseph Smith III and not Brigham Young was the true successor to church founder Joseph Smith Jr. Leaving the LDS Church would have put the Reinsimars outside mainstream Mormon society.

Peter paid $350 for half of a large lot on this block in 1866, which suggests there might have been some sort of house on it at the time. The family moved here from the Fifteenth Ward after information was gathered for the 1867 Salt Lake City directory, but before the city property taxes were calculated for the year. He paid taxes in the Ninth Ward at the end of 1867, and had a vehicle, livestock, and a watch or clock. Peter was working as a blacksmith at Sutton and Reinsimer [*sic*], where it seems his fortunes had improved dramatically. By 1870, he and Mary had a net worth of $1,250.[8]

The house is divided into apartments now, but the exterior is probably little changed from its original appearance. The rear lean-to appears to be a frame addition that transformed a central-passage house into a saltbox.[9] There are remnants of what may be original cornices beneath the eaves.

The Reinsimars must have been prominent members of the Josephite movement. Joseph Smith III stayed with the family during his visit to Salt Lake City in 1876. The *History of the Reorganized Church* mentions Brother Reinsimar several times in that context.[10]

Beyond that one event (and periodic appearances in census records and city directories), Peter Reinsimar escaped all public notice. By 1880 he was "at home" and had not worked for a year due to "nervous debility." The house remained in the Reinsimar family until 1884, when Peter's name last appeared in the city directory and tax records.[11]

Mary Reinsimar, along with most of Salt Lake City's prominent families, attended the wedding of her son John to Mayor Feramorz Little's daughter Nettie in 1885, but Peter was not on the guest list. Peter's death date and burial place are unknown, although he was reported to have died by April 1888.[12]

Mary died in October 1894 and is buried in Mount Olivet Cemetery, as was customary for non-Mormons.[13] Her gravestone, showing an incorrect death date of 1895, must have been placed sometime after her death.

Tenth Ward

The original Tenth Ward was settled by independent sorts like David Pettegrew, a veteran of the Mormon Battalion, who were untroubled by its steep slopes and its remoteness from the center of town. Several distillers, along with skilled tradesmen such as cabinet and clock makers, appeared in the 1860 census returns as well.

974 East 300 South—George and Eliza Parker Baddley, c. 1856 and 1871

George Baddley (1825–1875) and Eliza Parker (1821–1888) were born at Wolstanton, Staffordshire, England, where George worked in the well-known porcelain factories and Eliza was a china painter. They arrived in Utah in 1851 with their daughters Annie and Elizabeth. A third child, Maria, was born on the journey and died in 1853. The Baddleys very soon settled in the Tenth Ward at what became the corner of 300 South and 1000 East, where George farmed and raised grapes, made wine, and distilled whiskey. The couple eventually had nine children, all girls, two of whom died in childhood. John Alger, the other original owner of the lot, seems never to have lived here, and only Baddley's name appears on an early copy of Plat B.[1]

The oldest part of the existing house is the one-story south wing, a vernacular hall-parlor type which may have been built as early as 1856. Tax records for that year show that the family had livestock, a vehicle, and a clock or watch. Adobe bricks are still visible in the interior walls.[2]

George Baddley married Charlotte DeGrey (1842–1904) as a plural wife in 1861 when he was thirty-six and she was nineteen. They promptly moved to the LDS Church's Muddy Mission at St. George, leaving Eliza behind and pregnant with her last child. Within three years, the hard work and the hot desert climate had affected George's health. He and Charlotte returned to Salt Lake City in 1864 and built the adobe and brick two-story north wing of the house about 1871. Another Baddley residence was built somewhere on the north side of 300 South.[3]

By 1870, George and Eliza were living at this location with their five daughters. Charlotte lived with her four children, either in the south wing of this house or in another adobe that became 346 South 1000 East (demolished).[4]

Family stories describe George Baddley as a quick-tempered man who punished his children harshly, although that was likely true of many men at the time. He contracted tuberculosis, then called consumption, and died at age fifty in 1875. His obituary noted that at his death, "he was but little more than a live skeleton." Charlotte died at 346 South 1000 East, which was deeded to her after George's death.[5]

318 South 1000 East—Ephraim J. and Martha Baddley Swaner, c. 1880

The first part of this house was built perhaps a year or two after George and Eliza Baddley's daughter Martha (1857–1922) married Ephraim J. Swaner (1856–1907) in 1879.[6]

Ephraim was born in Salt Lake City a year after his parents, Jorgen and Julia Ann, arrived from Denmark in 1855.[7] Until about 1882, Ephraim, who was a well-known jeweler, and Martha, with their baby Ada, lived with Martha's mother Eliza in the Baddley household. When Eliza died in 1888, this became Martha's property. The Swaners raised seven children to adulthood here and lost at least one son to diphtheria.[8]

The south wing of the house was built first, its stone construction now obscured by a coat of stucco. The stone quoins made it a stylish house for the time. The newer north wing is adobe. But here the 1936 tax assessment cards disagree. These records identify the south wing as adobe and the north wing as brick. Photos show that there was once much more Victorian ornamentation, including Tuscan porch columns. Much of that was removed during a 1990 renovation, but the decorative barge boards remain.[9]

435 and 443 South 900 East—Pauli Edmund Balthazar, Julia Funk, and Mette Marie Nielsen Hammer, c. 1869

Remodeling, additions and renovations have given these two houses the appearance of mirror-image English cottages, but beneath their facades

they are simple adobe houses. The oldest accurate map shows that 435 South was perhaps a hall-parlor type with a porch on the west side, while 443 South was perhaps a double-cell type with its porch on the south side. Both houses seem to be shown on an 1875 map.[10]

When they were new, they belonged to Pauli (Paul) E. B. Hammer (1839–1929), who lived there with his first two wives, Julia and Mette Marie (Mary). Hammer, the son of a Danish goldsmith, was educated in the arts, music, and languages.[11] Converted to the LDS faith in 1860, Paul arrived in Salt Lake City in 1861 with an unidentified company.[12] He married Julia Funk in 1864 and Mette Marie (Mary) Nielsen in 1868. All are listed in a single household in the 1870 census. Mary died in June 1880 while Paul was in Europe on a church mission; four of her seven children died as infants and are buried in unmarked graves somewhere in the Salt Lake City Cemetery.[13]

When Paul returned from Europe in 1881, he either brought with him or was soon followed by a third wife, Anna Pauline Seliger. She may be the woman referred to by John Henry Smith, who wrote in October 1883 that "Elder J. Q. Cannon . . . says Paul Hammer was guilty of grave indiscretions when on a mission some years ago taking another mans wife home with him." Hammer returned to Europe on a second mission in 1883 and was back in Salt Lake City by 1884.[14] He married again, to Mary Marie Haney (Hanni) in 1885 and to Henriette Emilie Jeppesen in 1886.

Prosecutions for unlawful cohabitation or polygamy had begun under the Morrill Act in the late 1870s, so it was in the best interests of polygamous men to avoid drawing attention to their multiple wives. Paul Hammer sold both houses in 1874, and subsequently lived elsewhere with only one wife at a time.[15] If his other wives were in Utah, the census enumerators did not find them, and they are absent from directories and gazetteers. Such deception must have been terribly disruptive for the women and their children. Unlike many polygamists, Paul Hammer did not go to Mexico to avoid prosecution, and in 1890 he was arrested, tried, and fined $300. Hammer must have renounced Julia and Anna and was married only to Henriette when he died. Anna remarried, and Julia was living in San Francisco when she died in 1916.[16]

Hammer made his living painting portraits, chapel interiors, and theater scenery. He owned considerable real estate and traveled widely. Outliving three of his five wives, he died in 1929 at the age of ninety. All his wives, even Anna, are buried with him in the same plot at the Salt Lake City Cemetery.[17]

1010 East Linden Avenue—Christian Jorgenson and Emma Louise Burnett Swaner, c. 1867

When it was new, the adobe rooms of this hall-parlor house faced west toward 1000 East across a wide lot. At the time, there were only a few scattered homes here where the ground rises toward the foothills. The 1936 tax assessor's photograph clearly shows that the west wall is stuccoed adobe, although the gable ends are brick, perhaps sheathing that was applied to the original house. Today's entry faces Linden Avenue, and the house has had several addresses, including one on "Floral Lane" at a time when today's Linden Avenue led to a cluster of greenhouses.

East of 900 East, the gentle eastern slope of the Salt Lake Valley steepens abruptly. Cars and TRAX trains now climb readily toward 1300 East on a carefully engineered S-curve, but before the streets were graded and the contours of the land smoothed for modern buildings and easy travel,

this area was cut by gullies and was, in places, "impassable for teams." The Salt Lake & Fort Douglas Railway was built in the 1880s about 400 feet east of this house, crawling northeastward up a grade that only the most powerful Shay locomotives could master. By 1898 the railway was defunct.[18]

Christian (Charles) Jorgensen Swaner (1844–1881), with his parents and siblings, arrived in Utah from Denmark in 1855. His younger brother Ephraim was born the next year (see 318 South 1000 East, Tenth Ward). Christian married Emma Louise Burnett (1844–1913) in 1868. As a young girl, Emma came west from New York City with her family. Christian was a carpenter; his son Fred became an architect and builder in Ogden. After Christian died, Emma lived on in this house until her death.[19]

Kate Carter wrote that "Swaner's Gardens was the first outdoor playground in the 10th Ward." She could only have meant Fuller's Hill Pleasure Gardens, which opened in 1875, one block south of this house. In the 1870s and 1880s, when this was the very edge of Salt Lake City, William Fuller and his wife, Elizabeth, operated games, giant swings, slides, and other rides. Homemade ice cream and cakes were for sale and Fourth of July celebrations were advertised for weeks in advance. The Salt Lake City Brewing Company was directly south, on 1000 East. Only its bottling plant remains.[20]

Eleventh Ward

North of the Tenth Ward and also on sloping ground, the eastern reaches of the Eleventh Ward were occupied gradually as flat land became unavailable. South Temple Street, from the early days of settlement a desirable place to live, formed the northern boundary. Most of the ward's 60 households in 1860 were headed by tradesmen and laborers whose property was worth a few hundred dollars at most. The same occupations were common in 1870, when the number of households had risen to 149.[1]

844 East 100 South—Francis (Frank) and Charlotte Kjelling Sproul, c. 1872

The Sproul family—Francis Sr., his wife, Robenia, and seven children ranging in age from six to twenty-four, arrived in Salt Lake City from

Paisley, Scotland, crossing the plains with the Jesse Murphy Company in 1860. Francis Sr., a weaver, had borrowed from the Perpetual Emigrating Fund to make the journey and was living on this block in 1869. Young Francis, or Frank, enlisted in the militia during the Blackhawk War, marching to Moroni and serving one hundred days in 1866. He married Charlotte Kjelling, a Swedish immigrant, in 1874, and they raised four children here.[2]

The house is a vernacular hall-parlor type with one remaining gable-end chimney. The front porch, with its gable, is a later addition, but the cornices and cornice returns are typical of late nineteenth-century Utah architecture, and the first-floor windows retain their original size and shape. In spite of brick additions at the rear, the original structure is one of the least-altered adobe homes in Salt Lake City.

Frank Sproul bought this parcel, the west half of a ten-by-twenty-rod lot, in 1872 for $100 and received the Mayor's Deed for it the same year. None of the Sproul family was counted in the 1870 census, so Frank may have built this house somewhat later, probably soon after buying the land. He sold the east half to his mother, Robenia, in 1875, apparently building the larger adobe house (demolished) at 848 East and moving his family there. Henry Tuckett, Frank's brother-in-law, bought this house for $2,000 in 1886. His candy company factory, a large brick, wood frame, and metal-sided building, is shown as the "W. R. Servis Candy Fac." behind 848 East 100 South on the 1898 Sanborn Map.[3]

A teamster or express driver most of his life, when he and Charlotte moved to 1341 South State Street about 1893, Frank worked as a milk dealer.[4]

Frank may have been visiting his sister here at the old home in 1918 when he stepped in front of a streetcar to avoid an automobile and was killed. He was "known to have been almost totally deaf" and probably could not hear either vehicle.[5] Decades later, Frank's widow, Charlotte, died in an ambulance accident on her way to the hospital after breaking her hip.[6]

655 East 200 South—Jeremiah and Almira C. Beattie, c. 1880

Nicholas Rumel (1823–1904) probably built the first adobe house on this lot in the 1860s. The house may have been a hall-parlor type that faced

200 South, as seen on an 1870 map. Rumel was born in Philadelphia and may have traveled west with his brother John and their extended family in 1849. He stayed only briefly in Salt Lake City, returning to Omaha, Nebraska, by 1870, where he was a member of the Reorganized Church of Jesus Christ of Latter Day Saints.[7]

Rumel sold the property to Claude Clive, his wife, Mary Ann, and his sister, Charlotte, English immigrants of 1852 who paid $1,000 in 1871. Mary Ann and Charlotte received the Mayor's Deed in 1873. Claude, a tailor who made costumes for the Salt Lake Theater, was living in the original house by 1874 at the latest, but sold the property in 1877 and died in 1879.[8]

Almira C. Beattie (1843–1935), the wife of physician Jeremiah Beattie (1839–1913), bought the house, on what was then a larger lot, in 1880.[9] Rather than demolish the earlier house, the Beatties built the existing one-and-a-half-story, temple-form house as an addition. A faint outline on its west side shows where the two were joined.

Dr. Beattie could afford to have a stylish home, but still he had this one built of adobe and faced only the front wall with brick. It is one of two temple-form adobe homes still standing in Salt Lake City, examples of an architectural type that was already going out of style. Italianate stylistic elements in the window trim, bay window, and front porch update a traditional house form that had been common in the eastern United States in the mid-nineteenth century.

The Beattie family were well-to-do and socially prominent, appearing often in newspaper society pages, even vacationing in Hawaii in 1910. Perhaps in keeping with their status, the old wing of the house was demolished about 1893. That made room for a large, brick, two-story house at 653 East 200 South, where Dr. Beattie died in 1913. Almira lived there until 1930 when she joined her daughter Nellie in Chicago.[10] The fine brick house has been demolished, but the humbler adobe remains. Jeremiah and Almira Beattie, non-Mormons, are buried in Mount Olivet Cemetery.[11]

721 East 300 South—John Robert and Hannah Lark Bensley Oswald, c. 1874

John Henry Rumel, whose brother Nicholas built the earliest house at 655 East 200 South (above), was the original occupant of this lot, along with surrounding properties. After several changes of ownership, Brigham Young received the Mayor's Deed in 1873 as trustee-in-trust for the LDS Church. Richard Wright bought the south end of the 165-by-330-foot lot for $100 in 1874, and his widow sold this parcel to John Oswald for $125 the same year.[12] The original house was a hall-parlor type whose east gable end is still clearly visible in spite of several additions, including a curving exterior stairway to a second floor porch.

John Oswald was a farmer and later an iron moulder who had other property on 300 South before he bought this lot. City directories show that he lived between 700 and 800 East as early as 1874.[13] He was living at this address in 1884. The Oswalds came from England with five children and crossed the plains with the Daniel D. McArthur Company in 1868 (not with McArthur's Handcart Company in 1856, as his obituary states.) John and Hannah's youngest child, one-year-old Charlotte, died on the trail in Wyoming. Still, the Oswalds raised six of their ten children here, and both parents died in this house.[14]

The Big Cottonwood Canal once marked the northeast boundary of this lot. Envisioned in the 1850s as a water route for ox-drawn barges carrying blocks of stone from the Cottonwood Canyons to Temple Square, the canal was almost completed before its builders discovered that it did not hold water.

Its successor, the Jordan and Salt Lake City Canal, was an important source of irrigation water for farms 130 years ago. It still carries water, albeit in a conduit underground, but there is no longer any trace of it on this block. A walking trail is planned to follow the route from 800 South to 3300 South along approximately 1050 East (McClelland Street).

130 South 700 East—Ellenor Georgana Reed Jones, c. 1871

Now burdened with outsized pillars and porches, this home's first iteration likely was a two-story, central-passage type adobe built about 1871 for Ellenor and her children, Dewoody and Emma. At some point, an equal-sized one-and-a-half-story addition was built on the west side, followed by a brick addition. The building now is divided into apartments and has been heavily remodeled by later owners.

Ellenor Jones's story is full of gaps and difficult to verify. She appears to have been born Ellenor Reed in Tennessee about 1833, and to have moved sometime in the 1860s to California. She claimed to be the widow of a Californian named Anson Jones. The Eleventh Ward record

of members shows "Hugh Stevenson Jones & Emma [*sic*] Jones baptized May 3 1870. Arr. from Millberry [Millbrae] S[an] Mateo Co." No date was given for their coming into the ward.[15] If the Jones men were related, Ellenor offered no information.

Title to the property was put in the children's names when it was purchased in 1869, as Ellenor admitted in an 1876 letter to the Utah Territory Third District Court, to "keep my husband from taking it from me." Whether she referred to Anson or Hugh Jones in that statement is unknown. In 1871 a "Hugh S. Jones and E. Jones (wife)" together mortgaged the lot to build a house. The Salt Lake City tax rolls for the Eleventh Ward list Ellenor as the property owner in 1872, and gave a value of $1,000 in 1877.[16] Contradictions abound in Ellenor's story, and it may have been in part self-serving.

She claimed to have been a member of the LDS Church since childhood, although she had married "out in the World." Ellenor's son Dewoody asserted his ownership and right to sell the property in 1876, but Ellenor managed to retain title and lived in the house until 1882. At that point Dewoody prevailed and was able to sell the property to Frank Crocker.[17]

Dewoody Jones married into the prominent Godbe-Hampton family and later moved to Washington State. Ellenor seems to have disappeared until 1899, when she was serving the LDS Church as a sister missionary in California. In 1910 the census enumerator found her boarding with a Swanson family in San Francisco, where her birthplace was given as Virginia.[18]

Frank Crocker and his wife, Laura A. Ninde Crocker, paid $3,100 for the house and lot in 1882. Laura had been born in Salt Lake City in 1854 to a pioneer family; Frank was from Maine. When Frank died of cirrhosis in 1883, Laura married James W. Pitts, a retired brewer. They lived here with a blended family that came to include several children of their own. Like the Joneses, the Pitts family was also connected to the Godbes, in this case through partnership in the Godbe & Pitts Drug Store. James Pitts perhaps had too great a fondness for his own product, and like Frank Crocker, he died of cirrhosis. His funeral was held in this house.[19]

Once again, the house became the object of a pitched legal battle. Laura Crocker Pitts struggled to keep it after James died, even filing a "Declaration of Homestead," but ultimately she was forced to sell to W. N. Griffin. Laura moved, with six of her children, to a small house a few blocks away, at 746 E. Linden Avenue, where her neighbors were the widow and grown children of William Fuller, once the owner of Fuller's Hill Pleasure Gardens (see 1010 East Linden Avenue, Tenth Ward).[20]

51 South 800 East—Mahala Robbins/Septimus Wagstaff, Mary Ann Needham and Isabel Whitney Sears, c. 1871

The first house on this lot (demolished), perhaps built about 1853 by Edward Brain, probably stood approximately where the driveway is now. Brain, a mason who became a prominent builder, was one of the original occupants of the lot. He brought his first wife with him from England and promptly married again upon his arrival in 1852. Certainly he was living here by 1856, when he was assessed taxes not only on the land and improvements, but also on a cow and a clock or watch.[21]

In 1859 his taxes were delinquent, and Brain sold the property for fifty dollars to Mahala Briggs Robbins in 1860. Mrs. Robbins was an LDS convert from Massachusetts who had left her husband there to join two of her children in Utah. She was rebaptized in Salt Lake City in December 1857. Mahala had two cows and a wagon or buggy by 1861 and was listed in the 1867 city directory at this location, probably in the house

built by Edward Brain. Mrs. Robbins may have begun building some part of the existing house, but while she was working as a cook at Gardner's upper sawmill in Mill Creek Canyon, she was killed in an avalanche in April 1869.[22]

Mahala's children promptly sold the property for $1,300, a large sum in 1869, to Septimus W. Sears (1844–1903) and his wife Mary Ann. Sears had recently married a plural wife, Isabel M. Whitney, the daughter of a prominent family, and this house likely was built or completed for both her and Sears's first wife, Mary Ann.[23]

Two wives in a single house may not have been a comfortable arrangement. In 1871, Sears sold the property and subsequently maintained two households, one for each wife. The buyer was Alfred S. Gould, a mining agent and later the chief clerk of the Utah Supreme Court. He paid Sears $5,000, a truly princely sum that suggests an impressive house on a large lot. (Gould had been an owner of the *San Francisco Sun* newspaper and died an alcoholic in Sacramento in 1882.)[24]

Septimus Sears later became an executive of Zion's Cooperative Mercantile Institution (ZCMI), the LDS Church's grocery and dry goods emporium. He was prosecuted for "unlawful cohabitation" in 1885 and spent the rest of the 1880s out of state.[25] He died in 1903 and is buried in the Salt Lake City Cemetery, not fifty feet from Mahala Robbins's grave.

The original house appears to have been a side-passage type in the Greek revival style, as indicated by the position of the present entry and the remaining trim. A 1909 photograph shows part of the original porch with a second-story railing, and elaborate cornice returns. A 1920s brick addition obscures the west side of the house, and interior paneling covers the walls and whatever original woodwork might remain.[26]

157 South 800 East—James Ayres and Rhoda Parsons Cushing, c. 1876

Alterations and additions now surround the original house, which seems to have been a one-story, cross-wing type. Today it forms only the core of the first story. The second story is made of stucco-coated lumber. Brick and frame additions form the front and rear.[27]

Four members of the Cushing family came to Utah from England in 1866 on the ship *American Congress*, and then crossed the plains with an unidentified company.[28] By 1867 James Cushing (1844–1912) was working as a bootmaker with his father, Robert, whose adobe house was just to the north at 143 South 800 East (demolished). James bought this lot, the south half of his father's property, in 1877, but had likely already built the first room(s) by 1875 when he married Rhoda Parsons (1854–1908). Here, city property tax records give a precise construction date for the house. The assessed value of the full lot nearly doubled between 1874 and 1875, and the penciled note "two houses" appears on the assessment rolls for 1877.[29]

Rhoda Parsons did not leave England until 1874, on the ship *Wyoming*. She may have worked in the households of Daniel H. Wells and Brigham Young before her marriage, and James, who had almost no education, worked as a teamster for Brigham Young and then as a janitor at the president's office until May of 1912. The Cushings had ten children, seven of whom lived to adulthood. Rhoda's funeral in 1908 was attended by church president Joseph F. Smith. The couple lived in this house for their entire married lives, and both died at home.[30]

Twelfth Ward

East of the Thirteenth Ward, which was home to some of the most influential families in Salt Lake City, the Twelfth Ward was home to farmers, laborers, tradesmen, and at least one "gentleman."[1] It became a fashionable neighborhood, close to the center of town and bordered by South Temple Street on the north. Residents in 1870 included the attorney Zerubbabel Snow, part of whose 1874 adobe house can be seen behind the brick front of 350 East 100 South.

515 East 300 South—Joshua Hough and Annie Park Midgley, c. 1882

In 1889, every building on this block of 300 South was a residence, and every one was made of adobe. Today this is the last one. It stands on part of the much larger lot once owned by Joshua Midgley Sr., painter of the original interior of the LDS Temple, who came to Utah in 1852 with the James Jepson Company. Joshua married Jemima Hough, a young woman from the same company, and bought this lot from her mother, the widow Hough, in 1856.[2] Joshua and Jemima built a large adobe home facing 500 East (demolished) where they raised their children.

Their oldest son, Joshua Hough Midgley (1854–1945), married Annie Alexander Park (1858–1943) in 1876. Annie was born in Provo where her parents had fled when Brigham Young, anticipating the advance of Johnston's Army, ordered Salt Lake City evacuated in the spring of 1858. Joshua bought the southeast corner of his parents' lot in 1882 and probably built this house that same year. Joshua and Annie had thirteen children, including twins who died at birth and a daughter who lived to be 103. Joshua was a sign painter and wallpaper hanger, and several of his sons joined him in a successful business.[3] As of this writing, the property has been owned by the same family for 160 years.

The house is a Neoclassical-style, cross-wing type with cornice returns, tall, narrow windows, and a wide porch that would have been fashionable in the 1880s. Where the stucco has deteriorated on the east side, the stone foundation and adobe wall are visible.

72 South 600 East—George Finley and Hanna (Annie) Bowthorpe Brooks, c. 1867

From its east facade, this looks like many other brick apartment buildings. But the north and south facades reveal the massive walls, deep cornices, and original chimney of what was once a two-story adobe house. Before the lot was subdivided and later homes built around it, its address was 575 East 100 South.[4]

George Finley Brooks (1833–1911) was an English immigrant who came to Utah in 1856. He traveled with the James A. Hunt wagon company rather than the unfortunate handcart companies, and after a late start the wagon company was able to complete its journey in December, with help from men and wagons sent back along the trail from Salt Lake City.[5]

Hannah Bowthorpe, also from England, had arrived three years earlier with the Cyrus Wheelock Company. Both of their families had paid

for the journey with loans from the Perpetual Emigration Fund.[6]

At the time of the 1860 census, George was working as a common laborer and living with Hannah and their baby, Julia, in Moroni. He had improved his situation dramatically by 1867, finding work in Salt Lake City as a store clerk and purchasing the land where this house stands for $100. His brother Edmund owned a parcel to the north and soon sold part of that to another brother, Philip. The 1867 city directory places George at this corner.[7]

The Brooks family eventually grew to include seven (of twelve) surviving children. George continued in the grocery business, opening his own store at 50 West 100 South with his sons and expanding it to form G. F. Brooks & Sons. George died at this house in 1911. After his death, Hannah stayed on until 1914 and then moved into her daughter's house, where she died in 1923.[8]

Thirteenth and Fourteenth Wards

Prominent and wealthy men—among them Ezra Taft Benson Sr., Jeter Clinton, Erastus Snow, Daniel Spencer, Nicholas Groesbeck, and several members of the Young family—once owned homes or land in the Thirteenth and Fourteenth Wards.[1] Even before completion of the transcontinental railroad in 1870, their two-story adobe residences were being transformed into business offices and stores, a process that soon created a Main Street much like those the Mormons had left behind in so-called Babylon. Today not a single adobe building remains.

Left: East side of Main Street, between 100 and 200 South, by Charles W. Carter, about 1869. Most of the buildings in this scene were adobe. Utah State Historical Society photograph 19343, used by permission.

Fifteenth Ward

Like the Sixteenth and Nineteenth Wards, the Fifteenth Ward was on low, wet ground on the west side of Salt Lake City. Small farmers, laborers, and tradesmen predominated, and almost none of them owned property with an assessed value of more than a few hundred dollars. The Billings house is the only remaining adobe structure.

52 South 600 West—Lucius A. and Emma Parry Billings, c. 1870

Thomas R. Parry (1801–1886) arrived in the Salt Lake Valley in 1860 from Wales, accompanied by his wife, Ann Roberts Parry (1803–1882), and four of their children. For them, a three-month journey across the plains had followed a month's voyage on the *Underwriter* from Liverpool to New York.[1] Thomas, an illiterate stonemason, signed documents such as deeds with his mark, an "X."

Thomas was already fifty-eight, old by frontier standards, when he arrived in Salt Lake City. His name first appeared in city directories in 1869, when he was living in an adobe house (demolished) half a block south of this one. There is no record of his having title to the land until 1872, but he may well have had a sort of handshake deal with the seller rather than a written document filed with the county recorder.[2]

Thomas probably helped his daughter Emma (1850–1918) and her husband, Lucius Augustus Billings (1835–1923), build their hall-parlor house. Its asymmetrical facade is unusual for this house type, but the windows appear to be original, even to the six-over-six arrangement of their glass panes. The cross-wing, with its large gable-end window, was a later addition but also adobe. The young couple was living at or near this location by 1870, although not necessarily in this house. Title to the property was not formally transferred to them until 1884, when Thomas divided his original lot into parcels for each of his children.[3]

Little has been written about Emma Parry Billings, but Lucius Billings's (also known as Uncle Josh) personal history is a tale right out of the Old West. He was born in Ohio in 1835 but left for California via Cape Horn to look for gold. In 1860 he was working as a miner in Tuolumne County. Perhaps that was not as thrilling or lucrative as he had imagined, because in 1861 he joined the Union Army's Third Regiment, California Volunteers, and headed east to Camp Floyd, south of Fairfield.[4]

There, and later at Fort Douglas on Salt Lake City's East Bench, he served under Col. Patrick Connor until the end of the Civil War. He may have been connected with publication of the fort's newspaper, the *Union Vedette*, and he was its first carrier when he worked for the Salt Lake City Post Office. Billings lived in this house even after Emma died in 1918, and was still working for the post office in 1920, by which time he had worked there for fifty-two years.[5]

Sixteenth Ward

Until recently, there were nineteen adobe houses in the Sixteenth Ward. Seven—historically and architecturally significant—were demolished between 2011 and 2016. Several of those were built by residents who reflected the makeup of the ward before the Utah Central rails and Union Pacific depot separated it from the rest of the city and changed a community of tradesmen and small farmers into an area where small homes were widely separated by boarding houses, warehouses, and industry.

751 West 200 North—Peter and Sarah Julia Hepworth Olsen, c. 1880

Peter Olsen (1848–1908) was a common name in the 1870s and 1880s, as thousands of Scandinavian immigrants came to the Salt Lake Valley.

Had he married anyone but Julia Hepworth, it would have been extremely difficult to locate records that pertain only to him. Peter, however, had the good fortune to marry into the prominent Hepworth family, English butchers who had been in Salt Lake City since 1852.[1] A few houses east is John Hepworth's brick home at 725 West, built by Sarah's father in 1877. It is being restored to its original condition and is on the National Register of Historic Places.

Peter and Sarah married in 1872 in St. Mark's Episcopal Church and bought this lot from David Parry in 1875 for $300. By 1880, Peter and Sarah had two children and were living here, even though the 1884 directory erroneously lists their address as 754 West, which would have been on the opposite side of the street.[2] Peter mortgaged the property in 1883 and worked for the next several years as a clerk or porter at Kahn Bros. grocery store.[3] The house today has an added brick cross-wing with prominent quoins at the corners, but until at least 1911 its entry faced south across a full-width porch.[4]

Sometime before 1897, the Olsens moved to Juab County, Utah (Mammoth Precinct), where Peter labored in a quartz mill. Mines in the area produced both gold and silver, especially during a boom period from about 1900 to 1910. Peter, however, died in a Los Angeles hospital in 1908, of "peritonitos [*sic*] following an operation." His funeral notice gave no explanation as to why he might have been in California.[5]

Sarah (1851–1924) never remarried after Peter's death. She returned to Salt Lake City with her daughter, Mary, and Mary's husband, a miner named Harry Treloar. Eventually they moved back into this house, where Harry died in 1920.[6]

36 North 600 West—Octave and Josephine Ursenbach, c. 1865 (Demolished 2013)

One of Brigham Young's early designs for the earthly Zion was to promote local industry and agriculture, with the intention of disconnecting his people from eastern capitalism and imported goods. Mormons, who were after all Americans at heart, had other plans. They continued to buy not only sugar and stoves, but hats and bonnets, frock coats, and fashionable neckwear, often at very high prices.

Young proposed that development of a silk industry, raising silk-worms on mulberry leaves and producing silk from the cocoons, would limit church members' need for imported fashions. He advised in 1861, "Bring the seeds, the eggs of the silkworm, raise the trees for feeding the worms, and let us see if we cannot produce silk here." Silk was produced in this house, and although nearly every town in Utah Territory produced silk fabric, the work proved so difficult and time-consuming that it was never profitable. By 1905, the dream of silk production had faded away.[7]

Octave Ursenbach (1832–1871), a Swiss convert to the LDS Church, arrived in Salt Lake City in 1858, shortly before silk production began. A watchmaker at Godbe's drug store on Main Street, he offered lessons in German to supplement his income and also advertised his skills as a gold- and silversmith. He requested that a friend in Paris send him some silkworm eggs, which yielded the three thousand worms he exhibited at the Utah State Fair in 1863. By 1865 he was working with George D. Watt to promote the silk industry, encouraging the planting of mulberry trees along property lines. (Watt's two-story adobe house is still standing and in use on the Madeleine Choir School campus on First Avenue.) Ursenbach's first wife, Josephine Marie Augustine de la Harpe Ludert (1813–1878), should have received far more credit for her contributions to the silk industry than the brief report in the *Deseret News* of "the silk-worms so successfully bred in Utah, by sister Josephine Ursenbach, during six years."[8]

Josephine was French and had been married to Alexander Ludert, Russia's emissary to Cuba. Her daughters were both married to Russians. When Alexander died, Josephine took her young son, Joseph, and went to Geneva, Switzerland, heard LDS missionaries preach, and accepted their gospel in 1854. After a long ocean voyage, Josephine and her son walked to the Salt Lake Valley in 1856 with the Daniel D. McArthur Handcart Company. She never saw her daughters again. Josephine and Octave married in Salt Lake City in 1859. Octave was almost twenty years younger than Josephine, and they had no children together.[9]

Octave Ursenbach returned to France on a church mission in 1867. On the return voyage in 1869, he met an English divorcee, Eliza Durrant Whitehead.[10] Eliza had converted to the LDS faith, divorced her husband, and was bringing her baby daughter, Sarah Jane, to gather with the Latter-day Saints. She and Octave married in 1869, and their son, Octave

Frederick Ursenbach, was born in 1870. Tax records suggest that Ursenbach had built this house by 1865, and although his deed to the property was not recorded until 1869, the city directory shows he was living here by 1867.[11]

There seems to have been no good feeling between the two wives. Octave Ursenbach's will, written only a month before his death from tuberculosis in February 1871 but apparently not discovered until at least 1878, made it clear that Octave Frederick and not Josephine's son Joseph would be the eventual heir to this property. In the meantime, Josephine and Eliza were to divide the land and share the house. Josephine wrote plaintively that she had "worked, toiled and slaved" for her home, and that she had received the Mayor's Deed in 1873. She never referred to Eliza by name, but always as "the second wife."

An 1872 letter from Josephine to the probate court related that she was now ill with tuberculosis herself. She knew that a "gasometer" (gas plant) would soon be put on the block, and that she would have to "desert our home before it is ruined by the Gas." In 1892, after twenty years of legal wrangling, when both Josephine and Eliza were dead, Octave Frederick Ursenbach finally gained title to this house and the surrounding lot.[12]

Josephine lived here at least through 1874, and died of tuberculosis in 1878. Eliza remarried in 1874. For a while at least, she and her new husband, George Compton, lived in this house or one adjacent. Octave Frederick never lived here again. He moved to Los Angeles before 1940 and died there in 1951.[13]

The Ursenbach house, originally a hall-parlor type, had been extensively remodeled prior to demolition. A rear shed-roofed addition, like the rest of the house, was made of adobe, and the entire structure had a common fieldstone foundation.[14]

50 North 600 West—William and Naomi Orchard Sanders/Swen and Christina Johnson, c. 1869 (Demolished 2013)

Albert Bailey Griffin (1809–1896) was the original occupant of this lot. In 1848, he built a log cabin here near the corner of 600 West and North Temple Street, when this was the western edge of Great Salt Lake City. Albert and his wife, Abigail Varney, came to the Salt Lake Valley from

SOUTH ELEVATION

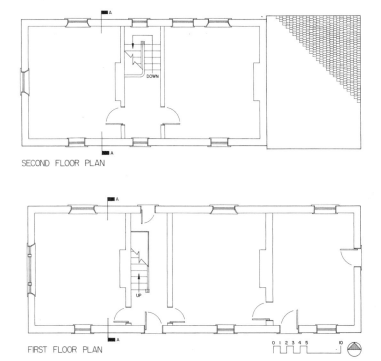

SECOND FLOOR PLAN

FIRST FLOOR PLAN

0 1 2 3 4 5   10

50 North 600 West, William and Naomi Orchard Sanders/ Swen and Christina Johnson. Architectural drawings, floorplans and south elevation, by Korral Broschinsky, Thomas Carter, and James Gosney. Used by permission, Western Regional Architecture Program Collection, J. Willard Marriott Library, University of Utah, all rights reserved.

Vermont by way of Nauvoo, Illinois, traveling with the Heber C. Kimball Company. The Griffins moved to the Church Farm (near present-day 800 East and 2100 South) by about 1856.[15]

There is no trace of it now, but before 1875 the north branch of City Creek meandered west along North Temple Street and across this property. Its water would have been an asset for the pioneer family and their livestock, although the ground along its banks would have been flooded in the spring and swampy year-round.

John Hepworth bought Lot 5 from Heber C. Kimball in 1866, paying $150 for what was then one and a quarter acres. Brothers John and Thomas Hepworth were butchers who had brought their wives and young children from England to the Salt Lake Valley in 1852. (Thomas's elegant two-story brick home at 725 West 200 North in Salt Lake City, built in 1877, is being painstakingly restored and is on the National Register of Historic Places.) Another butcher, George Davis (1840–1867), bought the lot from John Hepworth in September 1866, paying $600. He promptly sold the north end of the lot (which included the course of City Creek and its water rights) to the city for $550, recouping almost his entire purchase price.[16] Davis and his wife, Martha Filer, were living on the property by 1867, probably at what was 54 North 600 West (demolished 2013).[17]

George and Martha had two sons when George died unexpectedly in 1867, "killed by the falling of a bank of dirt." Martha was left to provide not only for her children but also for her mother, who had accompanied her from England in 1862.[18]

In December 1867, Martha Davis sold a three-by-ten-rod parcel of Lot 5 to William Sanders [Saunders], a clerk at William Jennings's store, for $470. Sanders (1836–1916) already had some prominence in the LDS Church, having been the president of the Kent (England) conference in 1863 and 1864. He sailed on the *Hudson* to New York in June 1864 (a voyage recalled in 1895 by John L. Smith) and reached the Salt Lake Valley the same year, traveling with an unknown company. His mother and three sisters were with him.[19]

William became a member of the Tabernacle Choir in 1865, married Naomi Orchard (1843–1912) in 1866 (with Heber C. Kimball officiating), and later became a traveling salesman for ZCMI. He was almost certainly living in this house in 1869, and was enumerated during the 1870 census.[20]

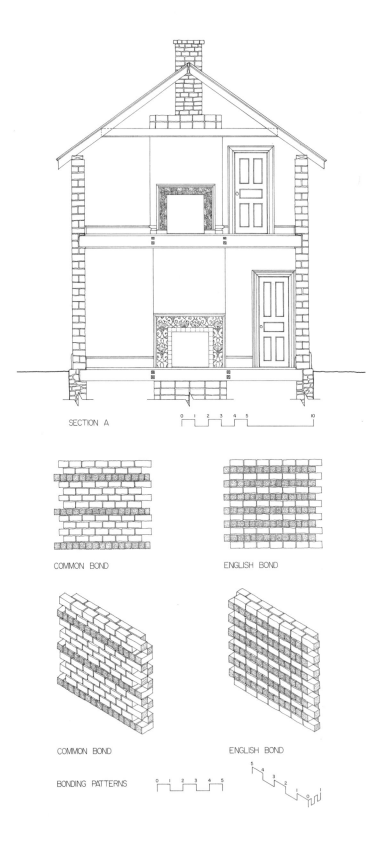

SECTION A

COMMON BOND

ENGLISH BOND

COMMON BOND

ENGLISH BOND

BONDING PATTERNS

Sanders probably began building this house about 1868 when he mortgaged the property heavily, borrowing exactly $2,007.61 from Joseph A. Young. Tax and census records provide further evidence for such a construction date. At the time of the 1870 census, William and Naomi, their two young sons, Naomi's mother, and a domestic servant were living in a house on this block. The assessed value of William Sanders's real property had been $800 in 1868, but by 1871, the total assessed value was $1,350. When he defaulted on his debt to Young in 1871, he moved his family to the Twentieth Ward.[21]

The next owners were Swedish immigrants, Swen Johnson (1841–1913) and his wife, Christina Johansen (1847–1940). Swen's arrival in Salt Lake City is undocumented, although in 1900 he reported arriving in the United States in 1865. Christina may have immigrated in 1869, and the couple married in 1870.[22] Swen's first documented residence was at this house, which was not far from the Salt Lake City Brewery, where he was a saloon keeper in the cellar of Godbe's drug store on Main Street.[23]

Swen and Christina Johnson bought this property from Joseph A. Young for $2,300 in 1871, again strongly suggesting that the large house was already complete. Yet in 1872, its assessed value was $800, as it had been in 1869. Within the next four years, Swen bought some additional land on the east and north, sold part of it, and obtained three mortgages. Swen and Christina received a Mayor's Deed in 1875 and, on the same day, sold the property to Louis Marier for $1,800.[24]

Louis Marier operated a bath house downtown on Commercial Street with his brother Clement during the 1870s, but it was not his only business.[25] He often provided financing for both real estate and mining interests, as evidenced by the frequency with which his name appears in the Salt Lake County title abstracts.

Left: 50 North 600 West. Architectural drawings showing the house in cross-section, with details of brick patterns or bonds seen in adobe construction, by Korral Broschinsky, Thomas Carter, and James Gosney. Used by permission, Western Regional Architecture Program Collection, J. Willard Marriott Library, University of Utah, all rights reserved.

Louis Marier apparently rented the house to various tenants, including James Bishop, a gas fitter. Bishop and two of his plural wives lived in this house in 1880, while his third wife, Ellen, lived in Cache County.[26] In 1882, Marier sold the property to John Lawrence for $1,600, taking back a $400 mortgage. Lawrence was a carpenter whose family lived in this house for many years, adding a large Victorian brick wing on the south side about 1905.[27]

The massing of this house strongly suggests a construction date in the 1860s. The house was a central-passage type with a south-facing entry. Its front door opened toward the base of the central staircase, which featured Eastlake-style Newell posts installed sometime in the late 1870s or early 1880s.

A group of local architectural historians was able to examine, measure, and draw the house before and during demolition in 2013, removing interior paneling and other modern materials. At the same time, a large area of the exterior stucco was removed from the north side of the house, revealing that the shed pantry on the east was an integral part of the original house, not an addition. Shed pantries were a common feature in English houses of the later nineteenth century.[28]

Throughout the building, the adobe bricks had been laid in a pattern called an English bond. Common fieldstone was used for the foundation of the house and to line the shed pantry's cellar walls (a later westward extension of the cellar was lined with brick). No cut stone or fired brick was observed in the original structure during demolition.

A roughly framed doorway on the north elevation probably led out to a drive or garden, and opened inward to a small area under the lower flight of stairs. The door and molding, like the interior woodwork, were probably part of a remodeling effort sometime in the late 1870s or early 1880s.

Other architectural features included large fireplaces of adobe, with corbeled tops and chimneys. To accommodate later stoves, all the fireplace openings had been partially filled in and lined with brick, probably during the 1880s. The parlor fireplace had a narrow surround of black tiles and a hearth of colored tiles. Eastlake-style wood mantels and surrounds finished the fireplace openings. Wallpaper had been applied to the plastered walls before the surrounds were in place. John Lawrence may have been responsible for adding these Eastlake design elements.

221 North 600 West—Jane Thornley Hamer/Samuel Jr. and Ann Albion Hamer, c. 1858

Jane Thornley Hamer (1802–1885) was already a widow when she arrived in the Salt Lake Valley in 1851. She and her husband, Samuel, had come from Lancashire, England, in 1842 and settled in Nauvoo, Illinois. Their baby, Joseph, died that September, and Samuel died of "ague and fever" in August 1843. Her oldest daughter, Martha, married John S. Haslam, and the two were still with Jane when they reached Winter Quarters in 1850. Jane, her four youngest children, her son John and his young wife, and Martha and her husband, probably came west together with the James W. Cummings Company.[29]

John Hamer received a large lot directly north of this one and built his house there. His brother, Samuel Hamer Jr. (1832?–1895), worked as a blacksmith and, at times, an inventor. He built this house, where he lived with his mother and, after 1857, his wife, Ann Albion (1835–1902). He paid his mother $60 for the land in 1857 and in 1858 was assessed taxes in the Sixteenth Ward on real estate valued at $500—almost certainly here.[30] Like many families in the Nineteenth Ward, the Hamers were related by marriage to neighbors—the Wilding, Haslam, and Player families—some of whose adobe houses are still standing.

Samuel was called to serve a church mission in Panaca, Nevada, in 1867, returning to "his old home" after the 1870 census had been completed and bringing with him a plural wife, Sarah Openshaw. He worked at the LDS Church blacksmith shop, for the streetcar company, and for the Union Pacific Railroad. By 1880, Samuel and Ann had nine children, Samuel and Sarah had five.[31]

The earliest part of this house is a small hall-parlor type that became a cross-wing by addition. Most of the early house is obscured by twentieth-century wood-frame additions on its east and west sides. Chimneys on the gable ends, as well as the deep, narrow windows, indicate its original form.

About 1883, Samuel built the hipped-roofed brick house at 227 North 600 West for his plural wife, Sarah Openshaw (1848–1927), and her children. Sarah was not a pioneer, having arrived in Salt Lake City via train in 1869, from the same town in Lancashire as the Hamer family. Samuel's name appeared twice in the 1884 city directory, at both 221 and 227. That and the fact that he was well known in the city probably led to his arrest for unlawful cohabitation under the Edmunds-Tucker Act in 1887. Although Sarah testified under oath that they had not lived together for the last three years and that he came to her home only to visit the children, Samuel was convicted in 1890 and spent ninety days in jail.[32]

Samuel died in 1895 and is buried in the Salt Lake City cemetery. Ann and Sarah continued to live next door to each other until Ann died of "old age" in 1902 when she was sixty-seven. She was memorialized by the *Deseret News* as "one of the few remaining handcart pioneers of this section." (She was not.) Sarah died in her home in 1927.[33]

264 North 600 West—George Henry and Sarah Ann Wright Spry, c. 1889

George Spry (1859–1899) was a latecomer to Salt Lake City, arriving in New York from England with his parents, Philip and Sarah, and three siblings in 1875 on the *Wyoming*, and taking the train to Utah. By 1880 the Spry family had settled on 500 West and soon bought land for an adobe house at 573 West 300 North (demolished).[34]

Philip Spry established himself as a gentleman's tailor. George lived with his parents until 1889, when he married Sarah Ann Wright (1857–1940) and bought this property from his parents, who had moved to

25 West South Temple Street, opposite Temple Square. George would have been twenty-nine, working as a laborer or teamster and active in the Democratic Party, when he built the first part of his house, probably a hall-parlor type. His work may have been dangerous, as evidenced by his membership in the Knights of the Maccabees, a fraternal organization (open only to white men) that paid insurance benefits to workers' widows. He probably felt fortunate to find work at Haslam Brothers' butcher shop about 1893, while his brother Philip worked in their father's tailor shop. His brother William was a clerk at ZCMI and lived in the elegant Forest Dale neighborhood.[35]

Salt Lake's west side had a dismal public health record in the late nineteenth century. The flat terrain, wet ground, and general unwillingness of the city to invest in infrastructure meant that sewage often was dumped or leaked into the streets. Wells were polluted and clean water was hard to find. Contagious diseases like cholera, diphtheria, scarlet fever, and especially typhoid were common and spread easily through drinking contaminated water or eating food touched by dirty hands. George Spry contracted typhoid fever and died in this house on October 13, 1899, at the age of forty. (George's younger brother, William, became Utah's third governor in 1909).

Sarah Ann Spry continued living here with her children, probably adding the brick south wing before 1911, and died in this house in 1940.[36]

854 West South Temple—John Clinton, c. 1878 (Demolished 2016)

John Clinton (c. 1826–1881) was one of those rare pioneers who arrived alone in the new Zion, never married, and had no known family. Born on the Isle of Man, he must have crossed the plains by 1850, although there is no definite record of his name in any company list. The 1850 census, taken in early 1851, found John Clinton in the household of William Watterson, another Manx pioneer, in Bountiful. Clinton's age was given as twenty-one, although that may not be correct.[37]

The name "J. Clinton" appeared in the LDS Church Journal History several times in 1866, but those records almost certainly referred to Jeter Clinton, a prominent doctor who held church and civic offices during that time. No other record dated between 1851 and 1872 was found, his name never appeared in a city directory, and the house is not shown on a detailed map drawn in 1875.[38]

Thomas Cannell, a laborer and 1868 Manx immigrant, sold this property to Clinton in 1872. Clinton obtained a small mortgage in 1878, possibly to build the house, and another mortgage in 1880. Clinton's occupation that year was "crushing ore," but he had been out of work for six months. On February 22, 1881, Henry Moore, another laborer who once lived adjacent to Cannell in the Fifteenth Ward, bought the property for $500, suggesting that some sort of house had been built.[39] John Clinton had by that time lost a total of about $120 in these transactions.

The remainder of Clinton's story is fairly well documented, but brief.

Four days after selling his property, the *Salt Lake Herald* reported that "a demented man, John Clinton, was arrested" on February 25, 1881. He was taken to the city Insane Asylum, located on Salt Lake City's east bench. Henry Moore recommended that the Probate Court appoint John J. Kelly, a stonemason, as his guardian. The asylum doctor, Seymour B. Young, sent word that Clinton was "not well enough to be moved or produced before this court," and Kelly was appointed to manage Clinton's meager estate—a few shares of mining stock.[40]

Clinton died in the asylum on April 30, 1881. No cause of death was given in the official record, which also lacked a birthdate, birthplace, and names of family members. He was buried in Mount Olivet Cemetery following a funeral held "from [city] Sexton Taylor's Office." In July, Henry Moore sold the property to Frank Crocker (see 130 South 700 East, Eleventh Ward) for $800.[41]

After all the asylum, funeral, guardian, and court costs were paid, the remainder of Clinton's small estate was sent to a sister, Ann Clinton, who lived near Manchester, England. She wrote to the court that she had brothers named John and Robert, and that their parents' names were John and Isabell Cachin [probably Kaghin]. Perhaps they were the John and Isabella Clinton who sailed from Liverpool to New Orleans with two young children on the *Swanton* in 1843.[42]

The house was one of only a few remaining examples of a double-cell type. Each of the two front rooms had a center front door that opened onto the porch, flanked by a double-hung window. Perhaps Clinton lived in one of the units while renting the other. Like much of the city's west side in the late 1870s, this was a mixed residential/industrial neighborhood. In 1874, narrow-gauge tracks for the Utah Western Railway were laid from the Union Pacific Depot, west along the center of South Temple Street in front of this house, and then across the Jordan River. The line opened for business on December 13, carrying passengers, the mail, and two carloads of ore.[43] Today the right-of-way belongs to the Union Pacific. The house was demolished in 2016 to make room for expansion of a restaurant parking lot.

Seventeenth Ward

The Seventeenth Ward was a desirable address, not only for its proximity to the Temple Block at its southeast corner but also for the water of City Creek, which flowed south and then west along North Temple Street. Influential figures—Albert Carrington, Orson Hyde, John Pack, William Clayton, and John Bernhisel—lived here in 1860 on land that rose above the valley floor and where the homes and offices of Brigham Young were only a few blocks away.

222 North West Temple Street—Alfred Jason, Emmerette Davis, Mildred Johnson, and Margaret Harley Randall/Nicholas and Elizabeth Thompson Groesbeck, c. 1865

Alfred Randall (1811–1891) was no ordinary pioneer, and this is no ordinary house. When it was new, its position on the lower south slope of Arsenal (Capitol) Hill gave it a clear view of Temple Square and the city to the south. The house has been made into apartments, but its remarkable story is intact.

Randall joined the LDS Church in 1840. He worked on the Nauvoo Temple, accompanied Joseph Smith to the Carthage Jail, and came west with the Heber C. Kimball Company in 1848. With him were his two wives, Emmerette Louiese Davis (1818–1898) and Margaret Harley (1823–1919), and Emmerette's three children—Charles, Sarah, and Alfred.[1]

A carpenter and builder, Alfred began soon after his arrival in the Salt Lake Valley to work on a mill for Heber C. Kimball in North Mill Creek and on Archibald Gardner's woolen mill on the Jordan River. He reported building a house in Salt Lake City in 1851, and then "built another house on another lot an[d] built a dobie school house 17th Ward" in 1853.[2]

But was this Alfred Randall's original home? The pioneers' characteristic vagueness about the locations and construction dates of their homes makes it difficult to pin them down before addresses were used. In this case, however, property and tax records, census returns, historical maps and photographs, newspapers, biographies, and reminiscences provide the full story.

The hilly area north of 200 North was included in Plat A when it was surveyed in 1847–1848, but the parcels were never distributed. Later it was resurveyed as part of Plat E, an area of odd-shaped lots and irregular streets following the terrain. About 1854, Randall acquired a "2 Story Adobie house," thirty-one-by-twenty-four feet, on the east side of West Temple Street, north of Temple Square. By 1856, Salt Lake City tax rolls show his property was valued at $2,500, a considerable sum for the time, and that he had livestock, a clock or watch, and household furniture. Newspaper articles from 1853 and 1854 advised the members of the Fifteenth Quorum of the Seventies, a church group of special missionaries, to meet at Randall's house, "first block north of the Tabernacle"—not the location of this house, but where?

An 1867 photograph shows that original two-story "adobie" house, north of Temple Square and adjacent to the very recognizable house of John Bernhisel, with the Randall/Groesbeck house overlooking them both. Randall's first house, then, was at what became 142 North West

Temple Street (demolished). When Edward Hunter, presiding bishop of the LDS Church from 1851 until 1883, bought it in 1871, the seller was Alfred Randall. A much later photograph shows a street view.[3]

In 1860, Randall was enumerated twice—in Ogden with his wife Margaret and four of their children, and in the Seventeenth Ward with "Emily" (Emmerette) and "Milda D. Johnson." Milda was described as a servant but was in fact Randall's third wife, Mildred Elizabeth Johnson. Born and educated in Virginia, Mildred (1827–1913) had gone to visit her brother in Council Bluffs, Iowa, and there joined the LDS Church. She traveled to Utah with the James S. Brown Company in 1859 and married Alfred in 1860. During the 1860s, she and Alfred served two missions in Laie, Oahu, where she taught at the LDS mission school. Mildred even became, in 1873, the first woman to serve a mission without her husband.[4]

But what of this house? Alfred Randall probably built it about 1865, shortly before he received a land certificate for the property in August 1866. With that paper in hand, he promptly sold house and lot to Nicholas Groesbeck. Alfred Randall left Salt Lake City and spent the rest of his life on his farm in North Ogden with his fourth wife, Hannah Severn (1841–1912). Margaret lived in Centerville, Emmerette (Louiese) remained in the Seventeenth Ward in Salt Lake City, and the Groesbecks lived here.[5] Mildred Randall lived independently and taught at Brigham Young's private school. Alfred Randall may also have lived with his fifth wife, Elsie Anderson (1830–1914), in Ogden, where she worked as a charwoman or janitor in an Ogden bank.[6] Alfred Randall died in North Ogden in 1891; all of his wives outlived him.

This house is a double-pile type, with its original entry off-center in the south elevation. First- and second-story porches ran the width of the house, and a stone and adobe barn was attached to the west side.[7]

Nicholas Groesbeck was a wealthy merchant who came to Salt Lake City in 1856 and very soon settled in a large house at 200 North and 300 West. He and his family fled south in 1858 before the advance of the U.S. Army's Utah Expedition, locally known as Johnston's Army. When he returned, he lived in the Thirteenth Ward for several years, and in August 1866 he bought this house from Alfred Randall for $6,250.[8] It was a huge sum of money, indicative of the large house and four lots.

The 1867 city directory entry is spare—"Groesbeck Nicholas, 17th wd." Groesbeck's name appears on tax rolls for 1868, and the 1869 directory places him on Crooked Street, an early name for North West Temple Street when it was only a winding path.[9] The Groesbeck name has become so linked with this house that Alfred Randall's is forgotten. Elizabeth Groesbeck died in 1883 and Nicholas in 1884; the property remained in the family for decades.

Eighteenth Ward

In 1860, most of the ward's population were members of the enormous Young, Kimball, Wells, and Whitney families, or their servants.[1] Four adobe homes survive, as well as three iconic adobe buildings: the early church office building and Brigham Young's Lion House and Beehive House. Two other large homes—that of Minerva White Snow, a wife of Apostle Erastus Snow, at 217 North Canyon Road, and one built for Helaman and Emeline Billingsley Pratt at 252 North Canyon Road—also remain. The two smaller homes are less stylish but certainly of equal interest.

36 East 200 North—Christeen Golden Kimball/Jonathan Golden and Jane "Jennie" Knowlton Kimball, c. 1875

Commonly known as the J. Golden Kimball house, it was actually built as a home for his mother, Heber C. Kimball's tenth wife, Christeen Golden (1823–1896). Christeen and her son had lived in Heber C. Kimball's household, remaining after his death in 1868 until at least 1870. Kimball had owned the whole block northeast of Temple Square where there were large adobe homes and a family cemetery that still attracts visitors.

J. Golden left school and went to work driving a freight wagon, and Christeen worked as a seamstress. In 1876, Christeen and her grown children moved to Rich County, and for the next fifteen years raised cattle and lived in obscurity. The 1880 census enumerator listed some two dozen members of Christeen Kimball's family at Meadowville.[2] Eventually Christeen returned to Salt Lake City and built this house on part of the Kimball block.

The 1883–1884 Utah Directory lists Christina [sic] B. Kimball on the north (probably south) side of 200 North between Main and State Streets.

At that time, J. Golden Kimball was serving in the LDS Southern States Mission, where he was later the mission president from 1892 to 1894. Between missions, he moved here with his wife Jennie in 1888. Christeen died in 1896. J. Golden Kimball lived here until his death in 1938, and Jennie died in this house in 1940.[3]

The original house had a single story on the north side and two on the south side, a sort of daylight basement that accommodated the sloping ground. The addition of a brick cross wing on the northeast corner sometime between 1898 and 1911 changed the house into a T-plan with a stylish front bay.

Photographs taken to show Brigham Young's homes in 1873 and about 1875 clearly show the excavation for this house and the construction of its lower walls from fieldstone set aside as excavation progressed.[4] The photographers probably had no idea they had captured these unique views. This house may have been left unfinished when Christeen and her family moved to Rich County, as census records and city directories offer no clues as to who might have lived here prior to 1883.

28 East Hillside Avenue—John Aird, James and Margaret Aird Robertson, John B. and Annie Robertson Cummock, c. 1882

Heber C. Kimball held the original title to much of the land on the south slope of Arsenal (Capitol) Hill. The chain of title to this property is incomplete, but there is a record of Kimball's estate selling it to Robert Grix in 1877 for $200.⁵ Grix, a Scottish LDS convert, sold his lot five years later to two relatives, James Robertson (1827–1893) and John Aird.

Today, the house appears to be a foursquare type, with its pyramidal roof and large front windows. In fact, it was built in stages, beginning as a single story said to rest on a granite foundation—certainly possible, because John Aird was a teamster and sometimes worked on the LDS Temple. The 1884 directory places John Aird, James Robertson, and Robertson's son-in-law, John B. Cummock, here, although Cummock was actually living in Almy, Wyoming, where he had been elected to the state legislature in 1886. Robertson's location was given simply as "Arsenal Hill" in the 1889 directory.

By 1890, Cummock had returned to Salt Lake City. His address then was 4 East 300 North, and Robertson's was simply "6 Second" (now 300 North), probably placing them in the east and west halves of this house. Later the address was "8 Second North" and finally 28 East Hillside Avenue. James Robertson died in 1893, and in 1895 his widow, Margaret

(1832–1905), obtained a large mortgage, presumably to enlarge and improve the house for her daughter Annie and husband, John Cummock.[6]

John Cummock arrived in Utah from Scotland in 1880, worked in the U.S. Marshal's Office, and then as a Salt Lake County deputy sheriff. He and Annie served an LDS mission to Scotland from 1921–1923; both died in this house. His great-great-grandson, also named John B. Cummock, died in the 1988 bombing of PanAm flight 103 over Lockerbie, Scotland.[7]

Nineteenth Ward

The oldest remaining houses in Salt Lake City can be found in the original Nineteenth Ward, north of 300 North and west of the approximate line of State Street. The Abraham Coon house (1850), the Charles Player and Nelson Wheeler Whipple houses (1854), the James and Elizabeth F. Smith (1855), Peter Nebeker (mid-1850s), and William Albrand houses (before 1860), all were built by pioneering families who not only knew each other but who often worked together as a community to survive the earliest days of settlement in the Salt Lake Valley. Anders Winberg (1854) and John Platts (1854, 1858) built their homes on hilly ground in the eastern part of the ward.

Close to what were then the marshes of Parley's Creek (along 700 West) and the Jordan River, the ground was soft and wet. Most of the earlier settlers (and more prominent families) had been allotted land farther south and east, but as more immigrants came to the valley these marginal lands became more sought after. Like the eastern part of the Nineteenth Ward, where the terrain was too steep for farming, lots on the west side often became the property of poor people.

The hilly east side of the Nineteenth Ward rose gradually and then steeply onto Arsenal (now Capitol) Hill, where the challenge of the landscape was not too much water but too little, as it sank quickly into the rocky, sandy soil. The usual farm crops—wheat, corn, sorghum, hay—were impossible to grow on the hillside. Property owners here grew fruit trees, grapes, and other small fruits, the kinds of crops—peaches, apricots, plums—that were reflected in the early street names.

324 North 200 West—Alonzo Hazeltine and Emily Player Raleigh, 1880?

John Gheen and Abel Lamb were the original occupants of this lot. (Gheen, a Mormon apostate who killed a man in Nauvoo, nevertheless came to Utah and was himself killed in 1859 by a gunshot to the head, perhaps a blood atonement at the hands of Porter Rockwell.)[1] In 1857, Alonzo Raleigh paid $100 to Heber C. Kimball for one-quarter of the original lot, and in 1872 he received the Mayor's Deed. The construction date of this house is largely speculative. Raleigh already had large adobe homes at 530 West 400 North, 303 North 200 West, and a small one at 594 North Center Street, and owned several other properties in the Nineteenth Ward.[2]

Alonzo Raleigh (1818–1901) was born in New Hampshire and came to Utah with the 1848 Heber C. Kimball Company. He was the second bishop of the Nineteenth Ward, a position he held from 1856 until 1877, and a mason who supervised construction of the adobe city wall through the area.

His first wife, Mary Ann Tabor, died at Nauvoo in 1843. Raleigh married Caroline Curtis in 1844. By the time she died in 1853, he had married two plural wives, who were soon followed by another, Julia Curtis, Caroline's younger cousin. Julia's brief biography tells a tale of family unhappiness that began in 1857 when Raleigh married two young wives, sisters Elizabeth (1839–1924) and Emily (1841–1921) Player, then eighteen and sixteen years old, respectively. They "never did understand the Gospel or the true Pioneer life," Julia's granddaughter wrote. By about 1869, family life had become so unpleasant that Julia petitioned Brigham Young for a better living situation, and for years she and her daughters lived with various other families. Eventually even that became intolerable, and "then there was another two roomed place provided" at an unspecified location.[3]

Alonzo, with various wives and children, was enumerated three times at three different homes in 1870. Comparison of the census with city directories suggests that he, Elizabeth, Emily, Julia, and their children were living in a large adobe house (demolished) on the west side of this street, at 303 North 200 West, but in fact Elizabeth was living with her children at 594 North Center Street.

In 1885, Julia was supposedly living at 530 West 400 North and was described as a widow, although Alonzo Raleigh was very much alive and living in California, where prosecutions under the Edmunds Act did not affect him. He had returned to 303 North 200 West by 1889, and in 1890 was apparently living here in the adobe at 324 North. Alonzo was the sole occupant in 1900 and died here in 1901.[4]

In his will, Alonzo Raleigh specified that his large house at 303 North 200 West should be given to the LDS Church. Although Emily, who had lived there for fifty years with "her demented son and my other children," filed suit to retain the property, she was evicted in 1905 and moved into this house. She died at the duplex next door (326) in 1921.[5]

The house was most likely built as a hall-parlor type. In 1889, Raleigh added two adobe rooms and it became the cross-wing type that it is today. An adobe "summer kitchen" at the rear was linked to the house by a wood-frame breezeway. At the time, it was directly south of Henry W. Hooper's mansion (demolished).[6]

527 North 200 West—Joseph Grafton and Sarah Currier Bailey Hovey, date unknown

Joseph Grafton Hovey (1812–1868) was born in Massachusetts but moved to Quincy, Illinois, in 1837 to work with his brother, Orlando Dana Hovey. He became a convert to the LDS Church, moved to Nauvoo in 1839, and left for Winter Quarters in June 1846. Joseph's first wife, Martha Ann

Webster, died there in September. In 1847, he married Sarah Currier Bailey (1806–1890), a widow. She accompanied him to Utah with the Heber C. Kimball Company in 1848, as did Joseph's two (of nine) surviving children. Sarah's five children with her first husband had all died by 1845.[7]

Hovey received this lot on the corner of 500 North and 200 West in 1848. On October 19, he "commenced to haul my dogies [adobes] sand, clay, and stone. . . . In twenty days I hauled all of my stuff for my house. . . . The dimensions of my house are sixteen feet by nineteen feet by eleven feet four inches high." Sarah and Joseph had one child, Sarah Elizabeth. Then Joseph married twice more, in 1850 and 1852, to sisters Sarah Louisa and Lousanna Emily Goodridge [Goodrich]. After that he spent most of his time with them in Cache County.[8]

Heber C. Kimball visited Joseph Hovey in Salt Lake City on the day Hovey died and spoke at Joseph's funeral in the original Nineteenth Ward meeting house. Kimball lived only a month longer himself. Joseph G. Hovey is buried in the Kimball family plot northeast of Temple Square, behind what was Heber C. Kimball's adobe home.[9]

Whether the existing house includes any part of the original house is unknown. An 1898 map shows a small adobe building downhill to the west of this one. It was still standing in 1950 but is now gone.[10] Even though neighborhood streets were poorly defined in 1848, lot boundaries were carefully surveyed and houses were meant to face the street, suggesting that the small adobe was an outbuilding, not a dwelling. The existing house is a simple cross-wing type. The south wing is adobe and the north wing is wood frame.

Sarah Hovey remained at this location until at least 1870, received a Mayor's Deed to the property in 1873, and in 1874 sold the current lot to Samuel Cooper, a real estate agent. The price, $400, strongly suggests that there was a house on the property. Sarah died in Davis County in 1890.[11] Subsequent owners sold part of the property to Gustave Johnson in 1875. Johnson owned other properties and seems not to have lived here.

560 North 200 West—Anders Wilhelm and Andrine Friese Winberg, c. 1854

Anders Winberg (1830–1909) and his wife, Andrine (1831–1912), were among the earliest Scandinavian immigrants, arriving from Sweden with the Hans Peter Olsen Company in 1854. In his detailed autobiography, Winberg recounted crossing the plains, shooting buffalo (and killing a Native American who had retaliated by shooting two of the pioneers'

cows), and finally making camp on the public square at 200 North and 300 West—today's West High School campus—in Salt Lake City. Andrine, who was pregnant, recalled walking all the way from the outfitting post at Westport, Missouri.

The Winbergs lived briefly with other pioneers in the Second Ward and built the first room of this house with local fieldstone. This may be the tiny stone room shown on an 1898 map. Soon after that room was built, Winberg added an adobe room, probably to the west side. Their first child was born here in March 1855. Winberg's recollection was that, when he and his family fled the city in 1857 to avoid Johnston's Army, he left behind "two city lots and a one room adobe shanty." The earliest known records for this property, dated 1861, show that by that time at least, Winberg did, in fact, own two adjacent lots. An 1869 photograph by Andrew J. Russell, who was in Utah to document the completion of the transcontinental railroad at Promontory Point, shows the Winbergs' house.[12] The ridge line of the early house and its south wall are still visible, but the fieldstone room appears to have been demolished.

The house grew through additions and alterations over the years. The full-length front porch had been built by 1875. Like other homes of this period, the earliest roof timbers are whole logs rather than sawn lumber.[13]

Winberg worked first as a blacksmith and later as a clerk. In 1876, he founded and began writing *Bikuben* (*The Beehive*), the first newspaper for Scandinavians west of the Rocky Mountains. The powder magazines high on Arsenal (Capitol) Hill exploded the same year, sending tons of rock and debris in all directions, shattering windows on Main Street, damaging hundreds of buildings, and killing several people, including the young men thought to have caused the blast. Among the victims was Mary Jane Van Natta, who was drawing water here at the Winbergs' well. A large rock thrown some three-quarters of a mile by the explosion hit her in the back, killing her instantly.[14]

Anders and Andrina had seven children, all of whom survived childhood. Anders married a plural wife, Elvina Nyman, in 1873, and they had eight children. Elvina had her own home or lived with one of her children as she got older. The *Salt Lake Tribune* reported that Elvina was "on the underground" while Anders was on trial for unlawful cohabitation in the 1880s. She died in 1915. Anders Winberg died in this house on August 9, 1909, and his first wife, Andrine, died here in 1912.[15]

625 North 200 West—George L. and Mary Pugsley Lambourne, c. 1877

George Lorenzo Lambourne (1856–1916) was born in St. Louis, Missouri. His parents were English immigrants who probably arrived in New York on the *American Eagle* in 1855 and then continued west. The 1860 census shows the family, which by that time included three children, living in St. Louis, where George Sr. worked as a tailor and owned property worth some $600. When George Sr. died in St. Louis in 1862, his widow, Rhoda, married Joseph E. Mullett (see 584 North Wall Street, also in the Nineteenth Ward).[16]

Together with Joseph's large family, Rhoda, with her sons George and Levi Lambourne, arrived in Salt Lake City with the Chester Loveland Company in 1868. The Loveland Company had assembled its wagons at Fort Laramie, Wyoming, then the western terminus of the transcontinental railroad.[17] The following year, the rails met at Promontory Point, Utah.

The house was built as a hall-parlor type that originally faced south. Sometime before 1911, a brick addition on the south made it a more fashionable cross-wing.

Very little is known of George Lambourne. He married Mary Pugsley, a daughter of Phillip and Clarissa Pugsley, in 1877, and bought this lot from Orlando D. Hovey. George and Mary were living here by 1879. They had three children, although two, Rhoda and George, died before they were two years old. Mary died of convulsions in 1884, and George sold the house to Ann Player, whose daughters were plural wives of Alonzo Raleigh.[18] (See 324 North 200 West and 594 North Center Street, both in the Nineteenth Ward.)

George married again, to Annie Newton, and had four daughters with her. Annie died of asthma and kidney disease in 1906 at the age of forty-four. Near the end of his life, which had been painful by any standards, George was discouraged and often out of work. He committed suicide by swallowing poison in 1916.[19]

60 West 300 North—Charles Frederick and Mary Ann Slater, c. 1867

Cemetery records indicate that Charles Frederick (Fred) Slater was born in 1821 and died in 1899.[20] Census records, on the other hand, show that both he and his wife, Mary Ann, were born in England about 1828.

Fred Slater came to Utah sometime between 1860 and 1867.[21] It is likely that he and Mary Ann were not then members of the LDS Church, so even if they arrived with Mormon immigrants, their names might not have been recorded on church lists or in the *Deseret News*. Frederick's death at the Episcopal St. Mark's Hospital also suggests he was not LDS.[22]

The earliest record of Frederick Slater in Salt Lake City is the 1867 city directory, in which his location is given as the north side of Currant (300 North) at Beet Street (now North Main Street). City tax rolls for 1867 also indicate he lived in this ward, and the 1869 directory placed him between Quince and Central. In 1870, the census enumerator found him, with Mary Ann and their children, living directly east of Ebenezer Beesley, almost certainly in this house, even though he did not buy the property until 1873.[23]

Fred was always identified in census records and city directories as a shoemaker. He lived at this house through at least 1885, when the address was 65 Currant (300 North), and then at various addresses on the city's west side. He became an American citizen in 1889.[24]

Mary Ann died in 1895 of debility and diarrhea. When Fred Slater died of kidney and heart disease in 1899, his death received only the briefest notice. With or without his consent, he became a teaching tool in a "school for undertakers" studying the art of placing a body in a casket.[25]

The adobe portion of the house, now stuccoed, seems to have faced west. Later frame additions, probably built after Slater sold the house to Lorenzo J. Aubrey in 1886, are Victorian in style, and the whole structure is in disrepair.

80 West 300 North—Ebenezer and Sarah Hancock Beesley, c. 1867

The Beesley house was built as a two-story central-passage type, with two rooms on each floor, separated by the entry hall and staircase. Its foundation is made of common fieldstone. The north wing of the house is a later addition, its granite foundation apparently made of rubble taken from the site of the Salt Lake Temple while it was under construction. This was a large and elegant house for its time, although it had little ornamentation and lacked even the cornice returns common to classical buildings of the time. The porches, with their turned railings and other trim, may have been added some time after the house was built.

Ebenezer Beesley (1840–1906) and his wife, Sarah Hancock (1840–1921), were English converts to the LDS Church. They were eighteen and nineteen years old and already a married couple when they arrived in New York City in 1859. Like many poor immigrants, they made their

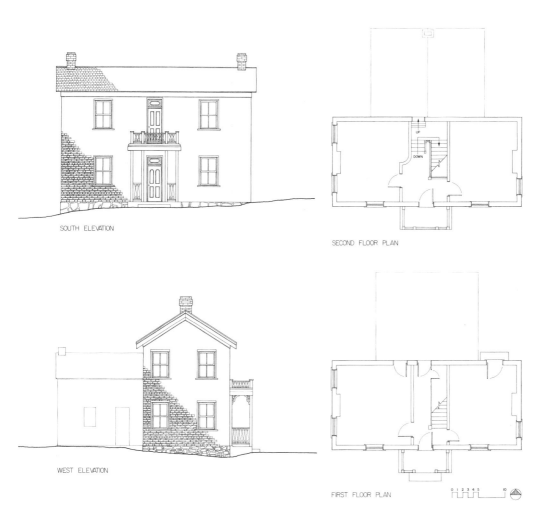

SOUTH ELEVATION

SECOND FLOOR PLAN

WEST ELEVATION

FIRST FLOOR PLAN

80 West 300 North, Ebenezer and Sarah Hancock Beesley. Architectural drawings by Thomas Carter and students, and James Gosney. Used by permission, Western Regional Architecture Program Collection, J. Willard Marriott Library, University of Utah, all rights reserved.

way to the Missouri River and joined the George Rowley handcart company, walking for three months from Florence, Nebraska, to Salt Lake City. Much later, Sarah reluctantly described their experiences as "dreadful" and refused to write her story of crossing the plains, saying, "My children have often tried to get me to write my handcart story but I will not." Sarah's mother came to join them in 1863, but lived only eight weeks after her arrival in the valley. Ebenezer had brought his violin with him on the journey and seems to have suffered far less than his wife. Soon after their arrival, he cheerfully set about recruiting other musicians for a band—using the musical talents that would rescue him from obscurity.[26]

When the census was taken in August 1860, the Beesleys, with their day-old son, were living in Tooele, but they had moved here by 1867. The house appears on a detailed map made in 1870, and on a similar map from 1875.[27]

The Beesley home is included here as a contrast to most of the others in this book and as an example of what could be done with adobe. Beesley became known in Utah as a pioneer musician, member of the Salt Lake Theater orchestra, composer of hymns, and, ultimately, director of the Mormon Tabernacle Choir.

Ebenezer married a plural wife, Anne (Annie) Frewin Buckridge (1845–1907), in 1869. Annie lived at this house only briefly in 1873 and thereafter in the Sixteenth Ward.[28] The census enumerator recorded Ebenezer twice in 1880, once here and once with Annie at a house on the corner of North Temple and 700 West. In 1900, Annie was living at 240 North 700 West, where she died in 1907. Annie and Ebenezer had six children, but only two survived childhood. Annie's daughter Clarissa was active in the LDS Church young women's movement. Annie herself remains largely a cypher.

For all practical purposes, this was Sarah Beesley's house. She gave birth to ten children between about 1860 and 1881, all but one of whom survived, and she raised them here. She died in this house at the age of eighty-one. An undated photograph, probably taken after Ebenezer's death, shows Sarah standing alone near the front door.[29]

Ebenezer Beesley's funeral was held in the Assembly Hall on Temple Square. He is buried in the Salt Lake City Cemetery together with Sarah and Annie.[30]

726 West 300 North—Charles Warner and Betsey Oades Player, 1854

A modern brick facade and smooth asphalt shingle roof conceal one of the oldest houses in the Salt Lake Valley. Its builder was Charles W. Player, a stonecutter who worked for thirty years on the Salt Lake LDS Temple. He intended his house to last. Rather than wooden sills and lintels for the windows and doors, he chose substantial stone. Instead of sawn lumber, which was rare and expensive, he cut small trees to use as rafters and door frames.[31] The house was built as a hall-parlor type, with a centered front door and windows symmetrically placed at either side. A third adobe room on the west, and one on the north that was probably a kitchen, add to the original footprint.

Charles Player (1827–1884) came from London, England, with his parents and siblings in 1842. They lived at Nauvoo for several years, even after the city was largely abandoned by the Mormons. Betsey (1829–1912), who was from Lincolnshire, sailed from Liverpool to New Orleans in 1848 on the *Erin's Queen*. She was eighteen, accompanied by her sisters Sarah, twenty-three, and Anne, twenty-five, and Anne's husband, Henry Jackson. Betsey married George Robbins in St. Louis, Missouri, in December 1848, but he must have died soon after. Betsey and Charles W. Player were married by the time of the 1850 census in Iowa.[32]

The couple remained for another two years in Iowa before joining the James C. Snow Company and traveling to the Salt Lake Valley, arriving in October 1852. Betsey gave birth to her first child, Charles Jr., while they were on the trail in Nebraska. Charles's parents, William and Zillah, did not reach the valley until 1862.[33]

Charles was the original occupant of this lot, and his name appears on one of the oldest known plat maps. In June 1854 he registered his brand in the Nineteenth Ward, about the time this house was built, and by 1856 he was assessed taxes on the property, his cattle, and household furnishings. Betsey's brief biography identified this house as a three-room adobe built soon after the family's arrival.[34]

Charles worked as a stonecutter on the Salt Lake Temple until he became too ill with silicosis to work, and died in this house in 1884.[35] Betsey succeeded in raising all of her thirteen children to maturity, a remarkable feat. Three of her descendants wrote about her disapproval of polygamy and the efforts she made to keep her house after Charles's death. Her older children found work, while Betsy sold parcels of the family lot to bring in money. She managed to remain independent for almost thirty years after Charles's death and, like her husband, died in this house.[36]

175 West 400 North—John and Anne (Annie) Underwood Flower, c. 1866

When Plat A was surveyed in 1847, this block was included in it and was laid out with the customary eight lots. Only the four lots on the west side of the block were distributed, probably because the steep and rocky terrain made those on the east side undesirable or even inaccessible before the streets were any more than footpaths. The east side of the block was much later included in Plat E, east of what is now Quince Street.

Two veterans of the Mormon Battalion, Abraham Day and James C. Earl, were the original claimants of this lot. Earl sold his interest to George Bryant Gardner in 1850. No persuasive evidence indicates that any of them built a house or lived here. Abraham Day sold the lot to Christopher Merkley in 1856 and Merkley sold it to another Mormon Battalion veteran, Benjamin Hawkins. In 1866, Hawkins sold the east half of the lot, where this house stands, to John Flower.[37]

John Flower (1818–1899) was a Welshman who departed Liverpool on the *Golconda* in 1854, with help from the Perpetual Emigrating Fund. From New Orleans he would have taken a smaller boat up the Mississippi River and then joined an emigrant company, arriving in the Salt Lake Valley by March, 1855. He was living alone in the 19th Ward in 1860, probably near here, and in 1861 he married Anne or Annie Underwood, recently arrived from England.[38]

This is one of several fieldstone houses on the slopes of Capitol Hill. Most have been stuccoed or otherwise obscured, and many others have been demolished. Like the John Platts house at 364 North Quince Street, it was built almost entirely of material that was available on or near the site. Also like the Platts house, but not as handsomely executed, there are stone quoins at the house corners.

The original house was a hall-parlor type with two rooms and an attic sleeping space. A later wood frame porch covers the west side. The house faced west and, like some of the oldest houses in Salt Lake City, its roof and ceiling timbers are not sawn lumber but whole logs. The house is visible in an 1869 photograph taken by A. J. Russell, who was soon to create the iconic image known as "Wedding of the Rails," showing the transcontinental railroad tracks as they were joined at Promontory Point.[39]

An addition facing 400 North, now faced with brick, is built of adobe and fired bricks, laid up so that there are two or three courses of one and then the other, visible because the house was undergoing renovation in 2013. This type of construction was also used in the Alonzo Raleigh house at 594 North Center Street.[40]

William Henry Hooper, Utah's first delegate to Congress, built his mansion directly west of the Flower house and facing 200 West, at about the same time. An early hand-drawn map of the Hooper house, made for fire insurance purposes, may also show this one.[41]

John and Anne divorced in 1875, and having no other property, he built the adobe hall-parlor house still standing at 365 North Quince Street. Multiple additions make it difficult to recognize, but it is on the south end of this same lot. When John married again, he lived there with his second wife, Mary Andrews. After their divorce, Anne Underwood raised grapes on trellises here, squeezing the juice into wooden tubs. She traded the wine she made for necessities like flour and always had a ready market for her product.[42]

236 West 400 North—Hannah Harvey Reese, c. 1874

Hannah Harvey (1826–1901) and her family were English converts to the LDS Church. They were in Buffalo, New York, while Enoch Reese (1813–1876) was the branch president there. Enoch and Hannah followed the church to Kirtland, Ohio, and then to Nauvoo, Illinois, reaching Utah in 1849 with the Allen Taylor Company. Hannah and Enoch married in 1843, and two young sons, James and Enoch Moroni, accompanied them to Utah.[43]

Enoch and his brother John were merchants, some of the first to reach the Salt Lake Valley. Together they went to the area of Carson City, Nevada (then part of Utah Territory), in 1850 to establish Mormon Station in 1851, a way station for trade and travelers to the California gold fields.[44] Nevada's Reese River is named for John Reese.

In 1859, Enoch Reese bought the parcel where this house stands from its original occupant for seventy-five dollars, and got a quit claim deed from Heber C. Kimball's estate for the same parcel in 1870. He probably never lived here. In 1860 he was living in the Seventeenth Ward with his later wives, Sarah and (another) Hannah. He lived with his youngest wife, Amy, in the Eighteenth Ward after their marriage in 1865.[45]

Although Hannah Harvey Reese's name never appeared on the deed, it may be that this house was built for her and her son James, who may have been living here as early as 1874. Enoch mortgaged the parcel for large sums in the 1870s, but likely invested the money in his commercial ventures rather than in improving Hannah's house. In 1877, Hannah's son Enoch Moroni and his wife, Zina, bought the property to the east. Hannah lived in this house through at least 1880 when it was sold to Israel Dewey and then to George B. Kelly.[46]

The Second Empire style of the house as it appears today did not come into vogue until the 1880s. The original house was likely a one-and-a-half-story, hall-parlor type. Later additions at front and rear, along with the mansard roof, almost completely obscure that structure. George B. Kelly, a son of John "Bookbinder" Kelly, probably made these alterations when he bought the house in 1884.[47]

Enoch Reese died in 1876, leaving an estate that was tied up in probate court until 1894. Hannah apparently received little or nothing—she was unable to pay even five dollars in taxes for 1896 and was declared indigent. She lived for many years at 561 North 200 West, in another adobe, and died there in 1901.[48]

George B. Kelly is usually credited with building this house, but most likely he simply updated its exterior. After mortgaging the property several times, he began selling off parcels of the lot in 1882, one of them to Andrew and Karen Hyrup, who built the cross-wing-type adobe house at 238 West 400 North.[49]

727 West 400 North—James and Elizabeth Fovargue Smith, 1855

Elizabeth Fovargue (1828–1902) grew up in Cambridgeshire, England, attending school until she was thirteen, unusual for a farm laborer's daughter. Her education and native intelligence made it possible for her to recall and record in vivid detail her experiences leaving home, marrying hastily, sailing to America, and living in Salt Lake City during the early pioneer period.[50]

Elizabeth and James (1823–1874) left Liverpool in February 1853, on the *International* for a nine-week voyage to New Orleans. There, Elizabeth recalled that some Mormon girls "did not behave themselves very good" (and went no further). A smaller boat took the Smiths up the Mississippi to Keokuk, Iowa, where they joined the Jacob Gates Company, arriving in the Salt Lake Valley on October 29.[51]

For the next two years, James and Elizabeth made do with very little, living with James's sister, Caroline, and her husband, Thomas Cottam. Then in 1855, triumph and tragedy came in quick succession. As Elizabeth wrote:

> Just before this time James had bought a half lot of one James Hall for 16 dollars. James and Father Smith hauled some rock from Red bute [Butte] Canyon they allso got some adobies and howled [hauled] them with Thomas Cottam ox team[.] I helped unlod them

and done all I could to help get a home[.] about a month before we left Mrs Cottams I was quite sick not able to go around when our house was so far finished so we could move into it.... My first child was born on the 13 of June, 1855, on the 10 of June James and I went to President Youngs Office and was sealed[.] we named our baby Joseph he was a delicate child.... he lingered on untill the 23 of August 1855 suffered considerable and died in convulsions we buried him in our Garden in a plain coffin with no one to follow him but our family.

Even when babies' deaths were common, they caused no less heartache for family.

James was a mason but often found work outside Salt Lake City. Elizabeth worked for "Mrs. Young," presumably Brigham Young's first wife, Mary Ann Angell, making dresses. Two more of Elizabeth's sons died as infants, but five children survived. The couple accumulated furniture, livestock, and even a clock or watch.[52]

James Smith died in 1874 at the age of fifty-one, and soon after that Elizabeth sold part of her lot (at the suggestion of Alonzo Raleigh) and was able to live a bit more comfortably. Elizabeth's children did well, and she found enjoyment in hearing Wilford Woodruff and George Q. Cannon speak at the Assembly Hall. She wrote of riding the streetcars, visiting Fuller's Hill Pleasure Gardens, until finally, in March 1891, she wrote her final entry. "I think that I will close my jurnal [sic] I neglect it so much[.] No more at present." Eleven years later, Elizabeth died of "old age and debility" at the age of seventy-six.[53]

Although the original north and east walls of the Smith house have been demolished, enough remains of the south and west walls to draw some conclusions about its architecture. It appears to have been about fourteen by twenty-two feet and was probably a hall-parlor type. Elizabeth and James would have lived in one room, and James's parents in the other. James, a mason, may have designed and built the house himself. Its west gable end shows the low roof pitch typical of the earliest homes, but most of the original roof has since been covered by later ones. The hipped-roof adobe rooms, built for Elizabeth Smith's son James and his wife about 1884, became the south side of the house, and a brick room with a Victorian bay front faces north. A wood-frame porch and a small room that were present in 1898 have been integrated into the east side of the house, and a rear wood-frame porch was added sometime after 1950.

423 North 600 West—William F. J. and Jane Ann Richardson Albrand, c. 1860

William Albrand (1828–1903) sailed from Hamburg, Germany, to New York in 1850 on the ship *Franklin*. He may have meant to continue west to the California gold fields, but when he reached the Salt Lake Valley, he attended a meeting at which Brigham Young spoke. He became a member of the LDS Church in 1852 and by 1854 was ordained a Seventy. Although he was called on a mission to the Eastern States in 1855, his name does not appear on the list of any company, either eastbound or westbound, after that time, so he may not have gone.[54]

The original occupant of the property was Henry Steed, a pioneer of 1850. No record was made of its sale to William Albrand, but in 1851 Henry and his brother, Thomas, moved to land they bought in Davis County, where they lived for the rest of their lives.[55]

Jane Ann Richardson (1831–1901) was an English immigrant who reached Utah with the Jesse B. Martin Company in 1857. She and William married in 1859, and by 1860 were living in this location. William gave his occupation during that year's census as "common laborer."[56]

Their real estate had an assessed value of $400, and they owned a pig and a clock or watch.

As they became more secure financially, the Albrand house grew in stages, beginning as a two-story, single-cell type that faced south, enlarged by a wrap-around, one-story addition on the west and north sides. By 1870, William was working as a gardener, a trade he practiced for many years afterwards.[57]

The Albrands ultimately had four children—Mary Amelia, William, Jane Ann, and Wilhelmina (who died when she was a year old)—but their married life must have been troubled. When William filed for divorce in 1879, he described the cause as "incompatibility of temper," admitting that their "life has been one of misery." He owned nothing beyond the house and lot. Jane agreed to forego a court trial if she could have possession of the house during her lifetime, along with their livestock and a buggy and harness. She also requested that William fix the doors he had broken.[58]

Jane and her children remained here, and her son, William, built his own house next door at 427 North 600 West. Daughters Mary Amelia and Jane Ann lived here with their families for many years, and Jane Albrand died in this house in 1901.[59]

William Albrand married again to Malvina Minna Scheffler in 1880 and had a small adobe house just to the north, at 433 North 600 West (demolished). They had two daughters, one of whom died in infancy. William lived at that house until his death in 1903.[60]

244 West 700 North—Cynthia Maria Wilcox Arnold, c. 1888

Cynthia Maria Wilcox (1846–1917) was one of nine children of Walter Eli Wilcox and Maria Wealthy Richards. Both parents were from Massachusetts and early converts to the LDS Church. Born at Council Bluffs, Iowa, only two months after her parents left Nauvoo, Illinois, Cynthia spent her first few years at Winter Quarters and in St. Louis, Missouri. She came to the Salt Lake Valley with her family in 1852, where until about 1860 they lived in the Seventh Ward near John B. Kelly (see 422 South 200 West).[61]

Cynthia's father had five wives, among them the young Matilda Watmough (see 348 North Quince Street, Nineteenth Ward). He worked in

various positions, often for Brigham Young as a mechanic or woodworker, operating sawmills in the Cottonwood Canyons and in City Creek, creating hollow log "pipes" to carry water, and building furniture. Later he managed a hospital.[62] Between 1866 and 1876 Cynthia's mother and her children lived in the original—and by that time thoroughly dilapidated—Warm Springs Bath House that stood on what is now Reed Avenue, near 300 West.

The family was well positioned in both the LDS Church and the community. In 1869, when she was twenty-three, Cynthia married Henry Arnold as his sixth wife. Henry (1822–1888) was forty-seven and English. He had come to Utah in 1852 and spent the next fourteen years at various forts and settlements, fighting Native Americans and serving in various military actions.[63] He took over management of the new Warm Springs Bath House, which stood at the north end of 300 West, in 1866. Cynthia [Sintha] was reportedly living with her parents in 1870, and Henry was "in charge" at the adjacent bath house. They had ten children, five of whom died in early childhood, between 1876 and 1884.[64]

Brigham Young owned the bath house property, and after his death in 1877, its buildings were demolished. The property was sold and subdivided. Evaline L. Young Davis bought the parcel where this house stands in 1878.[65] Whether Cynthia Arnold ever held the title is unclear.

Henry Arnold relocated to the Globe Bakery on Main Street in 1877. Soon after that he bought a stone house which is still standing at 630/632 N. Wall Street, and enlarged it for his growing families. By

1885, prosecutions under the Edmunds Act had begun in earnest and "it was the general understanding that he [Henry] was in England or some other foreign country." In July 1888, Henry was arrested and charged with unlawful cohabitation under the Edmunds Act but died in September before a trial could begin. Two of his widows, Christina and Elizabeth, stayed in the Wall Street house after his death, and Cynthia moved into this house.[66]

None of this provides any real insight into Cynthia Arnold's life. One of her great-granddaughters attempted to write a biographical sketch but was forced to admit, "There was not a history of Cynthia Maria Wilcox Arnold found." A brief obituary revealed nothing more.[67]

The house, which has some attractive Victorian eclectic elements such as an arched entry and windows and a pillared porch, is no more than a single-cell or shotgun type, which was extended with a wood-frame room on the north end sometime between 1911 and 1950.[68]

322 North Almond Street—Edwin, Ann Marsh, and Marie Cowley Rawlings, 1871

Edwin Rawlings (1838–1914) and his wife, Annie (1839–1914), left England in 1862 and sailed for America on the *William Tapscott* with more than nine hundred other passengers. From New York City, they made their way to Florence, Nebraska, and joined the Horton D. Haight Company, arriving in the Salt Lake Valley in mid-October. Their journey had lasted five months.[69]

The house was built in 1871, after Edwin and Annie had lived elsewhere in Salt Lake City for nearly ten years. They bought the lot from Henry Dinwoody for $100 and apparently had saved enough money to complete the house without needing a mortgage.[70] Almond Street—then known as Crooked Street—was no more than a winding path in the 1870s. The deep setback of the house from today's street may reflect its position near the original path.

Because Edwin was a skilled cabinet maker, he was able to add decorative architectural details that were rare in adobe homes. There are turned spindles and scrollwork trim on the porch, and the adobe bricks are entirely covered with clapboard siding.

Edwin and Annie had no children, but Edwin had five children with his plural wife, Marie Cowley (1847–1923), between 1880 and 1889. Capitol Hill historian Hermoine Jex reported that although the children were Marie's, Annie took care of them all and served as president of the Nineteenth Ward Relief Society. When prosecutions for polygamy were being conducted under the Edmunds Act, Edwin Rawlings was charged with and convicted of unlawful cohabitation in 1888. He served seventy-five days and paid a seventy-five-dollar fine.[71]

Annie, Marie, and Edwin, with their children, lived here together until Edwin died in 1914. Marie's son Edwin James lived in the house all his life and never married. The house remained in family ownership until 1998, when Edwin's granddaughter Gladys Bullock sold it to a friend. In its current dilapidated condition the house is worth only $1,600, one-tenth of its assessed value in 2014.[72]

328 North Almond Street—Richard G. and Mary Hancock and Sarah Linnell Collett, c. 1874

Richard Collett (1842–1904) bought this lot from the estate of Heber C. Kimball in 1872, almost ten years after he and his wife, Mary (1842–1921), left England on the *Amazon* for New York City. They arrived in the Salt

Lake Valley with an unidentified pioneer company in 1863, accompanied by their son, Lorenzo George. Richard and Mary, whose sister was Ebenezer Beesley's wife, Sarah, eventually had thirteen children, of whom eight reached maturity. They lived briefly in the Seventeenth Ward and then at the corner of Center and Quince Streets in 1869, presumably saving money to build a home of their own. Richard was a shoemaker who worked for Zions Cooperative Mercantile Institution (ZCMI) and other large stores. He was also a musician who sang in the Tabernacle Choir, and, like John Platts, played cricket.[73]

The earliest section of this house, perhaps only a single room, had been built by 1874, when Richard Collett [Callet] appeared in the city directory on Crooked (Almond) Street between 300 North and Apricot (Cross) Streets and paid property taxes. When the powder magazines on Arsenal Hill exploded in 1876, Collett's son was injured by a falling wall, "bruising the boy—not serious."[74]

In 1880, Richard was living here with Mary and his plural wife, Sarah Linnell (1844–1896), whom he had married in 1872. Sarah had six children with Richard, of whom four died in childhood between 1875 and 1879.[75]

Collett and his neighbor Edwin Rawlings both appeared before Commissioner McKay on charges of unlawful cohabitation in 1887. Rawlings pleaded not guilty, but Collett was convicted and was sentenced to six months in the penitentiary plus a $100 fine.[76] Richard Collett, his wives, and several of their children are buried together in the Salt Lake City Cemetery.[77]

A building permit for the two-story brick addition on the rear was issued in 1895.[78]

122 West Apricot Avenue—John Platts, c. 1874

When John Platts built this hall-parlor-type house, it joined two others already on his property (see 364 and 368 North Quince Street, a half block west in the Nineteenth Ward). It may have been built for a particular tenant, Sarah Marinda Bates Pratt (1817–1888), the first of ten wives of LDS apostle Orson Pratt.

Sarah Bates met Orson Pratt when he was a young missionary in her home village of Henderson, New York. They married in 1836 and began the peripatetic life common to most early Latter-day Saints. Several moves and several children later (they would ultimately have twelve, although six died in childhood), they reached Nauvoo, Illinois. There, the unwanted attentions of Joseph Smith, rumors of Sarah's infidelity, and of Smith's multiple relationships were circulated by John C. Bennett in 1842. Bennett was excommunicated. He wrote inflammatory letters to the *Sangamo Journal* excoriating Joseph Smith and the LDS Church, and accusing Sarah Pratt of adultery. Orson Pratt himself was excommunicated in 1842, although that action was invalidated in 1843.[79] The taint of scandal followed Sarah for the rest of her life.

Orson Pratt married his first plural wife in 1844. When the Latter-day Saints began leaving Nauvoo in early 1846, he packed up his families and moved them to Winter Quarters, where they remained while he accompanied the first pioneers to the Salt Lake Valley in 1847. Returning to Winter Quarters that fall, Orson left again, on a mission to Great Britain, taking Sarah and her children with him. Sarah finally reached the Salt Lake Valley in 1851. Pratt acknowledged the practice of polygamy in 1852.

Because Orson Pratt was, in spite of his many later marriages, supportive of Sarah, he often found himself in conflict with Brigham Young, who dealt with the obstinate apostle by sending him away on missions.[80] Pratt's families, Sarah's included, were left to support themselves and suffered during his absences.

Orson Pratt deeded his large adobe house and part of his lot on the corner of South Temple and West Temple Streets to Brigham Young in 1861 when he, Sarah, and their children accompanied Erastus Snow to St. George, Utah. After an unhappy three years in St. George, during which Orson was for the most part absent on a mission to Austria, Sarah and her children returned to Salt Lake. Orson returned from Austria in 1868, not having seen Sarah since 1862, and married his tenth wife. Sarah had had enough.[81]

With Young's permission, Sarah moved back to the Pratt family house on the corner of South Temple and West Temple and stayed there until 1873, when Brigham Young had her evicted, claiming ownership. While the court proceedings were in progress, Sarah Pratt lived in this unornamented two-room house on Apricot Avenue, now expanded by multiple additions at the rear. Its roof is not original, as indicated by the insubstantial rafters, and the porch may not be original.

The 1874 city directory listed Sarah Pratt as a widow (although Orson Pratt was very much alive) living here on the north side of Cross [Apricot] between Central and Quince Streets. She was excommunicated for apostasy in 1874. When subsequent court rulings upheld Sarah's claim to the property on West Temple Street, she returned to her old home.[82]

Sarah Marinda Bates Pratt was Mitt Romney's great-great-grandmother.

328 North Center Street—Elijah Francis and Grace May Marks Pearce, c. 1875

Elijah Pearce (1835–1922) was an English basket maker who arrived in Salt Lake City with the Ira Eldredge Company in 1861. He and his business partner, Job Smith, first advertised their wares that fall. Grace Marks (1852–1879) came from England with her mother and siblings in 1866. She married Elijah in 1867 when she was fifteen and he was thirty-two.[83]

By 1870 they were living with two young sons in the Sugar House Ward, on the corner of what is now 500 East and 1700 South. Wilford Woodruff's 1856 log farmhouse (still standing at 1604 South 500 East) was across the street to the west. (The census enumerator incorrectly reported Elijah's birthplace as New York, and his wife's name as Jane.) Elijah's real and personal property was valued at $2,600, a substantial sum for a tradesman.[84]

Elijah bought this property from the architect E. L. T. Harrison in 1875, along with rights to use the private street at the rear "for bringing any materials required thereon," suggesting that there was as yet no house on the lot. He mortgaged the property for $550 and built what was, for the time, a spacious home. But things must have soured quickly; he lost the property in a sheriff's sale in 1878 and sold it at a loss to Richard G. Lambert.[85]

In October 1878, Pearce was called on a mission to New Zealand. Presumably, Grace would have been left to fend for herself, but she may have had help from her family. When she died in 1879, her son Brigham was adopted by her brother, Stephen R. Marks, who was living in this house in 1884. Her son Robert lived with a shoemaker and his family on Main Street, attending school.[86]

When he returned from New Zealand in 1880, Elijah was cut off from the church for adultery and other improper acts. He was not considered for restoration to the priesthood until 1894. By then he had remarried, to Jemimah Wiggill Ellis (1838–1922), a widow and the daughter of a South African convert. The couple lived in Logan for the rest of their lives, and Eli seems to have reconciled with his children. He died at his son Brigham's home in Salt Lake City in 1922, and was buried in a plot owned by his younger son, Robert.[87]

The house is a one-and-a-half-story T-plan with classical elements and carpenter's Gothic embellishments. Pearce apparently had the resources to build a relatively large and comfortable house for his family.

444 North Center Street—Edward Evans and Catherine Vaughan Jones, c. 1870

A rectangular log cabin, now covered with stucco, was the original room on the north end of what has become a cross-wing-type house. The cabin's age is unknown, but it was almost certainly here when Edward Jones (1842–1927) bought the lot from Moroni Pitt in 1870.[88] A few pioneers built log houses in the late 1840s and early 1850s, including one built by William Hawk between 1848 and 1852 that is still standing (although not at its original location) at 458 North 300 West. The Osmyn Deuel cabin, now adjacent to the LDS Church Family History Library, was an extension of the first pioneer fort and stood at the rear of Albert Carrington's home at 176 North West Temple until about 1902.[89] The south wing of the Jones house, which turned the cabin into a cross-wing type, is made of adobe.

Edward Jones's name was a common one, making it difficult to be certain that any particular record relates to him. He may have left Wales with his family in 1856, worked in Colorado, and come to Utah in 1865. Catherine (Kate) Vaughan (1848–1872) left Wales alone at the end of May 1866 on the *John Bright*, and arrived in Salt Lake City with the William Henry Chipman Company in September. Edward and Kate were married in 1870 and were living here in July of that year. Edward was working as a miner.[90]

Even though it seemed that their life in Salt Lake City might have been off to a good start, with land, employment, and a house, the couple's fortunes quickly deteriorated. Edward had been arrested for helping a friend escape from the custody of a police officer and was bound over for trial in May 1869. There were other problems as well. Their first child, Edward, was born and died in 1871. For reasons unknown, the attorney general of the territory, Zerubbabel Snow, passed the house and lot to Catherine in May 1871, remarking, "Katherine [*sic*] Jones is to have use of the property to the exclusion of her husband, or to any future husband. If she die without issue the property is to go to said Edward E. Jones if he survive her then to his heirs in fee." If that ruling actually benefited Catherine, its effect was limited. She died in September 1872, and her month-old baby girl died a week later. They are buried together in the Salt Lake City Cemetery.[91]

Of course, the property reverted to Edward, who received the Mayor's Deed in 1875. He kept it only until 1877, when he sold it to Susan Frances Williams for $650. She probably used a mortgage of $200 to improve the house, and lived there until at least 1885. Edward Jones moved to Stockton, Tooele County, where he lived in a boardinghouse and continued working as a miner. He remarried in December, 1873, and was living in Salt Lake City at the time of the 1920 census with his wife Letitia. He died in 1927 at the age of eighty-five.[92]

467 North Center Street—Daniel and Jane Wing Powell Cross, 1882, 1890

Daniel Cross (1816–1895) was from Banbury, Oxfordshire, England. He came to the Salt Lake Valley with his wife, Jane Wing Powell (1818–1874), and their two teenage children in 1868, sailing from Liverpool to New York on the *Minnesota* and continuing on from Laramie, Wyoming, then the western end of the transcontinental railroad tracks, with the Joseph Rawlins Company.[93] Their journey, like that of all the other company members, was financed by the Perpetual Emigrating Fund Company.

The family first lived in the Eleventh Ward near the intersection of South Temple and 700 East Streets, but the 1870 census found them all in Ogden where Daniel and his son, Nephi, were working on the railroad. Jane died of cancer of the mouth and jaw, after what must have been a grisly surgery and a great deal of suffering, in 1874.[94]

Daniel's whereabouts for the decade after Jane's death are unknown. He probably built this double-cell house at 467 North Center Street in 1882, placing a stone in the north gable-end that reads "Banbury Cross." His name first appeared at this address in the 1884 city directory (when it was 257 Centre Street) and he probably died here in 1895.

The small building at 455 North Center Street, also on the Cross property, was built in 1890, a "one-story two-room dwelling" costing an estimated $500.[95]

505 North Center Street—Anders (Andrew) Beck, Catherine Wickel, Mary Jones Mitchell, and Susan Williams Benzon, 1868

The Benzon adobe is one of the most thoroughly camouflaged in Salt Lake City. The original structure, a hall-parlor type that faced Center Street, is surrounded by frame and brick additions of various dates, including a store on the south side. Much of it is covered with siding and faux stone. Although its historic architectural character has been damaged, its history remains intact.

Andrew Beck Benzon (1835–1901) was born in Maribo, Denmark. He probably arrived in the United States in 1860. His obituary reported that he worked in the mining trades near Philadelphia and enlisted in the Union Army, that he had some medical training, and that he was wounded near Wilson's Creek, Missouri. His military record shows only that he was a private in the Missouri Infantry for three months in 1861.[96]

Benzon married his first wife, Catherine Wickel (1840–1915), in St. Louis in 1862. They made their way to Florence, Nebraska, where they joined the James Wareham Company and arrived in the Salt Lake Valley in late September. By 1869, the Benzons were living here at the corner of what was then "Central & Peach."[97]

Andrew married again in 1870, to Mary Jones Mitchell (1851–1917), and in 1871 to a third wife, Susan Williams (1850–1898). He seems to have been a man of many talents, among them medicine, sales (at ZCMI, among other stores), and superintending construction of the American Fork Railway. Although he was called by the LDS Church to go on a mission to Scandinavia, there is no record of his having made the journey. His life in Salt Lake City seems to have been uneventful.[98]

Almost nothing has been recorded about Andrew Benzon's wives. Census records show that Andrew, with Catherine, Mary, and Catherine's children, were living in this house in 1870, and that Andrew was living with Susan in 1880, while Catherine (Kate) had a separate house nearby.[99]

Susan (Susie) died at 244 Center Street in 1898. After that, Andrew lived with his children until he died at Holy Cross Hospital of cystitis and general debility in 1901. Susan and Andrew are buried together in the Salt Lake City Cemetery, along with twelve of Andrew's children. Catherine married again after Andrew's death.[100]

594 North Center Street—Elizabeth Ann Player Raleigh, 1861

What began as a single adobe room has become a lesson in the architectural history of Salt Lake City, as seen in a single house. The original room, a single-cell adobe built in 1861, faced south. Sometime before 1870, a brick one-and-a-half-story addition, more stylish but only a bit larger than the original room, was built on the west side. Three wood-frame additions on the north side of the house were built before 1898, completing the historic structure. By that time, one entry opened onto a west-facing porch, giving the house its address on Center Street. Recent additions on the east side complete the house.[101]

Alonzo Raleigh (see also 324 North 200 West, Nineteenth Ward) received three lots here at the north end of Center Street in 1865. The house
was built for his plural wife Elizabeth Ann Player Raleigh (1839–1924).
Elizabeth was a Welsh immigrant who reached Boston on the *Enoch Train*
in 1856 with her parents and three siblings and continued west with only
her sister Emily on the John A. Hunt wagon company. She married Raleigh in 1857 when he was thirty-nine and she was eighteen. Emily Player
also married Raleigh in 1857, when she was sixteen.[102]

Elizabeth and Alonzo had eight children. The last, born in 1880, lived
only a year. At the time of the 1870 census, when Elizabeth was living
here with six children and a servant, Alonzo Raleigh was also reportedly
part of the household. He was enumerated at two of his other homes that
year as well, and may never have resided here. Cora, a Native American
child adopted by the Raleighs, died in September 1870, after the census
was taken, but was not listed at any of the Raleigh households.[103]

At his death in 1901, Alonzo had "no legal wife," and it was not until
1902, when his estate was being settled, that Elizabeth's name first appeared on the deed to this house. She lived here, at times with her daughter Annette or her son William, until she died in 1924. Although she was
literate, Elizabeth seems to have written nothing about herself. By 1990,
the house had been condemned, but careful restoration by the current
owner has preserved its character and its history.[104]

66 West Girard Avenue—James J. and Eliza Wyatt, c. 1883

At one time, this house was a duplex whose smaller unit was on the east side (demolished). It shared the lot with another adobe duplex to the west (demolished).[105] The widening of West Capitol Street probably forced demolition of the east unit before 1950.

Not much is known about James Wyatt (1847–19?) or his wife, Eliza Jane (1845–1920). They were not pioneers, but they were in Utah by 1872 when their daughter Eliza Jane was born, and in Salt Lake City by 1874. Both Eliza Jane and her baby sister, Maud, died of diphtheria in September, 1878. Later census records indicate that the Wyatts were English, had several other children, and had emigrated in 1870 or 1874.[106]

James was an ambitious man. A plasterer, he also tried to make money in mining stocks, even buying some in Eliza's name, although several delinquent notices in 1875 suggest that he was not able to make his payments on them. Yet, somehow, he not only built the houses here on the corner of Girard and West Capitol Streets, but also a six-unit brick row house about a block north (136–146 West 600 North) in 1884. In the process, he borrowed heavily and transferred ownership of this house to Eliza, perhaps hoping to avoid legal problems.[107]

Life in Utah was difficult for James Wyatt. He must have had experiences, in addition to the deaths of his children, that soured him on living as an outsider in a Mormon community. For whatever reason, he attacked a boot black and then got into a long-running dispute with another man in the summer of 1878. Details on both sides were aired by newspapers with opposing viewpoints, often quite bitterly. He was denounced as a "spotter," someone who spied on polygamists at a time when the Edmunds Act was being enforced actively, and as a "hero of lies."[108] It was enough to drive the family away.

They moved to San Francisco in early 1886, where James continued to work as a plasterer, apparently at peace with his neighbors. They lived at the same address in the Bernal Heights neighborhood for many years. The Wyatts lost this property in a court action in 1889. James died sometime before the 1920 census, and Eliza Jane died in San Rafael, California, in November 1920.[109]

334 North Quince Street—Joseph Moralee and Annie Davis Watson, c. 1866

Joseph M. Watson (1840–1895) left a large footprint in Salt Lake City, both as a builder and as a "leading citizen." He emigrated from England and arrived in Salt Lake City with the Robert Neslen Company in 1859.

For a short time he lived in the Fourteenth Ward with Henry Woolacott, a stonecutter, until he married Anna Maria Thompson (1841–1864) in 1861.[110]

Their marriage was brief. After bearing two children who died in infancy, Anna died in May 1864. Watson did not remarry until 1881. His second wife was Annie M. Davis (1845–1926), also from England.[111]

Watson probably built the original house, a hall-parlor type, before 1866 and was living here in 1867. The rear lean-to may have been a later addition.[112] Recent two-story additions dwarf the adobe house, whose windows and door have been altered. Even the chimney has been enlarged. Joseph and his older brother, James, who reached Utah in 1863, formed Watson Brothers in 1864.[113] Some of the firm's major projects were the ZCMI shoe factory, the Hooper-Eldredge block, and construction of the red sandstone buildings at Fort Douglas, beginning in 1875.

The Watsons lived here through 1885 and then moved to a larger house on West Temple Street opposite the Temple Block.[114] They had no children, and when Joseph died, Annie administered his estate.[115] She lived another thirty years, a benefactor of LDS Church projects, active in the Genealogical Society, and a frequent traveler. Annie died at the house on West Temple Street in 1926.[116]

348 North Quince Street—William and Mary Ann Elizabeth Dyas Watmough, c. 1868

William Watmough (1808–1879) was a watchmaker from Lancashire, England. Even though his wife, Mary Ann Elizabeth Dyas (1815–1895), became a convert to the LDS Church in 1847, William remained a Methodist all his life. Still, he sailed for Boston with his wife and daughters, Matilda and Amanda, in 1856. By the time the Watmoughs arrived in Utah in 1862, they had already spent several years in Boston, presumably saving money for the journey west and entertaining visiting LDS apostles at their home.[117]

The Watmoughs' daughter Matilda was permitted to leave for Utah in 1856 or 1857. Reaching Salt Lake City, she married Walter Eli Wilcox, whom she had likely met in Boston. He was thirty-six and she was fourteen, the third of his five wives. Matilda died giving birth to twins in 1860, before her family could join her. One of her babies died, but one, named for her mother, survived and was raised by Walter Wilcox's first wife, Maria Wealthy Richards Wilcox. That little girl lived in this house with her Watmough grandparents, where she was joined by her husband, Charles Henry Bliss, in 1879.[118]

William continued to work at the watchmaker's trade all his life, and seems to have done well. His shop was downtown at First South and Main Street. By 1870, the assessed value of the family's real and personal property was $1,200. The Watmoughs' house, built by 1869, served both as a home and as Mary Ann Elizabeth's schoolroom. She was an educated woman who brought with her from Boston the tools of her trade—maps, books, and slates. She was a member of the County Teachers' Institute in 1877.[119]

Like most of its neighbors, the house was originally a hall-parlor type, with a stone shed on the east side that seems to have been built after the front rooms. Prior to 1879 the house had not been stuccoed, but today it is covered in wood siding.[120] Then, as now, it sat above Quince Street, buttressed by a sloping stone wall.

Joseph Openshaw (1857–1940) wrote of attending Mrs. Watmough's first school beginning when he was eight or nine, "in the 17th Ward about 260 North 2nd West." His sister, Esther Ellen (1851–1940), also attended that early school.[121]

The Watmoughs' surviving daughter, Amanda, married John Chamberlain in 1865. They lived in Cedar Fort, but when Amanda died in April 1879, their sons, Mark and Charles, also came to live with the Watmoughs.[122]

William Watmough died in October 1879, the result of a fall he took while pruning one of the fruit trees on this property. Two-year-old Mark Chamberlain died on the day of his grandfather's funeral and was buried in the same grave.[123]

After William's death, Mary Ann Elizabeth Watmough lived for a time with John Flower and his second wife, Mary, at 365 North Quince Street (see also 175 West 400 North, an earlier John Flower house on the same block), but she continued teaching. Supporting her grandchildren must have been a great financial burden. As a widow, she claimed an abatement of property taxes three times during the 1890s. Shortly before she died in 1895, she transferred this property to her granddaughter, Carrie Chamberlain, who had taught music at her grandmother's school.[124]

364 and 368 North Quince Street—John and Emily Price Platts, c. 1858 and 1854

John Platts (1827–1889) and Emily Price Platts (1832–1901) were first cousins, born in Coleorton, Leicestershire, England, and married there in 1850. Coleorton was a village of 549 people that year, including three bricklayers, one of whom was probably John Platts.[125] In the mid-1850s, the English Midlands were fertile ground for Mormon missionaries eager to find new converts among tradesmen and others who had been left behind by the Industrial Revolution and the economic breakdown of traditional farming.

In February 1854, John and Emily and their three children, along with Emily's parents and three siblings, boarded the *Golconda* in Liverpool and arrived in New Orleans about six weeks later. Then cholera struck. What was described as a "delightful" ocean voyage became a desperate struggle to reach Salt Lake City alive. The family went up the Mississippi River to St. Louis and then to Kansas City. They joined the William A. Empey wagon company to complete their journey, but by that time, their two daughters had died and only their son, Orson, survived.

It may be that 368 North Quince Street was the Platts's first house, possibly the "cabin" described by a granddaughter, Emily Platts Smith.[126] Recent work on the building revealed that its southwest corner, at least, was built of adobe on a fieldstone foundation.[127] That section is now covered by stucco, and multiple additions have obscured the building's original form.

About 1858, Platts began building the house at 364 North Quince as a one-story hall-parlor or central-passage type. Its front door faced south. Adobe bricks form the interior walls, and the unusual exterior walls are of fieldstone, with dressed sandstone quoins. When the first fired brick became available, Platts added a full second story to the original home, and then other extensions built of brick and lumber.[128] Platts was identified as a master mason in the 1860 census; he probably designed and built these two houses himself. He had other talents as well; he managed to bring his cricket bat all the way to Salt Lake City, where cricket became a popular sport among British immigrants.[129]

John and Emily left the LDS Church in 1870. Family stories put the responsibility on Emily, asserting that she had refused to let her husband marry in polygamy.[130] A contrasting version is found in the journal of Nelson Wheeler Whipple, whose 1854 adobe house is still standing at 564 West 400 North. Whipple recorded that John Platts acknowledged at the "19th Ward Fellowship meeting, Mar. 1, 1870...that he had fallen in with Godbeism and believed their teachings....[Following] a motion by N. W. Whipple, seconded by Robert Smith, he was cut off the Church of Jesus Christ of Latter-day Saints, by unanimous vote."[131] John Platts's support of Sarah Bates Pratt (see 122 West Apricot, Nineteenth Ward) when she left polygamy in 1874 agrees with this latter explanation.

442 North Quince Street—Thomas and Elizabeth Slight Kiddle/ Hyrum, Sarah Johnson, Annie Wooley, and Matilda Brockway Bull, c. 1881

Thomas Matthew Kiddle (1860–1940) was not a pioneer. His mother, Eliza, an LDS convert, left her husband Edward in London, gathered her seven surviving children (of thirteen), and sailed from Liverpool on the steamship *Idaho* in 1877.[132] They took the train to Utah. Edward Kiddle remained in England, married again, and died in 1891. Once in Salt Lake City, Eliza identified herself as a widow.[133]

George Willis was Eliza Kiddle's son-in-law, and the family's first home was with him, in the Seventeenth Ward on the east side of West Temple Street, where the LDS Church Conference Center stands today. Both Thomas and his brother Walter were working "in Shoe Fact.[ory]." Thomas became an engineer (mechanic) and at times played the flute, although probably not quite as well after 1896, when his right middle finger was torn off while working at ZCMI.[134]

WEST ELEVATION

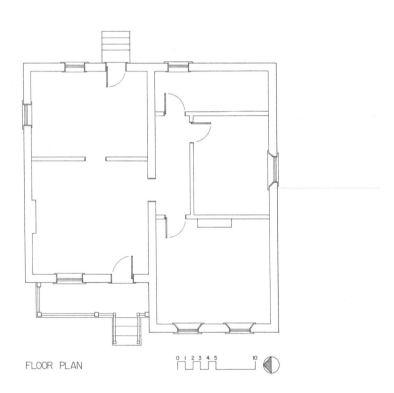

FLOOR PLAN

0 1 2 3 4 5   10

442 North Quince Street. Architectural drawings by Thomas Carter and James Gosney. Used by permission, Western Regional Architecture Program Collection, J. Willard Marriott Library, University of Utah, all rights reserved.

Thomas and Walter bought property here on Quince Street in 1880.[135] Walter built his house at 450 North Quince Street, and Thomas built here. The first floor of the house looks much as it did when it was new, a cross-wing type with a large porch. The upper half-story, with its imbricated shingles, is a later addition, as are the other Victorian details—fans, spindles, and balusters—on the porch.

Elizabeth Slight married Thomas Kiddle in 1882 when she was almost twenty and he was twenty-two. Elizabeth was a latecomer herself, arriving in Salt Lake City from England with her parents and siblings in 1873, with a loan from the Perpetual Emigrating Fund Company. (Elizabeth's obituary states that her father was Thomas Sleight, called from England in 1860 to take over the printing of a new edition of the Book of Mormon. Her father was actually Thomas Slight, a laborer.) Thomas and Elizabeth had seven children. Their son Thomas Benjamin died in 1888 but the others lived long lives.[136]

Thomas sold this house in 1884.[137] He stayed near his mother, who remained at 450 North Quince until her death in 1899, simply relocating to a brick house (demolished) on its north side. Then, in 1900, Thomas moved to Stirling, Alberta, Canada. His family joined him the following year.[138]

Stirling today is one of only three communities in Canada that are National Historic Sites. Settled in the late 1890s and early 1900s, Stirling was laid out according to what was, even then, an old pattern—Joseph Smith's 1833 "Plat of the City of Zion." Thomas may have been called as a settler by the LDS Church because his skill as a mechanic was crucial to construction of an irrigation system that supported farms, rail lines, and coal mines during Canada's western expansion. Town lots and surrounding farms were also available to poorer church members who paid for their homes in work for the railroad.[139]

The buyer in 1884 was Hyrum Bull (1852–1931), an English immigrant, a shoemaker, and an 1873 latecomer to Utah. He paid Thomas Kiddle $900, then mortgaged the property five times through 1890. Bull's life was a difficult one. Between 1871 and 1896 he married three times in succession, and each of his wives died, of pneumonia or tuberculosis, while living in this house. Of his fourteen children, six died before they were two years old. Hyrum went on living here until he died in 1931. He is buried in the Salt Lake City Cemetery with his wives and the children who predeceased him.[140]

Only a few cross-wing-type adobe houses, in which the two wings meet at right angles to form a T- or L-shaped floor plan, remain in Salt Lake City. This design became popular in the 1880s, and it helps to confirm the construction date of the Kiddle/Bull house. Here, the windows are stylishly tall and narrow, widening into the home's interior to let in maximum light.

215 West Reed Avenue—Catherine Mary Cowley Anderson, 1887

Until about 1886, the lots on what became Reed Avenue were held by LDS Church presidents as trustees-in-trust for the church. Then they were platted on an unnamed street. In 1887, Catherine bought the property and probably began building the house.[141]

Catherine Mary Cowley Anderson (1834–1913) was the daughter of Matthias Cowley and Ann Quayle, immigrants from the Isle of Man. The Cowleys were early converts to the LDS Church, arriving in New York in 1841 and proceeding to Nauvoo, Illinois, where they lived until the Mormon exodus in 1846. From there, it was a long and halting journey. Matthias died in St. Louis in 1853, leaving his wife to accompany Catherine and her siblings to Utah in 1854.[142]

Catherine married James Anderson, an iron and brass molder, in 1856 and had ten children, all but one of whom lived to maturity. James, a Scottish immigrant of 1849, made some of the earliest iron castings in Utah and, in 1870, held the final spike on the Utah Central Railroad when its tracks reached Salt Lake City.[143]

The Anderson family lived for many years at 342 South 400 West in the Sixth Ward, but Catherine was living in this house on Reed Avenue by 1893. Although James lived until 1899, Catherine began referring to herself as a widow about 1898.[144]

Catherine's son Franklin was killed by a train while crossing the Rio Grande railroad tracks in late December 1891. Already having served a mission to Indian Territory and then "paying his addresses" to a daughter of George Q. Cannon, Franklin's loss would have been devastating to the family.[145]

This hip-roof cottage may have been built as a rental property. Its only decorative elements are the flat arched window heads. The porch roof is original, but its supporting columns have been replaced. Although Catherine lived here briefly, she sold the house to Wilson Pratt, and in 1900 was living with her daughter Elizabeth on 400 West.[146]

241 West Reed Avenue—Emma J. Hamson Whitecar, 1887

Emma Jane Hamson (1825–1893) made her way to Utah at the end of a journey that had lasted for six decades. Born in England, she came to New York on the ship *Ganges* in 1827 at age two. Almost a quarter-century later, the 1850 census enumerator found her, with a five-year-old daughter, living in Philadelphia. Her first husband's name may have been Robert Jeffries. Probably a widow, she married Isaac Atkinson Whitecar [pronounced Whitaker] in November 1850 and went to live with him in the area of Camden, New Jersey, where he was the proprietor of the Flat Iron Tavern at the corner of Broadway and Ferry Road. At some point, Emma's son George went to Salt Lake City, joined the LDS Church, and returned to New Jersey. Emma too became an LDS convert and, after her husband died in 1883, made the decision to move west with her son.[147]

Emma's son's name, George Brinton Whitecar, appeared in the 1885 Salt Lake City directory, but Emma herself was not listed until 1893.[148] George Whitecar bought this property from Angus Cannon for fifty dollars in 1887, and ultimately he and his brothers, Arthur and James, lived on the same block. Salt Lake City was Emma's final destination, and her stay here was unfortunately brief. She died of septicemia on October 30, 1893.[149]

This tiny, hip-roof cottage is devoid of decoration and probably had only two rooms.[150] The double-hung windows have plain wooden sills and lintels. Even on a street of small houses, it is dwarfed by its neighbors.

270 West Reed Avenue—George Washington and Cynthia Stewart Hill, c. 1876

The history of this house is by any measure one of the most unusual in Salt Lake City. In 1874, Brigham Young received a Mayor's Deed to this and much of the surrounding property, and from him it passed to President John Taylor as trustee-in-trust for the LDS Church. Probably because of his many services to the church, the house was built for George W. Hill and his family. It was not until 1888 that he bought it for $2,000.[151]

When it was new, the house faced west; its earliest address was 770 North 300 West. Before the brick apartments were built between this house and 300 West, there was a full-length porch extending across the west side. The front door is original, as are many of the windows. An early adobe extension on the north side, and later additions of various

materials, give the house its present form. A half-inch layer of brick tile now covers the adobe walls, which rest on a foundation of granite and concrete.[152]

George W. Hill was born in Athens County, Ohio, in 1822 and spent his youth moving around the state, to Illinois, and eventually to Missouri. When he met Cynthia Stewart, already a Mormon convert, he joined the LDS Church and they married in 1845. George and Cynthia, together with her mother, uncle, and brothers, joined the Smoot/Wallace Company in 1847, arriving in the Salt Lake Valley in late September. George was one of the hunters in the company. He returned east in 1850 to bring his mother and younger brother to the valley, but got lost at South Pass, Wyoming, on the return trip and ended up in the area of what became Ogden instead.[153]

In the early days of settlement, Brigham Young needed interpreters who knew the languages of Native Americans, and George Hill learned to speak several. His family lived in Ogden for many years while George served in the LDS Church Salmon River Mission. He met with other tribal groups, serving also as ambassador to the Eastern Shoshone in Wyoming. This last was a secret assignment, the federal government having put the Methodist Church in charge there.[154]

Dimmick Huntington, who had been a Danite (a group formed in 1838 that operated as vigilantes) and "high constable" in Nauvoo, was the previous LDS Church Indian agent and interpreter. He died in Salt Lake City in 1879. "J W Hill, Indian interpreter" was living at this location in 1883. It was an ideal place, no doubt chosen for its proximity to the Warm Springs and the traditional Native American camping grounds nearby. At the time, this was open country; the city wall ran east-west on the north side of the Hills' house and then turned southeast along what is now Wall Street. A block east of the Hills' house may be what family histories refer to as an "Indian house" built of adobe (see 761 North Wall Street, Nineteenth Ward).[155]

After decades of service, George Washington Hill was released by the LDS Church and died in 1891. Cynthia lived here until she died in 1908, and the house remained in the family until 1975. It has been divided into apartments and was used, briefly, as a brothel in the 1980s.[156]

584 North Wall Street—Joseph E. and Rhoda Amelia Lambourne Mullett, c. 1876

Joseph Edward Mullett (1838–1922) was an English immigrant who came to Utah with Rhoda and her sons George and Levi, children from her earlier marriage to George Lorenzo Lambourne. They were among the last of the pioneers, members of the Chester Loveland Company that arrived in 1868. (For Rhoda's story, see 625 North 200 West, Nineteenth Ward.) Joseph's mother and his siblings accompanied them, and like many poor people, they financed their journey through the Perpetual Emigrating Fund Company.[157]

The family lived in the Fourteenth Ward before moving here. This house may have been built as a hall-parlor type, but the asymmetrical facade with its door on the north end is certainly not typical. It may represent an alteration of the house after it was built. There are also additions built in 1891, and a later stone porch. Joseph's name first appears in the chain of title for this property in 1873, and he received a Mayor's Deed in 1875. The house was almost certainly built by 1876.[158]

Joseph was a general laborer and sometime soap maker who probably worked at the Nineteenth Ward Soap Factory. By 1880, the Mulletts had four surviving children, including Joseph Jr., who was born soon after the family arrived in Salt Lake City. Not much is known about the family's life before the summer of 1888. On March 7, Joseph Sr. had been named the librarian of the LDS Salt Lake Stake library and the family was considered "highly respectable." Only a few days later, he was arrested and taken to jail. He was charged with molesting children, then released on bond. He promptly fled. Rhoda divorced him in 1892, claiming desertion and failure to support her since 1888.[159]

Yet by 1900, Joseph had reappeared in Bluffdale, at the south end of the Salt Lake Valley, where he was charged with molesting a neighbor's child in 1912. Joseph lived at the County Infirmary (which also served as a poorhouse and asylum) from about 1916 until he died in 1922.[160]

Rhoda never remarried. She made her home on Wall Street with her adult children and near her son Joseph Jr., and worked as a tailoress. She died at 572 Wall Street in 1916.[161]

620 North Wall Street—Franklin and Elizabeth Peck Merrill, c. 1873

Franklin Merrill (1843–1896) was born in Connecticut. His father, Albert, a hatter, joined the LDS Church in 1841 and for the next three years served a mission in the Eastern States. The family went to Nauvoo in 1844 and from there crossed Iowa during the terrible winter of 1846–1847. Three of their children died and were buried together, and most of their animals were lost or stolen. After five years of subsisting in the temporary

camps in Iowa, the family finally managed to get to Salt Lake City with the Thomas Howell Company in 1852. They lived briefly in Provo, and then in the Seventeenth Ward in Salt Lake City.[162]

Franklin, or Frank, did not join his father in the hatter's trade. He married Elizabeth Peck (1845–1919) in 1868 and worked as a laborer, living near his parents in the Seventeenth Ward. Frank and Elizabeth ultimately had twelve children, but only five lived to maturity.[163]

The Merrills lived here only a few years while Frank worked as a bartender, selling the house in 1876 to Christopher Stokes and moving to the Cache Valley. They returned shortly before Frank died in 1896.[164]

The house probably appears much as it did when it was built, a two-room hall-parlor type, although the porch is a twentieth-century addition. Its most unusual feature, and probably one unique among Salt Lake City adobes, is the later addition with its truncated northeast corner, built to fit just inside the lot line.

688 North Wall Street—George Alfred and Isabella Roe Boyd/ Thomas and Priscilla Boyd Bircumshaw, c. 1866

George Alfred Boyd (1841–1918) arrived in Salt Lake in 1863 with an unknown company. He may have returned east to assist the William Hyde

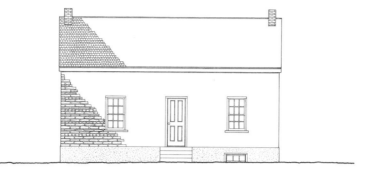

WEST ELEVATION

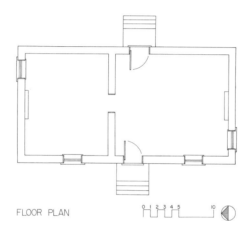

FLOOR PLAN

0 1 2 3 4 5   10

SOUTH ELEVATION

620 North Wall Street. Architectural drawings by Thomas Carter and James Gosney. Used by permission, Western Regional Architecture Program Collection, J. Williard Marriott Library, University of Utah, all rights reserved.

Company in 1864, escorting his sister, Priscilla Seymour Boyd (1847–1915), and their mother, Ann, to the valley. In 1866, George became the first "lawful claimant" of this lot, a month after he married Isabella Jane Roe (1847–1902).[165]

Isabella's father had died in England in 1853. Still, her mother, Elizabeth, crossed the Atlantic with her children on the *Germanicus* in 1854. They got as far as Mormon Grove in eastern Kansas, where Elizabeth died. The children went on across the plains without her in 1855 and were adopted by other families in the company.[166]

George and Isabella may have lived elsewhere in the Nineteenth Ward for a time and built this house as their resources allowed, probably beginning with a single-cell type to which three adobe rooms were added by 1898, followed by brick and wood-frame rooms, one of which forms the cross wing. Tax assessment rolls from 1868 and 1872 show that they owned horses and a wagon which, together with the property, were valued at only $150. Still, of their eleven children, all but one lived to maturity, and one lived to be ninety. Their daughter Alice was christened in Salt Lake at St. Mark's Episcopal Church in 1880, indicating that the family had left the LDS Church by that time. Their youngest children were born in Plain City, Weber County, where the family lived in 1900.[167]

George Boyd sold this property to his sister Priscilla (1847–1915) and her husband, Thomas Bircumshaw (1846–1925), in 1881. Thomas worked as a grocer or butcher who was living in the Eleventh Ward with Priscilla and their baby, Thomas, in 1870. Of their five children, only two lived to maturity.[168]

Thomas also worked in a saloon, and as a porter at various hotels for many years. His working life nearly ended in 1898 when he fell on the stairs of the Knutsford Hotel and broke three ribs, but he remained employed until at least 1920.[169]

After Priscilla died, Thomas moved to his son's home in California and died there. His body was returned to Utah, and he is buried with Priscilla in Mount Olivet Cemetery.[170]

761 North Wall Street, unknown builder, c. 1875

Now a mix of styles and building materials, this house was built initially as an elongate adobe pair house or double-cell type. This earliest portion is best seen from the northeast, where one gable end is exposed and the central chimney is visible. The rest is obscured by subsequent additions.

Until 1906, this lot was public property, part of a larger space originally granted to "Salt Lake City and Inhabitants" by surveyor Jesse Fox in 1874. It had no individual owner, and I speculate that it may have been a communal building constructed by or for members of Native American tribes who traditionally camped near the Warm Springs.[171]

George Washington Hill, the Indian agent, lived a few hundred feet west of this house (see 270 West Reed Avenue, Nineteenth Ward) and welcomed Native Americans to the area. The city wall for which Wall Street was named turned to the west here. A nearly forgotten part of Salt Lake history may be preserved in this building.

598 North West Capitol Street—George Roy and Mary Thompson McClure, c. 1889

George McClure (1847–1929) and his wife, Mary (1851–1928), were Scots immigrants who sailed from Liverpool to New York in 1882. George's name appears on the passenger list for a ship that sailed earlier that year, but he likely delayed their voyage so they could travel together. Mary was pregnant; the young family arrived in September with a new baby and four-year-old Violet.[172]

For a few years, the family lived in the Twentieth Ward, but by 1889 they had moved to this house, where they remained for the rest of their lives. Of their nine children, only four survived childhood. George worked consistently for Silver Brothers Iron Works as a machinist.[173]

The original owner of this property was James H. VanNatta, who received a Mayor's Deed in 1868. VanNatta never lived here, but he got a mortgage for $1,000 in 1874, then sold it for $1,800 in 1875, which suggests that other property was included in the sale. Yet when George McClure bought this lot in 1888, the purchase price was $75.[174] The current house appears to be brick. It was only when recent owners undertook a remodeling project that they discovered a fifteen-by-fifteen-foot adobe room inside, probably the original structure. It had a door on the south side and windows on the north and west and had been completely enclosed in the existing structure.[175] It seems likely that when the McClures bought the property, rather than demolish the adobe room, they simply built around it.

Twentieth Ward

Some of the simplest adobe homes in Salt Lake City, as well as some of the most elaborate, were built in the neighborhood now known as The Avenues. The area was not originally a residential neighborhood, although the smaller lots—half the size of those in most of the city—suggest otherwise. In fact, the hilly terrain and lack of water—it was known as the "Dry Bench"—were simply incompatible with large gardens and livestock, but nearly every home had an orchard. The first residents were small farmers, herders, and tradesmen, and many property owners in the 1850s, who lived elsewhere, grazed their livestock here.[1] Not until about 1880 were the small lots further subdivided and the fine homes that now characterize The Avenues built in large numbers.

When the Twentieth Ward was formed in 1856, its western boundary was set in the middle of what is now A Street, and its southern boundary was South Temple Street. On the north and east, the Twentieth Ward had no defined boundaries but simply extended as far as there were inhabitants. As settlement progressed, such a large ward became unmanageable for a single bishop, and the Twenty-First Ward was split off in 1877, its western boundary running the length of H Street.

157 North B Street—William Bell, Ellen Birchall, and Sarah Foster Barton, c. 1862

William Bell Barton (1836–1923) was an early English convert to the LDS Church who had served in several positions there before emigrating. He married Ellen Birchall (1835–1918) on March 13, 1860, and two weeks later they boarded the *Underwriter* in Liverpool and sailed for New York. The passenger list included William's twin brother, James, so the three

pioneers crossed the plains with the James D. Ross Company, arriving in Salt Lake City in September. William's parents, John and Elizabeth, and three of his younger brothers followed in 1862 and settled in Kaysville.[2]

William Barton was a carpenter, cabinetmaker, and bookkeeper. He built this house in 1862, although purchase of the property was not recorded until 1869. The seller was Eric M. Caste, a Swedish sailor who had come to the United States on the *Golconda* in 1853.[3]

Sarah Foster (1846–1917) came to the Salt Lake Valley with her family in 1866. She found work in the Barton household assisting Ellen and became William's second wife in June 1867.[4] All three lived here together until 1874, when William left to serve a church mission in England. His father died in August and his mother probably moved into this house at that time. By the time William returned two and a half years later, the powder magazines on Arsenal (Capitol) Hill had exploded, breaking windows, dishes, and lamps in the Barton home. To support themselves in William's absence, Ellen and Sarah sewed and made hats for sale, made all their clothes, rugs, and bedding, and preserved food from their garden.

About 1885, Sarah and her youngest children fled Salt Lake City, allowing William to avoid a fine or prison sentence for polygamy while he continued to support both his families. When Sarah returned, William built a small house for her at 276 I Street where she lived as a widow, though William was very much alive.[5] William outlived both his wives and six of his nineteen children, and both he and Ellen died in this house.

This well-preserved house is an example of the Gothic Revival style, with its steeply pitched roof, transverse gable, original finial (the drop and second-floor balcony have recently been replaced), and tall, narrow windows. The style was typical of the eastern United States from the 1830s until the 1860s, and there are still a few rare examples in Salt Lake City. The original house probably had very little "style," even in 1870 when it was valued at $500. Joists made of split logs support the first floor of the original rooms.

One of the earliest homes in the Twentieth Ward, the Barton house sits at a slight angle on its lot, suggesting that the streets had not yet been precisely laid out. It may also reflect the position of the Twentieth Ward Ditch, which carried water from City Creek southeast across the Barton property and the "Dry Bench."[6]

280 North B Street—David Wooley and Elizabeth Alldridge Evans, 1873

David (1833–1876) and Elizabeth (1842–1906) were English immigrants. David sailed for New York in 1860 and crossed the plains with the William Budge Company. His widowed mother, Mary Edna Wooley, followed in

1862, bringing five younger children with her on the *Manchester*. Mary Edna died near Florence, Nebraska, in mid-July. Her children—Emily, Annie, Mary Jane, and Arthur, and Minnie, a little girl she had raised from birth—continued on with the Ansil P. Harmon Company, arriving in Salt Lake City on October 5, 1862.[7]

News of his mother's death did not reach David until the pioneer company got to Salt Lake Lake City. In the meantime, David married Elizabeth Alldridge in June 1862. They ultimately had five children and lived most of their married lives in a small adobe house (demolished) near the corner of B Street and Third Avenue.[8]

David purchased this lot in 1870. The house, described as "a square adobe house, two stories…ten rooms…hip roof," was designed and built by architect William Paul Jr. in 1872 and 1873. It can be seen in a photograph of the neighborhood taken about 1875, and in a bird's-eye map published the same year.[9] Details such as the iron-trimmed hipped roof, the cornice with its paired brackets, the porch, and south bay window contribute to its Italianate appearance.

David Evans worked as a phonographic reporter (taking notes in an early form of shorthand) for the LDS Church and the *Deseret News*, and he played the violin in the Salt Lake Theater orchestra. He died of kidney disease at the age of forty-three in 1876. Elizabeth was first listed as residing here in the 1883–1884 directory.[10]

David and Elizabeth's son John fell from a streetcar and fractured his skull, lingering for a month before he died in June 1906. Elizabeth, who had been "more or less an invalid for some years," never left her bed after John's death and died in this house on July 30 of that year.

Annie Isabella Evans Lamberson inherited the house when her mother died in 1906, and lived in it with her husband and her sister Elizabeth. They converted it to apartments in 1917 and continued to live here until 1923.[11]

86 North C Street—Charles and Mary Ann Lewis Sansom, c. 1875

Henry Lewis was an English blacksmith who sailed from Liverpool to New Orleans late in 1850 with his wife, Jane, and four children, one of whom was Mary Ann. They brought with them on the ship *North American* "4

Boxes of apparel, 1 Hamper of Clothes, 1 Barrel & 2 Beds." Jane died in
St. Louis, but Henry and his children reached the Salt Lake Valley, where
he married Harriet Porter in 1855. Henry built his first adobe house about
1860 at what became 78 North C Street (demolished). He bought this lot
from Brigham Young in 1867.[12]

Charles Sansom (1826–1908) entered the picture when he married Henry's daughter Mary Ann (1835–1906) in 1853. Charles was also
an English immigrant whose first wife had died in Kanesville, Iowa, in
1851. After her death, Charles married again, to a woman whose name
he seemed not to recall years later. That marriage was very brief, as "she
would not go the Valley herself" so Charles left her some money and departed, reaching Salt Lake City in 1852 with the John Tidwell Company.[13]

Charles worked as a clerk in several stores, and was a member of the
original Salt Lake Theater orchestra in 1862. Before this house was built,
he and Mary Ann lived on F Street where all but two of their eleven children were born. By 1879 they were living here.[14]

Charles was called on a church mission to Great Britain in 1873 and
returned in 1874. His father-in-law, Henry Lewis, died in 1876. Henry's
widow and surviving children, including Mary Ann, sold this property to
Charles Sansom for $1,500 in 1882, probably well after the house was built.[15]

The Sansom house—a two-story Federal style facing north—seems to have been a central-passage type. It may even have been built initially as a single-story house. Later alterations to enlarge the windows and cover the porch have obscured many details, but it retains its early character. A late addition on the south side now forms the entry.

117 North C Street—Samuel and Eunice Francis Neslen, c. 1874

Samuel Neslen (1807–1887) was a well-to-do carpenter and a Methodist preacher in his native Lowestoft, Suffolkshire, England. He and Eunice Francis (1808–1891) married there in 1829. Both converted to the LDS Church in 1849 and, with their nine children, sailed from Liverpool to New Orleans on the *Golconda* in January 1853. They crossed the plains with the Claudius V. Spencer Company in 1853, a journey richly documented by Hannah Tapfield King, who had become a close friend during the ocean voyage.[16]

The Neslens settled first in the Seventeenth Ward, but Samuel soon acquired property on South Temple Street between A and B Streets and was living there in 1867. He bought this property in 1874, paying $500 to Patrick Lynch.[17] Most of the Neslen children were grown by that time and had their own homes. Samuel lived here until he died in 1887, and Eunice remained until she died in 1891. Even though the Neslens were prosperous and well known in the community, very little was written about them, and only the briefest obituaries appeared after their deaths.[18]

The south wing of the house, and probably the earliest, seems to have been a one-story hall-parlor type with at least one gable-end chimney. It may have been built even before Samuel Neslen bought the property. The two-story north wing has an Italianate, floor-to-ceiling second-story window with a first-floor bay window below it.

167 North C Street—Edward and Emma Maria Sims Shoebridge, c. 1873

Edward B. Shoebridge (1842–1897) came from England to the Salt Lake Valley sometime before 1867, when his name appeared in the first city directory. Emma Sims (1846–1908) came earlier, with the Jacob Gates Company in 1853, accompanied by her parents and sister Julia. Her sister Henrietta had died near New Orleans after the ocean voyage from Liverpool on the *International*. Emma's family was living in the Twentieth Ward by 1860.[19]

Edward and Emma's marriage date is uncertain, but their son Edward was three years old in 1870. At that time, the Shoebridge family lived in the Seventh Ward, adjacent to Emma's aunt Elizabeth, who was the plural wife of John B. Kelley (see 422 South 200 West, Seventh Ward). Two of the eight Shoebridge children died young. Edward bought this property in 1872 for $825 and built the front section of the house that year or soon afterward. It seems to have been a hall-parlor type, although the entry was off-center and the two windows are markedly different, possibly a result of remodeling. When the rear adobe section was added in 1887, a new entry was built on its east side, under a small porch with decorative railings. The house now is overgrown and in poor condition.

The family moved to the Tooele County mining town of Stockton in 1880, where Edward opened a drugstore, but when a fire damaged the store in 1887, he bought this house back and returned to Salt Lake City.[20]

Edward lived in this house for the rest of his life. He had a plumbing supply company and interests in the mines in Bingham Canyon, but was not associated with the fabulous wealth of the Shoebridge Bonanza mine in Juab County. Emma was socially active, so her children married well but outside the LDS Church. Her daughter Dolly married P. J. Moran, the contractor who paved Salt Lake City's streets and built its water supply system. Edward was only fifty-six when he died in this house in 1897. Emma lived here until 1907 and died at her daughter Dolly Moran's house on South Temple Street in 1908.[21] Unlike many pioneers who sold or demolished their adobe homes as soon as they could afford to replace them with more fashionable and convenient brick or frame houses, the Shoebridge family chose to stay put.

177–181 North C Street—William Henry, Mercy Hodgson, and Christine Nielson Robinson, c. 1867

William Robinson (1832–1888) and his wife, Mercy (1830–1878), reached the Salt Lake Valley in 1853, after two months on the *Falcon* from Liverpool to New Orleans and another six weeks on the Mississippi River to reach Keokuk, Iowa, the starting point for the Appleton Harmon wagon train. They arrived safely in the valley after four months on the trail, perhaps sending word back to William's parents and siblings in England that they should begin their journey. George and Margaret Robinson, with their children Dorothy, Elizabeth, and George, sailed on the *Horizon* in 1856, reaching Iowa City in time to join the ill-fated Edward Martin Handcart

Company. But young George, who was fourteen, refused to go west and ran away. Unwilling to leave his son, the elder George stayed behind, only to die a year later in Iowa. Margaret and her daughters survived the cold, snow, and starvation that killed nearly one-fourth of the handcart company and reached Salt Lake City on November 30, 1856.[22]

William Robinson first built a house in the Ninth Ward where his mother joined them after her arrival. In 1865, he bought this lot from Brigham Young for $100 and built the adobe (south) portion of his house no later than 1867. A carpenter who worked for the Public Works Department of the LDS Church while the Salt Lake City Temple was being built, William probably was paid in food and goods. William and Mercy Robinson had eleven children between 1854 and 1872, but only five survived early childhood.[23]

William and Mercy's son William Henry Jr. recalled playing on the city wall that formed the north side of the family's property along what is now Fourth Avenue, and the explosion of the powder magazines on Arsenal Hill in 1876. Beyond the wall were bears, Indians, sawmills, and a gristmill, all in City Creek Canyon. Inside the wall, every lot was planted in gardens and fruit trees that fed the settlers.[24]

Mercy died in a fire at the city's Insane Asylum where she was a resident in 1878. Her youngest child, Alice, was four years old. Family histories do not mention Mercy's death or her confinement in the asylum. Even Mercy's nephew Oliver Hodgson, a meticulous record keeper (see 425 East Second Avenue, Twentieth Ward), wrote nothing in his journal. The asylum keeper was exonerated of any blame.[25]

William married again in 1881 to Christine (Kirsten) Nielson, a Swedish immigrant. They had three sons, the youngest born only four months before William died of chronic asthma in November 1888. Christine and stepdaughter Alice Robinson went on living here even after Alice married in 1898 and brought her husband, Sidney Francis Bowman, to live in the house.[26]

The original adobe structure, 177 North C Street, has a symmetrical facade (an entry door flanked by two identical windows) and a single brick chimney at the south end. A later addition, probably concrete, extends to the north, and there are both wood-frame and brick additions on the west side. The house is in such poor condition that these last are not visible. Other houses on the block, including the brick cottage at 185 North C Street, were also built by William Robinson.

218 North C Street—Esther Neslen Dean, 1889

The original quarter-block lot at 218 North C Street passed through several hands after it was first allotted to Adam McKenzie in 1866. Mercy Bennett Shoebridge bought it in 1869, and then the lot was subdivided repeatedly, but not until 1889 was this parcel sold to Esther Neslen Dean.[27]

Esther (1837–1916) was born in Lowestoft, Suffolk, England, the daughter of Samuel and Eunice Neslen (see 117 North C Street, Twentieth Ward). She came with her parents and eight siblings to the Salt Lake Valley in 1853 with the Claudius V. Spencer Company and three years later married Thomas Francis Parsons (1834–1918). There is no record of a divorce, but Thomas and Esther soon parted company. Thomas remarried and lived in Salt Lake City until his death in 1918. Esther Neslen appeared in the 1860 census, working as a domestic servant in the Nineteenth Ward household of Richard Margetts.[28]

Samuel Dean (1830–1873) had come west from Connecticut in 1855 with an unknown company. For several years he worked at Fort Bridger (then part of Utah Territory) as an accountant.[29] He and Esther married in 1860, and Samuel, at least, returned to Fort Bridger where he was appointed clerk of the probate court. His name appears on the treaty with the Eastern Shoshoni tribe, dated 1863, a document that established the "perpetual peace" necessary to allow construction of the transcontinental railroad.[30]

In 1870, the couple were living together in Junction City, Kansas, where Samuel worked as a bookkeeper. The *Deseret News* reported in December 1873 that Samuel, who had gone to get water, had somehow fallen into a neighbor's well and drowned. Esther returned to Utah and by 1880 was again living in her father's household at 117 North C Street.[31]

Esther's father died in 1887. The money he left to his children allowed Esther to buy this small lot for $600 and build a home in 1889. She made her living as a nurse and lived here for the rest of her life.[32]

The house is a T-form, cross-wing type with many Victorian elements such as arched windows and corbeled drip molding. It was built at a time when the Twentieth Ward saw an increase in building by widows and by women whose husbands had, following passage of the Edmunds Act, renounced polygamy. By 1889, brick and frame construction had become the norm and this house was the only adobe structure built in the Avenues neighborhood that year.

277 North C Street—Thomas A. and Louisa Gobel Horne, c. 1874

Thomas (1821–1898) and Louisa Horne (1818–1907) sailed from Liverpool to New York on the *Belle Wood* in 1865. Also on the passenger list were Thomas Jr. and Annie Horne, presumably their children, but a Thomas Horne Jr., was also on the passenger list for the *David Hoadley* later that year. Thomas Sr. and Louisa entered the Salt Lake Valley in 1868 with the William S. Seeley Company, but there is no record of Thomas Jr.'s or Annie's overland travel. Both did make the journey—a brief 1898 death notice in the *Latter-day Saints' Millennial Star* noted that Thomas left "a wife and two children." Thomas, Louisa, and their son were living in the Fourteenth Ward in 1870, and in 1874 Thomas Sr. received the Mayor's Deed to this property. Both father and son were laborers, meaning that they had no particular skills, but Thomas Sr. was working as a gardener by 1884, and his son eventually became a streetcar conductor. Thomas and Louisa lived here the rest of their lives.

Very little is known about the Horne family, perhaps because both Thomas and Louisa were illiterate. They signed the deed with an "X" when they sold their house in the Fourteenth Ward to Clarence Allen in 1891.[33]

The original home was probably a hall-parlor type with a front door that faced south.[34] Recent remodeling and the addition of a second story resulted in the collapse of most of the adobe structure. At this writing, only the south end of the front wall is original.

215 North D Street—George and Amelia Jane Schofield Reynolds, 1881

George Reynolds (1842–1909) made an unconventional entrance into Salt Lake City in 1865. He had traveled west, not with hundreds of others on an immigrant train, but via stagecoach, then on a wagon bought in Denver, and finally, with a string of pack mules. His only fellow travelers were the merchant William Godbe and a missionary returning from England.[35] Also, unlike most immigrants from the British Isles, Reynolds came from a middle-class family, had a good education in languages, history, and literature, and had already served in several important church positions.

He met his first wife, Mary Ann (Polly) Tuddenham (1846–1885), in England. She came to Utah in 1864 with her parents and siblings.[36] George and Polly were married soon after his arrival and lived first in the Thirteenth Ward. George worked briefly for William Jennings, owner of the Eagle Emporium, and at the church tithing office. Then he was hired as a clerk in the office of the LDS church president, where he worked in various roles for most of the next forty-four years. He was both clerk and secretary to Brigham Young, and later to his successors. He became a scholar of the Book of Mormon, writing dozens of articles, including a catalog of names found in the book, and an interpretation of its geography.

In 1866, George became the "lawful claimant" of this lot on the northwest corner of D Street and Fourth Avenue. His wife Polly's father, a contractor, probably built their first small house (demolished) in 1867; it was gradually enlarged for members of George's extended family. George married a plural wife, Amelia Jane Schofield (1852–1908), in 1874. George and Polly had eleven children, four of whom died in childhood. George and Amelia had twelve, two of whom died in childhood.[37]

George Reynolds's name is best known in connection with his 1874 indictment and 1875 prosecution for bigamy in Utah's Third District Court. His conviction was upheld by the Territorial Supreme Court in 1876 and then appealed to the United States Supreme Court. George's conviction was again upheld in 1879, and he was sentenced to two years in the penitentiary and a $500 fine.

Polly and Amelia were living in the original house with ten children and George's brother and sister in 1880. (His mother had returned to London in 1875.) George served his sentence at federal penitentiaries in Lincoln, Nebraska, and at Utah's Territorial Prison in Sugar House, near what is now the intersection of 2100 South and 1500 East Streets.[38] He was released in early 1881.

After his release from prison, this house was built for Amelia Schofield Reynolds and her children, directly north of the original house. It was known in the family as "Amelia's house," and title to the property was in her name.[39] There was sometimes animosity between Polly and Amelia, and among their children, but George Reynolds could afford to have a house for each wife, making everyone's life, including his, more peaceful. The earlier house became "Mary (Polly)'s house."

For its time, this was a fashionable house of two stories, built in the Greek Revival style with heavy cornices and cornice returns. Originally a cross-wing type built in the form of a T with one gable end facing the street, it was altered sometime between 1898 and 1911 by the addition of an adobe two-story north wing.[40]

Later, when the Edmunds Act of 1882 attempted again to mitigate against polygamy, George went "on the underground," hiding in the LDS Church offices that were then in the Gardo House on South Temple Street between State and Main, or in the Social Hall on State Street. Then, in 1885, he married again, to Mary Gulliford Goold (1859–1936), a domestic servant to church president John Taylor. Their marriage was performed in the Endowment House but was kept secret from the rest of the family. George and Mary eventually had nine children.

The families moved often in the 1880s, hiding from federal marshals. Polly's last pregnancy, her eleventh, ended with her death in December 1885. She was buried in the family plot with her baby, and because George was still in hiding he attended her funeral dressed as a woman.

By 1900, George and Mary Goold Reynolds were living on Wall Street in the Nineteenth Ward with twelve children. Amelia had sold this house to her daughter Margaret and was back in the original house, 333 Fourth Avenue, with ten children aged five to twenty-four, and a boarder.[41] Amelia lived until 1908. By that time, George's health had declined dramatically, culminating in a stroke on his sixty-fifth birthday in 1906. Mary went with him to Hawaii where he improved physically but not mentally, and in 1908 he was committed briefly to the state mental hospital in Provo. When Amelia died of kidney disease in 1908, George was unaware of her death. He died in August 1909, survived by twenty-six children.[42]

George Reynolds paid a high price for his devotion to his church and the principle of polygamy. But his wives and children, even though they were far better off financially than most families in Salt Lake City during the last half of the nineteenth century, also suffered, from his absences and from the stress of moving and hiding from authorities, but also from the inability of one man to share his time with so many people. While George gained public and ecclesiastical stature from his work and from his multiple wives and many children, privately he had little time to spend with them and was unable to prevent the conflicts that often arose among plural wives.

Polly and Amelia were literate, yet we know virtually nothing about them. Whether they had nothing to say or simply no time to say it is unknown. Even Alice Louise (1873–1938), who may have been closer to her father than any of his other children, wrote almost nothing about the women in her family.[43] On the other hand, George Reynolds's writings, including his journal, would fill a library shelf.

236 North D Street—Henry and Ann Selina Earney Puzey, c. 1869

Henry Puzey (1828–1896) and his first wife, Mary Ann Wateridge, had ten children, at least half of whom died in childhood. Henry left Mary Ann and their surviving children behind in England when he came to the Salt Lake Valley in 1866. Mary Ann died in the Southampton poorhouse in 1886. Their son Henry William had joined his father in Utah by 1870, the only one of Mary Ann's children to do so.[44]

Well before that time, Henry had married again, in 1867, to Ann Selina Earney (1841–1920). Selina sailed from London to New York on the *Hudson* in 1864, and probably traveled overland with her parents with the William Henry Chipman Company in 1866.[45]

The one-story adobe portion of the house faced Fifth Avenue and would have been built soon after Henry bought this lot in 1868. As the family prospered, they added the wood-frame two-story south wing about 1874, facing D Street. The couple had four children of their own, including five-year-old William, who was ill with diphtheria at the time of the 1880 census, but who recovered and lived until 1925.[46]

Henry was a blacksmith who built wagons and carriages at his shop on State Street between 200 and 300 South.[47] His early poverty had forced him to borrow from the Perpetual Emigrating Fund to pay for his passage from England, but he became friends with the photographer C. R. Savage (86 North D Street), served as a school trustee, and was a director of the LDS Twentieth Ward Institute. He testified on behalf of George Reynolds at his polygamy trial in 1875.[48]

About 1894, when he was sixty-six, Henry suffered a series of strokes that affected his speech and his personality, leaving him "morose and suspicious." Leaving his home on May 7, he evidently wandered away and fell into Red Butte Creek near Fort Douglas. His body was recovered from the fort by his son Edwin. Perhaps Henry had already sensed that his health was failing, because he had transferred ownership of this property to Ann Selina in 1893. Her sons were able to build their own homes south of the family home at 222, 230, and 234 North D Street, and her daughter, Ann Selina Chipman, inherited this house.[49]

234 North E Street—William Richard and Zina Stuart Lambourne, 1874

William R. Lambourne III (1844–1915) was an English immigrant who had reached St. Louis, Missouri, by 1860. He and eight family members traveled with the John D. Holladay Company in 1866.[50] The original owner of this lot, William Cahoon, sold the west half to William R. Lambourne in 1871, but Lambourne may have built the house by 1869, when he and his brother Alfred were listed at this corner in the city directory. It was large for its time, only a single story but probably intended to house the whole family. It appears to have faced north across the lot towards Fifth Avenue, the ridgeline running east-west, and is now almost completely engulfed by later additions on its north side.[51]

Even by the standards of nineteenth-century Utah, William Lambourne's family life was highly unusual. His father had married in England to William's mother, Diana Simms (1809–1894), in 1843, and then, in Salt Lake City, married her daughter by a previous marriage, Martha Wernham (1835–1912), in 1868. Both Diana and Martha were identified as "wife" in William Sr.'s household. A family history acknowledges only that "Martha's mother, who lived with them, helped to raise her (Martha's) family."[52]

The Lambourne family settled in the Ward, where by 1880, seventeen family members were living within a few blocks of each other.[53] William worked at various times as a store clerk or carpenter, but many in the family were artisans—paperhangers, decorators, florists—and painters.[54] William's brother Alfred painted scenery for the Salt Lake Theater and later accompanied photographer Charles R. Savage on his journeys around the West, painting the same landscapes that Savage photographed. William's sister Caroline married into a prominent family, becoming the plural wife of Miles P. Romney.

The younger William married Zina Agnes Stuart (1853–1930) in 1872. She was born in Salt Lake City to Daniel Stuart, a pioneer of 1850. William and Zina had seven children, all but two of whom died before they were six years old. Although no records survive, William and Zina may have divorced in 1886, when he sold her this house and lot for one dollar. By 1892, she was again known as Zina Stuart. She promptly bought the adjacent property, got another mortgage, and sold the two lots to David P. Anderson for $1,000. Through a series of transactions that may not have been correctly recorded, the property was returned to Zina's ownership; she sold it in turn to Daniel Stuart (either her father or her brother) in 1898.[55]

Zina married again, to Frank B. Watkins, in 1906 and then divorced him for cruelty in 1908. Economic necessity may have driven them back together; by 1910, both were living in her son Joseph's household. Zina's father died in 1904, leaving an estate of $67,000 to be divided among his three children. That undoubtedly allowed her financial independence, but still she seems to have lived with her son Joseph for the rest of her life.[56]

William Lambourne apparently continued to live in this house, dying of cancer at the county hospital in 1915. His obituary focused entirely on his brothers and sisters, his one surviving son, and his skill as a violinist. Although Zina was still alive, William's obituary dismissed her with the phrase, "his wife died some time ago." Zina's obituary identified her as Zina Watkins, the "widow of the late William Lambourne."[57]

275 and 283 North H Street—William J. and Kate Roberts Castleton; Charles L. and Mary Ann Luff Castleton, c. 1880

These two houses, very similar in age and appearance, illustrate a shift in the use of adobe to satisfy builders' desire for more fashionable homes. The basic hall-parlor type had been superseded by the cross-wing during the 1870s, and by 1880, hipped or pyramidal roofs were taking their place.

James Joseph Castleton (1829–1882) brought his family from Lowestoft, Suffolk, England, to the Salt Lake Valley in 1862, when William

(1856–1940) was six years old and Charles (1854–1923) was eight. James received the lot where these two houses stand in 1866, at a time when the family lived in an adobe house (demolished) at the corner of L Street and Second Avenue. When James became ill in 1879, he divided this lot between his sons William and Charles. Their mother, Frances, set up a small store in front of the family home and began selling food, dry goods, and notions to support her children.[58]

The brothers built these houses soon after receiving the land. When their father died in 1882, William became very much involved in running the store, which expanded in 1893 as Castleton Bros., carrying toys, fruits and vegetables, hay, grain, flour, and potatoes.[59] The store building is still standing at 736 Second Avenue.

Charles married in 1879. He worked as a carpenter and lived in the house he built at 283 North H Street with his wife, Mary Ann (1860–1949), for the rest of his life. Three of their adult children were still living with them in 1920. William married Kate Robertson in 1880. He and Kate sold their property to Charles in 1890 and moved into the house attached to the store. Kate died of diabetes in 1902, leaving seven children; William remarried in 1908. [60] The property at 275 H Street remained in Castleton family ownership and was probably a rental property.

Both houses are vernacular one-story buildings with truncated hipped roofs and projecting front bays. The various architectural styles suggest that both may have been built in stages as the brothers' financial conditions improved and their families grew.

73 North I Street—Hans Olof and Ann Elizabeth (Amelia) Randal Pike Jynge [Young], 1876

Andrew MacFarlane bought this lot from Brigham Young in 1872, built his own house in the northeast corner, and sold this parcel in 1873. It passed through several hands before Hans [Hance] O. Young [Jynge] (1838–1919), an immigrant from Norway, bought it in 1876. He mortgaged the property twice, probably to build this house. By that time, Hans had married Amelia (1842–1919), who was from Norfolk, England, and a pioneer of 1860. Then Amelia bought the property from Hans in 1877 for $800.[61]

Beneath these superficial elements of Amelia Pike's story, and more difficult to evaluate, are details that offer further insight into the lives of pioneer women and plural marriage. In 1862, Amelia had married John Young Greene (1826–1880), a nephew of Brigham Young who as a young man had driven his uncle's team to the Salt Lake Valley in 1847. John and Amelia had at least one child, Rhoda Mabel, born in 1864. John was a polygamist, enumerated with an earlier wife, Anna Spencer, and their four children (of twelve born between 1850 and 1871) at the time of the 1860 census.[62]

At some point, Amelia left John, although there is no divorce record, and married Hans Young. Hans had a colorful past and, like John Young Green, was probably a polygamist. He had been a company commander of the home guard at Rockport, Summit County, in 1866, where he lived with his wife Hilda (Henrietta) and several children. Later, he ranched in Uintah County, Wyoming, was the LDS bishop of Parley's Park, and had interests in mining. (The historic Wallin Barn at Kimball Junction stands on part of another of Young's ranches, now part of the Swaner Nature Preserve.[63])

City directories continued to list Hans as a resident at 73 I Street until at least 1885, although he may have been living with his wife Henrietta. In 1889 he was reportedly living on 800 South; the 1904 directory again gave the I Street address. Henrietta had died in 1896. When Hans died in 1919, he was living on Third Avenue, and his wife's name was Ellen.[64]

Amelia's daughter, Rhoda Young Lippman, was killed in 1899 in a stagecoach accident near Yellowstone National Park. For several years after the accident, Amelia lived with her daughter's family to help raise Rhoda's three children, but returned to live out her life here. The house appears to have been built as a cross-wing type that faced south with the gable end facing the street. Wood-frame additions at the rear have enlarged the house, and the arched entry gives it an English cottage appearance.

Amelia left no known records in her own hand; she may even have been illiterate. Her brothers Walter, John, and Edward, who also came to Utah, were educated men and had interesting careers. Amelia's obituary noted her "womanly qualities" and "splendid character."[65]

123 North J Street—Thomas S. and Harriet Medlock Goodman, c. 1873

Thomas (1834–1894) and Harriet (1827?–1912) Goodman were English immigrants who sailed from Liverpool to New York on the *William Tapscott* in 1862, arriving in Salt Lake City on October 5 with the Ansil P. Harmon Wagon Company.[66]

In 1869, the Goodmans were living in the Twelfth Ward and Thomas was working as a gardener. They had no children of their own, or at least none who left England with them, so there were no descendants to write the family's history. Even the spelling of Harriet's maiden name and her birthdate are uncertain. What is known is Thomas's fondness for music.[67]

In 1869, a four-year-old girl named Rebecca Hampton sailed from Liverpool to New York on the *Colorado*, her passage paid by the Perpetual Emigrating Fund Company. There is no record of her whereabouts until the 1880 census was taken, when she was sixteen and living here as the Goodmans' daughter. Thomas was a store clerk at the time, and had been out of work for seven months that year.[68]

Title and tax records offer only a general idea of when this house was built. Thomas first paid taxes on the lot in 1872, and city directories list the family at this location by 1874. Yet Thomas did not hold title to the land until 1879, when he paid a two-dollar executor's fee to receive one-quarter of this block from Brigham Young's estate.[69] That action may have cleared up an earlier informal deal that had allowed him to build a house here without paying for the land.

The original Goodman house was built as a vernacular hall-parlor type and was expanded with an 1892 adobe addition at the rear.[70] An asymmetrical facade with three windows and an off-center door may not reflect the original configuration. A gable-roofed porch with turned columns also postdates the original house.

About 1884, Thomas subdivided the lot, sold the parcels for considerable sums of money, and then moved to St. Johns, Arizona, to start a nursery. Harriet probably remained here, and Thomas was still listed in the Salt Lake City directory.[71]

Thomas may have become ill and returned home, where he died on October 31, 1894, from an attack of "creeping paralysis." Harriet, about whom nothing more was written, died in 1912 of "general debility" at the home of her adopted daughter, Rebecca Hampton Eaby, on P Street.[72]

233 North L Street—Elijah Henry and Elizabeth Caffall White, c. 1874

What began as a simple hall-parlor type adobe that faced south has been surrounded by brick and frame additions. A later brick addition with a hipped roof faces the street, embellished with a porch whose turned columns give the house a Victorian appearance. However, the original adobe room or rooms were in place by 1875 when the *Deseret News* reported on the superb potatoes grown by its owner, "north of the [city] wall" which followed what is now Fourth Avenue.[73] At the time, this was roadless, open country where the Whites had few neighbors.

Elijah (1848–1881), who went by Henry, and Elizabeth (1845–1914) were English immigrants. Elijah sailed from Liverpool in 1867 on the *Manhattan* and Elizabeth made the voyage in 1868 on the *Constitution*.

They met in the Salt Lake Valley and married in 1869. They were living in the Twentieth Ward at the time of the 1870 census, not far from Charles Sansom's house at 86 C Street, with baby Edith. Eventually they had nine children, but five died as babies or in early childhood, and only one lived past the age of thirty.[74]

Over time, Elijah improved his situation, beginning as a day laborer, becoming a teamster, and then an expressman. After he died of a stroke in 1881, Elizabeth lived on in this house until the end of her life, often with one or more of her surviving children.[75]

1216 East First Avenue—John Harris Picknell, c. 1866

John Picknell (1813–1878) was a butcher when this area was known as Butcherville.[76] Today it is the exclusive Federal Heights neighborhood, but in the mid-nineteenth century its slaughterhouses supplied meat to butcher shops on Main Street, and after 1861, to the soldiers at nearby Fort Douglas. During the 1880s, a narrow-gauge railway linked the city with the fort, crossing the East Bench a few yards from this house.

Creating an area of slaughterhouses here away from more densely settled areas suggests that the city was already undergoing an important transition from the earliest days of settlement. The pioneers had typically butchered livestock on their property, but as Salt Lake residents became more concerned with comfort and gentility, the convenience of backyard butchering was outweighed by distaste for the unpleasant sounds, smells, and waste.

First built as a five-bay, hall-parlor type with two original rooms, this house grew through the addition of a full-length porch and rear lean-to. Both gable-end chimneys are still intact. The shutters are a later addition.

John and his wife, Elizabeth Parsons (1813–1854), were English converts who bought passage from Liverpool to New Orleans in November 1854 on the *Clara Wheeler*. Elizabeth and the children embarked as planned, but John was arrested for an unpaid debt and detained. The ship sailed before he could board. Elizabeth and two of her six children died at sea, and three more children died after reaching St. Louis.[77]

John, knowing none of this, reached Philadelphia alone in March 1855. He may have been reunited with his one remaining child, twelve-year-old Sarah, in St. Louis and perhaps took her to Utah with the John Hindley Wagon Company.[78] But by Sarah's own account, she was left in St. Louis with a family that proved to be abusive, so when John sent for her in 1860 she took the opportunity instead to marry William A. Reid, a stagecoach driver who had been in Salt Lake City at the time of the census. Their oldest child was born in Utah, and together they lived in frontier towns around the West. They owned a ranch near Medora, North Dakota, where Theodore Roosevelt visited them. Sarah died in 1902 in Dickinson, North Dakota.[79]

After reaching Utah, John Picknell married three women and had three more children, only one of whom survived to adulthood. In 1860, the census enumerator found him in this house with his wife Elizabeth, and also in the Fourteenth Ward with his wife Ann (Hannah). He seems to have done well, accumulating property worth over $1,000.[80]

Picknell was an active LDS Church member, serving as counselor to the president of the Deacon's Quorum in 1876. He died of pneumonia in 1878 and was buried in the Salt Lake City Cemetery.[81]

315 East Second Avenue—William Francis, Eleanor Mitchell, Eliza Westerman, and Mary Evans Neslen, c. 1877

The original owner of this property was Edward Brain (see 51 South 800 East, Eleventh Ward), whose two-story adobe house stood at 303 East

Second Avenue until it was demolished sometime after 1898. Brain sold part of that property to William F. Neslen (1841–1918) in 1877, and construction of this house probably began soon after. It seems to have been designed as a cross-wing type, with an adobe-filled wood-frame addition on the north side. Neslen mortgaged it repeatedly through 1883 for a total of $5,000.[82]

William was the youngest son of Samuel and Eunice Neslen, one of whose houses is just around the corner at 117 North C Street. He came to the Salt Lake Valley with his family in 1853. Ten years later, he married his first wife, Eleanor Mitchell (1842–1914). Between 1865 and 1870, they lived in Nephi, Juab County, where William worked for S. P. Teasdale as a store clerk and served in the home guard during the Black Hawk War. By 1874, they had moved back to Salt Lake City and a house on Fourth Avenue.[83]

The couple had eight children, but by about 1880 William wanted a second wife. Eleanor announced, "A new wife can't come under this roof," so he divorced her in 1884. William cited her "systematic ill treatment" of him over a period of at least four years. He was awarded custody of their children, and Eleanor was forbidden to use the Neslen name. She received, for use during her lifetime, a small frame house at 922 East 100 South (demolished), where she lived until her death.

One of her granddaughters recalled stories Eleanor told of crossing the Atlantic from England about 1860, being run over by a wagon on the plains, and her long, painful recovery. When she reached the Salt Lake Valley, Eleanor was placed with William's parents, Eunice and Samuel Neslen, probably as a domestic servant, and that is where she met William. The elder Neslens were not entirely pleased when William and Eleanor married.[84]

William married Eliza Westerman (1852–1892), "about 1880." Very little is known about Eliza—she was English but not a pioneer, and her name appears in no document except the death and burial register. She and William had two daughters, one of whom died in infancy, before Eliza died of heart failure at age forty.[85]

William married again about 1895 to Mary (Polly) Evans (1857–1935), who had come from England in 1882. Mary was about thirty-eight and William was fifty-four when their only child, Ethel, was born in December 1895. Then, about 1903, William was severely injured when he was thrown from a buggy. He spent the rest of his life in a wheelchair.

Eleanor, whose name for William after their divorce was "Old Buck," liked to say, "That's what Old Buck gets." She left the LDS Church but apparently enjoyed the company of her grown children and her grandchildren, as well as the sixteen dollars that William was required to send her each month.[86]

Both William and his third wife, Mary, died in this house.[87]

323 East Second Avenue—John and Mary Sorensen Snowball/ George Edward Percy and Lavinia Triplett Careless, c. 1867

John Snowball (1840–1921) came from England with his family in 1854. His parents and one of his sisters died on the journey, leaving him, at age fifteen, the oldest of the four remaining siblings. He and his brother Ralph both lived in the Twentieth Ward in 1867. By the time of the 1870 census, John had married Bodil Maria (Mary) Sorensen (1848–1920) and was living here with their first two children. Mary was Danish, although some census records show her country of origin as England, and with her family, had reached the Salt Lake Valley in 1857.[88]

John Snowball sold the house to George Careless and moved to Randolph, Rich County, in 1871, becoming a prominent stock raiser. The

price suggests that the house had been enlarged and improved by then.

George Careless (1839–1932) paid $1,200 for the house and soon got a mortgage of $250, perhaps to add living space. George was born in London, England, and grew up with many advantages, including a fine musical education with the Royal Academy of Music and the experience of performing in London theaters. But when he arrived in the Salt Lake Valley in 1864, he struggled to make ends meet until Brigham Young named him overseer of the Tabernacle Choir and director of the Salt Lake Theater orchestra. Careless also went into the music business with David O. Calder, who lived a short distance west at 69 C Street (demolished).[89]

Lavinia (Lovenia) Triplett, George's first wife, was also an English immigrant and a singer who had performed with George in the London (LDS) Conference choir. She reached Salt Lake City in 1863, a sixteen-year-old girl with a baby listed as "Ann Jane Triplett" on the Daniel D. McArthur Company. Ann Jane may have been George and Lavinia's illegitimate child, but in any case the couple were married in 1866 and had two other daughters, Adelina (1875–1966) and Charlotte (1878–1878). The family lived here only until about 1875. Lavinia, who often sang at the Salt Lake Theater, returned to London for voice lessons in 1879 and at some point became addicted to morphine. When she died of an overdose (or suicide, as shown in the death record) in July 1885, George admitted that she had been using the drug "for some years."[90]

John Snowball probably built the house as a hall-parlor type, which was then enlarged and made more stylish by subsequent owners. It is now a cross-wing type with a front bay, a cornice and cornice returns on the gable end, and paired brackets under the eaves. A wood-frame addition, twice the size of the adobe house, extends from the north side and is flanked by wooden porches.

Later owners of the house included William H. Rowe, who operated one of the electric railway lines in Salt Lake City, and Lydia and Susan Alley Wells, plural wives of Mayor Daniel H. Wells, both of whom moved here after his death in 1891.[91]

425 East Second Avenue—Oliver and Mary Etta Simmons Hodgson, 1883

Once they reached Salt Lake City, many pioneers seemingly lost interest in telling their precise whereabouts. Perhaps they felt that once they were in Zion, that was description enough. In this, Oliver Hodgson (1851–1932) was the exception. Not only did he give this home's precise address in his memoirs, he described its plan (five rooms and a bathroom) and gave the seller's name and the date of purchase.

Oliver came from Halifax, West Yorkshire, England, with his entire family, parents and eight siblings (although baby twins died en route), in

1866. They settled at the northeast corner of C Street and Fifth Avenue in a lime concrete dugout house that was still there in 1898.[92]

His aunt, Mercy Hodgson Robinson, had emigrated in 1853 and lived only a block south (see 177 North C Street, Twentieth Ward) until her death in 1878. Oliver did not mention the Robinsons, and perhaps they had little contact, as the city wall along Fourth Avenue separated their houses. He started work immediately in the LDS Church carpenter shop, learning a trade he would follow for the rest of his life as a builder and contractor.

Oliver Hodgson married Ann Pickard Hollingsworth in 1871. The couple stayed with Ann's parents in their log cabin at 800 South and Main Street. Ann lived only a few months, dying of heart failure or "Inflam. Bowels." In 1875, Oliver married Mary Etta Simmons (1856–1928), and they moved to a two-room adobe cottage he had built at 938 E. 300 South (demolished). The couple eventually had twelve children, four of whom died in childhood.[93]

The family moved to this house "about October 1, 1883." Oliver paid $925 for the land, purchased from John Lyon, whose log cabin stood on the corner of Second Avenue and F Street in the 1860s. Lyon had incorporated the cabin into an adobe house at 431 East Second Avenue (demolished). Oliver Hodgson's house appears to have been built as a hall-parlor type and grown to become a cross-wing with an elaborate porch and window treatments.

Oliver went on to supervise construction of several LDS Church buildings, including the Church Office Building at 47 E. South Temple. By 1898, the family had moved to 28 North 300 West.[94]

No obituary was printed when Mary Etta died in 1928. Oliver was hit by a streetcar in 1930 at the corner of 300 South and 900 East, dying instantly of a fractured skull. His obituary noted that he had had two wives, "both of whom are dead."[95]

482 East Third Avenue—George and Mary Ann Thorne Anderson, c. 1865–1871

This was the childhood home of Utah photographer George Edward "Ed" Anderson. His father, George Anderson (1837–1906), was born in

Scotland and came to New York in 1855 on the *S. Curling* with a loan from the Perpetual Emigration Fund. He reached the Salt Lake Valley with the Milo Andrus Company. Seven unrelated Andersons were with the company, but George seems to have been eighteen years old and alone.[96]

Ed Anderson's mother, Mary Ann Thorne (1835–1926), also sailed from England in 1855. She came with two friends, all of them "plaiters," women who wove straw for hats, on the *Siddons*. Osmyn Merritt Deuel was a fellow passenger; he wrote that Mary Ann was sick during much of the voyage. An early convert to the LDS Church, Deuel was a prosperous blacksmith and farmer from upstate New York. He first went west in 1847 and was returning from a mission to England. Both Osmyn and Mary Ann arrived with the Jacob F. Secrist–Noah T. Guymon Company late in 1855.[97]

Deuel was more than thirty years Mary Ann's senior and already had one wife. They married when they reached the valley, Mary Ann no doubt pleased that her husband offered her the security of his wealth and position. (The Deuel log cabin, originally part of the 1847 fort in Pioneer Park, has been moved to West Temple Street, opposite Temple Square.) Osmyn and Mary Ann had no children (nor did any of Deuel's other wives), and their marriage did not last.[98]

In February 1860, Mary Ann married George Anderson, a "fancy gardener" living in the Eighth Ward. Anderson bought this property—at the

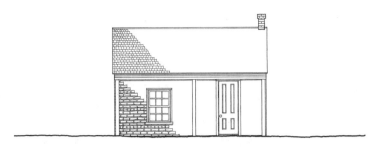

EAST ELEVATION

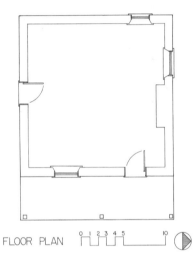

FLOOR PLAN   0 1 2 3 4 5   10

NORTH ELEVATION

Architectural drawings showing the original single-cell house at 482 East Third Avenue as it appeared c. 1867. Drawings by Thomas Carter and James Gosney. Used by permission, Western Regional Architecture Program Collection, J. Willard Marriott Library, University of Utah, all rights reserved.

time, one-quarter of the block—from Brigham Young in 1867, although the original room of the house may have been built somewhat earlier. He described himself as a herdsman, but he may have been a gardener for Brigham Young's first wife, Mary Ann Angell Young. By 1870, the family had grown to include four children, of whom George Edward was the oldest. Nine children were born to George and Mary Ann Anderson, but three died in childhood.[99]

George Edward Anderson (1860–1928) became the prolific and talented photographer who captured landscapes and scenes of life in Utah during the late nineteenth century. He wrote nothing about his childhood or his home. It was described, probably long after the fact, as "a humble home, immaculately clean, and breathed an atmosphere of beauty and culture."

Other sources paint a very different picture. Ed Anderson's father attacked his mother with a butcher knife in 1867, and although the marriage lasted for another twelve years, testimony in their divorce proceedings detailed the beatings and abuse suffered by both Mary Ann and her children. Mary Ann's witnesses testified to the brutality, while George's male friends testified to his fine character. Regardless of the facts in this case, George was something of a crank. He complained of the "descendants of Jehu around here at present, who frequently drive along the public thoroughfares with exceeding great speed . . . and dash recklessly through hapless herds of cattle . . . to the detriment of the interests of herdsmen and cattle owners generally."[100] The divorce was granted in 1879. Mary Ann received the south half of the lot, where there was a small house, along with a milk cow and the household furnishings.

George Edward Anderson began working for the photographer Charles R. Savage when he was a teenager and by 1879 had opened his own shop on Main Street, employing his brothers J. Stanley and Adam. In 1880, Mary Ann and her children were counted twice by the census enumerator, both at the Main Street shop and here on Third Avenue.[101]

Ed Anderson bought land and a picturesque home in Springville, Utah County, in 1881 and went on to produce some thirty thousand images of people, landscapes, homes and businesses, LDS temples, and historic sites, many taken and developed in portable studios on horse-drawn carts that he hauled around Utah. Some twenty thousand negatives survive, most of them now in the Harold B. Lee Library at Brigham Young University.

One shows his parents at Ed's wedding to Olive Lowry in 1888. They are seated next to each other but looking in opposite directions.[102]

Ed's adult life was far from peaceful, as his obsession with photography trumped his interest in making enough money to support his family. Like his father, Ed had a bad temper and was physically abusive when he was displeased. His diary indicates that he was "disgusted" with himself when he lost control. His father, who never remarried, joined him in Springville about 1888, remaining there until his death in 1906.[103]

Mary Ann Anderson identified herself as a widow after her divorce. She remained in Salt Lake City, for a time with her daughter Lillie (Lillian) in a large brick house that is still standing on the south half of the original lot, at 123 North G Street. She was declared indigent in 1896 and her property taxes were abated. Her children scattered and gone, she died in an apartment on North Temple Street in 1926.[104] No published death notice or obituary was found.

William Everill and his wife Ellen bought this house from George Anderson in 1879, although the sale was declared "fraudulent and void" by the court because the Andersons' divorce had not been finalized. Everill finally got legal title in 1881, then repeatedly mortgaged the property as he struggled to build and maintain his butcher shop next door (474–476 East Third Avenue).[105]

The store closed in 1893 when William was gravely injured by a runaway horse; he never recovered and died in March 1895. Only two months later the Everills' sixteen-year-old daughter collapsed and died at school. Ellen Everill lived here with her daughter Mabel until 1898, struggling to pay her property taxes and repeatedly losing the house in tax sales. She died in 1916.[106]

The original north room of the house, a single-cell type, has been much altered by later owners, who enlarged the north window and converted the adobe fireplace to a coal-burning, brick fireplace. The front door faced east across the lot toward G Street. The covered porch may not be original, but it does reflect the earliest orientation of the house, as does the earliest street address—133 North G Street.[107] Details of the foundation and sash saw marks on the floor joists seen in the cellar also suggest an early construction date.

The one-and-one-half-story addition was built soon after the original room, about 1870, as indicated by the simple hand-turned balusters

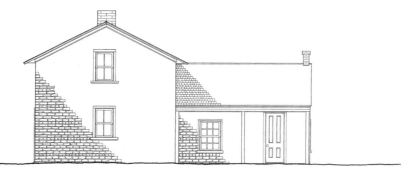

EAST ELEVATION

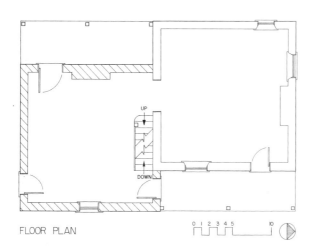

FLOOR PLAN

0 1 2 3 4 5   10

Architectural drawings showing 482 East Third Avenue as it appeared c. 1870. Drawings by Thomas Carter and James Gosney. Used by permission, Western Regional Architecture Program Collection, J. Willard Marriott Library, University of Utah, all rights reserved.

and newel post on the stairway, and by the increase in tax valuation.[108] An adobe fireplace on the west wall of the first floor provided the only heat for the addition.

580 East Third Avenue—Henry and Betsy Clark Williams Fewens Tempest, c. 1865

The oldest part of this house may have been built as early as 1865, when Henry Tempest paid property taxes on unspecified land valued at $600 in the Twentieth Ward. Certainly there was a house here by 1867, when Betsy's name appears at this location in the city directory.[109]

Both Henry (1824–1890) and Betsy (1821–1911) were English, and both had left their spouses behind to gather with the Latter-day Saints in Salt Lake City. Henry brought his sons John Henry and James with him, claiming he was a widower, but his wife, Mary, lived on in England until her death in 1881. Betsy left her husband, William Fewens, taking their son, William. They may have sailed on the *George Washington* from Liverpool to Boston in 1857.[110]

Betsy and William continued their journey west in 1860. By that time, she had met, and presumably married, Henry Tempest. The blended family was listed by the 1860 census enumerator at both Genoa, Nebraska (in June) and Omaha (in August). They joined the Daniel Robison Handcart

Company at Florence, Nebraska, leaving on June 6 and arriving in the Salt Lake Valley in late August 1860.[111]

Betsy was living in this house in 1867, and Henry lived here for at least a short time prior to Betsy's divorcing him. No reason for their separation was given, except that the couple could not live together "in peace and union." In the settlement, Betsy received the east six-tenths of Henry's original lot, and her son, William, received the west four-tenths.[112] The original house was an unornamented hall-parlor type; a brick addition on the east side makes it appear to be a cross-wing.

Henry married Mary Ann Giles in 1874 and moved to Fort Herriman. Betsy too married again, in 1872, to a blacksmith named James Glover (1823–1905) who lived in West Jordan. She sold this house and lot to Soren P. Neve in 1876 for $2,000, and eventually it became the property of two of Neve's plural wives, Marintha and Mary, who owned it for many years. Betsy's son, William, was killed in an accident in 1875. His property was tied up in the probate courts until 1892 when it was distributed to relatives "for use of family." Betsy seems not to have lived with James Glover, as city directories and federal censuses placed her in the Twentieth Ward until 1910. She died at the County Infirmary in 1911, when she was nearly ninety.[113]

457 East Fourth Avenue—Harriet Husbands Bell, c. 1868

Harriet Husbands (1832–1899), a "spinster," sailed from Liverpool, England, to New York in 1860, accompanied by her widowed mother, Margaret, and two brothers. They joined the James D. Ross Company at Florence, Nebraska, and arrived in the Salt Lake Valley in early September.[114]

Within ten weeks of her arrival, Harriet had married Millard P. Bell. Bell (1814–1868) was a recent convert to the LDS Church. He left his family in Ohio, where he was a sawyer or lumber mill worker, and worked at the same trade in Salt Lake City. He became the "lawful claimant" of this lot in 1867, mortgaged it for ninety dollars in 1868, and then died the next year. Harriet was left with three children, and a fourth who was born in 1869. The house may have been built by that time, but census records and city directories are silent on Harriet's whereabouts. In any case, the mortgage went into default in 1869.[115]

Although the house is now a cross-wing type, that form was apparently achieved by the addition of a south room to an earlier hall-parlor type. A large front window on the gable end has a simple transom, another indication that the room was built after the original house.

Harriet married Collins Eastman Flanders (1814–1881) as his fourth (plural) wife in 1871 and had at least two more children. For a time, at least, they may have lived here, but Harriet was again calling herself Harriet Bell by 1880. When Flanders died in 1881, Harriet regained ownership of the property, as well as the west half of the large lot to the east, on the corner of Fourth Avenue and G Street.[116] She sold part of that lot in 1887 to David P. Anderson, who built a large adobe home for Henry T. McEwan in 1889 (473 East Fourth Avenue).

City directories place Harriet Bell here until her death from "paralysis" in 1899.[117] There was no published death or funeral notice, and no obituary. Harriet's son Hyrum sold the house as soon as he inherited it.

Harriet and her brother William may have had a falling out over religion. In 1871, the year Harriet became a plural wife, William testified to a representative of the U.S. Congress that he no longer believed in Mormon doctrine, and that Utah should not become a state because he had heard Brigham Young preach violence against the "Gentiles." William and his wife, Sarah, were buried in Mount Olivet Cemetery, which was nondenominational.[118]

Twenty-First Ward

Only five adobe houses were built in The Avenues after the Twenty-First Ward was formed in 1877, including the two described below.

186 North M Street—Marion Robertson Pringle, 1884–1887

Robert (1847–1884) and Marion Robertson Pringle (1844–1929) were Scottish immigrants but not pioneers, arriving from Liverpool in 1872 on the *Minnesota* and taking the newly completed transcontinental railroad train to Salt Lake City. Their two young children, Robert and Jessie, made the journey with them. Eventually the Pringles had eight children, all but one of whom lived long lives.[1]

For most of the next ten years, the family lived on C Street between Sixth and Seventh Avenues, and Robert worked as a stone cutter. They had bought the C Street property but were evidently unable to pay for it, and it was sold at a marshal's sale in 1875. Finding work must have been a constant challenge for Robert, at one point moving to Reno, Nevada, where their daughter Marion was born in March 1875. Then Robert lived in Logan from late 1880 until 1883, working as an agent for a sewing machine company. That venture seems not to have worked out, and he left Ogden with a crew of men to work on the Oregon Short Line in October 1883. He did not return. Robert drowned in the Snake River near Huntington, Oregon, while working on a bridge for the railroad.[2]

Marion built this house after Robert died, even though his estate was not settled until 1893. The adobe rooms, which form the south side of the house, appear to have been built as a hall-parlor type with a porch that covered the entry. A stone or concrete addition forms the north half of the house, and there are wood-frame additions at the rear.

Marion's situation must still have been precarious, as she soon applied for tax relief. She lived briefly with one of her daughters about 1900, but then returned here, where she lived until her death.[3]

573 East Third Avenue—James Orson and Clara Brown Ellerbeck, c. 1884

Brigham Young was the original owner of the block bounded by Third and Fourth Avenues, H and I Streets. He sold it to William Godbe in 1868, who quickly sold it to Thomas Witton Ellerbeck, Brigham Young's chief clerk. The first house on the block, facing Third Avenue, was built about 1873 for Thomas Ellerbeck's mother-in-law, Sarah Jarrold Hyder Free (1800–1897). Sarah was the second LDS convert baptized in Cambridge, England. Widowed in England in 1838, she had come to the Salt Lake Valley with three of her daughters in 1851, and married Absalom Free in 1856.[4]

Thomas Ellerbeck went on to work for the Union Pacific Railroad, then took charge of construction of the first waterworks in Salt Lake City, and oversaw the finances of Utah's first gas plant (see 36 North 600 West, for its location near the Octave Ursenbach home, Sixteenth Ward). His family lived in a spacious adobe home at 233 West 200 North (demolished). Of Thomas's four wives, the first, Martha Birch Hyder, was James's mother. She died in June 1863 when James was less than a year old.[5]

James Orson Ellerbeck (1862–1927) married Clara Brown (1861–1930) about 1882. He bought half of the southeast corner lot on this block in 1884 and soon built the initial adobe wing of this house. A $300 mortgage taken out in 1889 probably paid for construction of the brick rooms on the west side. The original door seems to have faced east toward his grandmother Sarah's house, and his ownership was "subject to occupancy of house on east side during life of Sarah Hyder." Sarah died in 1897.[6]

James worked first as a collector at the gas works but was for most of his life a blacksmith. By the 1920s, he had entered the automobile age and was the manager at a tire company. When James died of stomach cancer in 1927, he was identified as a sportsman, suggesting that he enjoyed considerable leisure time. Clara died in an automobile accident in 1930. Their sons, Clarence and James, lived relatively short lives, dying not long after their parents.[7]

Conclusion

The Houses

In selecting the houses and histories featured in this book, my choices were influenced by factors that may not always be obvious. Most of the remaining adobe buildings in Salt Lake City began their existence as two- or three-room, single-story homes of the hall-parlor type, and therefore these modest homes predominate in the descriptions. Second, although they are rare now, I chose a few larger homes to illustrate other characteristic types and styles of architecture, or because of their owners' connections to events and trends in the city's history. And third, I chose the small and often humble homes that illustrate what is missing from our collective history, the great trials and small joys experienced by those on the social and economic underside of the nineteenth-century city.

Twenty-first-century residents of Utah may find it difficult to imagine that their capital city, known as Great Salt Lake City until 1868, began as a cluster of log and adobe buildings and was, for its first twenty years, almost entirely an adobe city. For the pioneers, who had traveled thousands of miles, for the most part on sailing ships, horse- or ox-drawn wagons, or on foot, it was their Zion. In the first years of settlement, members of the Church of Jesus Christ of Latter-day Saints anticipated the end times, the millennium, to be fast approaching. Their purpose and their energies were bent towards the day when they, and no other people, would be deserving of salvation. Their city was meant to provide a short-term physical refuge, and at the same time, to exemplify their special relationship with God and each other.

The Builders

In the early years, the most basic tasks somehow had to be accomplished, beginning with finding water, building shelter, raising or gathering enough food to survive, cooking, and staying warm and dry. The settlers accomplished their goals only through superb organization and hard work that was done entirely with hand tools and with implements driven by domestic animals or moving water. In an unfamiliar landscape, plagued by pests, injury, drought, and disease, the effort might have seemed unbearable. A child's death, or even a minor accident without any effective medical help, must have been heartbreaking, but events like these were familiar to people everywhere at that time. Most of us in the United States are generations removed from such experiences. We should be astonished and humbled by the pioneers' devotion to establishing their spiritual and physical home, and by the price they paid to do so.

A Material Change

Brigham Young extolled adobe for what he saw as its durability and practicality, but it was clear that most of the Latter-day Saints came to disagree. At least, they offered little praise for the stuff. Not one owner expressed regret upon moving to a brick or frame house as those became available. Once they had served their immediate purpose, providing shelter in a landscape of grass, and once the pioneers realized that their stay in Zion would be longer than expected, adobe homes were abandoned or remodeled for more comfortable and genteel quarters by almost everyone who could afford to do so.

Getting to Zion was the great equalizer. Prior to 1869 (and completion of the transcontinental railroad) everyone, rich and poor alike, had to spend months crossing more than a thousand miles of wilderness, and most had already endured thousands more miles on ships crossing the Atlantic. Being in Zion was another story. After the first few years, people who arrived with good health, ambition, intelligence, and needed skills found ways to obtain the better things—white flour, sugar, velvet, lace, and fashionable hats that arrived on freight wagons. These same pioneers organized bands and theater groups, sports teams, and ward dances. They found opportunities to enjoy music, attend plays, and write poetry. If the owners of the small adobe homes seldom joined them, that did not mean they were any less aware of what refinement meant. It was on display for any man who went to hear church leaders speak and for every woman who was a servant in a large house. Fine furniture, china, and fabrics were available, but at a price few could afford. In spite of early efforts at social and economic equality, superficially at least, life in Zion began to resemble life in the eastern United States.

Ordinary people, when they could, acquired fashionable things and enjoyed them as indicators of their individual rise in economic status. As Thomas Carter writes, earthly success came to be seen as indicative of spiritual favor. Elizabeth Fovargue Smith, who helped her husband build their house in 1855 (727 West 400 North), recorded every purchase—a hat, new blankets, dress fabric—and its cost, even thirty years later.[1] She stayed in her adobe house until the end of her life but she added a stylish brick front room. Her son James built a brick house next door.

All the fine adobe homes that once lined South Temple Street—a few remained, even in the 1950s—are now gone. They had been downgraded from mansion to house to shed, and finally to fill dirt, and replaced with larger and finer homes made of more stylish and durable materials. At least no one puzzles over their owners' stories, since they were often privileged to write them, or to have someone else write them.

Of the remaining adobe buildings, many are crumbling because they are worth less than the cost of repair, or because they are so resistant to modernization. A few have been placed on the National Register of Historic Places; most remain because they are utilitarian at best. Having seen adobe houses fall to track hoes and excavators, I can tell you that they do not go down easily. Large sections of walls, the mortar still holding tight, often fall in a single piece. The adobes may break, but they do not crumble to dust.

My hope is that a little knowledge will inspire the reader to understand, to respect, and to preserve what remains. In Utah, words like "heritage," "pioneer," and "legacy" have special meaning, especially to members of the LDS Church. We should use those words, too, in describing Salt Lake City's architectural past, its tangible link with what, for western American settlement, is the "deep past." Salt Lake City's last few adobe houses, unassuming though they may be, embody tales of courage and fear, success and defeat, and like the old benches in the Mormon Tabernacle they should be hailed as "the real thing."

Appendix

Other Extant Adobe Buildings, Salt Lake City

These buildings were not described in detail either because they were not built as homes, because they are generally larger or more elaborate than the vernacular structures featured in this book, or because reliable and detailed information about them was unavailable.

First Ward
764 South Lake Street, builder unknown, post-1898

Second Ward
775 South 300 East, Hans and Elena Larson, date unknown
768 South 400 East, James Peterson, c. 1887
446 East 700 South, Jacob and Catherine Heusser, 1871 (some remnants
    of the 1850s Charles Northrup Woodard adobe may remain)
461 East 800 South, Peder C. Johnson, c. 1874

Ninth Ward
407 East 600 South, Joshua and Delphia Pendleton, by 1874

Tenth Ward
756 East 500 South, Andrew E. and Julia Brooks Busby, 1884
872 East 500 South, Isaac R. and Mary Jane McRae Pierce, c. 1869
    (southeast room)
550 South 800 East, Caroline Pettegrew, c. 1870 (northeast room)
563 South 800 East, James E. and Margaret Malin, c. 1865
517 South 900 East, Frank W. and Sarah Earl, by 1887

Eleventh Ward
753 East 200 South, George and Elizabeth Horrocks Coulam, c. 1872
113 South 700 East, Jabez W. and Sarah Ann Ellis Taylor, c. 1874

Twelfth Ward
350 East 100 South, Zerubbabel and Mary Snow, c. 1874 (at rear)
522 East 100 South, Almon Babbitt and Amelia Brooks Palmer, c. 1869
     (at rear)

Sixteenth Ward
613 West 200 North, Gammon and Sarah Ann Cripps Hayward, c. 1869
837 West 300 North, builder unknown, c. 1900
767 West 400 North, John R., Margaret, and Annie Haslam, by 1861
147 North 600 West, Thomas and Sarah Ann Bouck Powell, c. 1883
205 North 600 West, John Thomas Thompson, c. 1879
215 North 600 West, John Thomas Thompson?, c. 1891
260 North 600 West, Edward King, c. 1885
135 North 700 West, Charles Smith Harman, c. 1862
844 West South Temple, Alexander Ledingham, c. 1873

Eighteenth Ward
63 East South Temple, Lion House, 1854–1856
67–69 East South Temple, LDS Church offices, 1852 and 1854
75 East South Temple, Beehive House, 1852–1854
Temple Square, LDS Church Tabernacle, 1867 (lower walls)
217 North Canyon Road, Minerva White Snow, c. 1885
252 North Canyon Road, Helaman Pratt/Franklin R. Snow, c. 1875

Nineteenth Ward
613 North 200 West, Orlando D, Abigail and Frederikka Hovey, 1869?
633 North 200 West, Joseph Askie and Mary Eleanor Watson Silver, 1878?
112 West 300 North, James W. Brown, 1882–1884
229 West 300 North, Milando and Elizabeth Rich Pratt, c. 1876
239 West 300 North, Milando and Elizabeth Rich Pratt, c. 1881
238 West 400 North, Andrew and Karen Hyrup, 1888
259 West 400 North, Michael Sargent and Mary Thomas Katz, 1880

318 West 400 North, Frederick Crowton, c. 1880

320 West 400 North, Frederick Crowton?, c. 1880

564 West 400 North, Nelson Wheeler Whipple, 1854

224 West 500 North, John H., Abigail Smith, and Caroline Calkins Tippets, by 1874 (at rear)

364 West 500 North, Alfred J. Ridges, by 1884

604 West 500 North, John Lees, c. 1880

616 West 500 North, John Lees, c. 1880

213 West 600 North, Richard and Mary Collett, 1885

250 West 600 North, John Oscar and Mary Maria Lowe, c. 1869

351 North 600 West, Edwin Pettit, date unknown

468 North 600 West, Daniel Whipple, date unknown

525 North 600 West, Joseph H. Player?, date unknown

232 West 700 North, Susa Young Gates, c. 1887

236 West 700 North, Charles W. Olson, c. 1889

260 West 700 North, Frederick C. and Margaret Emma Arnold Rich, 1883

365 West 800 North, Carl Morris and Maren Harder Madsen, 1884

321 North Almond Street (rear), Ebenezer, Jr., and Emily Cooper Beesley, 1882

349 North Almond Street, William C. and Isabella Stewart Campbell Clive, 1883

271 North Center Street, Henry and Charlotte Perkes, 1873 (store)

314 North Center Street, Fergus Coalter, 1880

390 North Center Street, Sven J. and Marie Jonasson, 1870

1258 West Clark Avenue, Abraham and Elizabeth Coon, 1850

160 West Clinton Avenue, Benjamin and Harriet Cross Johnson/Francis Williams, 1891

314 North Quince Street, Richard Vaughan, Lavinia Robins, and Harriet Jones Morris, c. 1865

365 North Quince Street, John and Mary Flower, c. 1874

450 North Quince Street, Walter and Margaret Kiddle, post-1880

680 North Wall Street, Charles J. and Elizabeth Mullett, c. 1876

528 North West Capitol Street, Thomas Grieve and Annie Geddes Sutherland, 1886

66 West Zane Avenue, Atkinson and Agnes Boyd Whitworth, 1874

343 North 600 West, builder unknown, c. 1873

344 North 600 West, Peter and Maria L. Davis Nebeker, c. 1855

Twentieth Ward

205 East First Avenue, George and Elizabeth Golightly Watt, 1861 (west side of Madeleine Choir School campus)

268 East Second Avenue, Anna Mackay Calder, by 1885

136 East Third Avenue, Orson P. Arnold, c. 1888

183 East Third Avenue, Mathoni W. and Elizabeth Sheets Pratt, c. 1885

474–476 East Third Avenue, William R. and Ellen Everill, c. 1881 (southeast part)

473 East Fourth Avenue, Henry T., Lusannah Hardy, and Margaret Sharp McEwan, 1888

414 East Fifth Avenue, Abraham R. Wright/James M. and Edith Pyper, 1878?

259 East Sixth Avenue, John and Sarah Latimer Timms, 1890

263 East Sixth Avenue, John and Sarah Latimer Timms, 1890

522 East Sixth Avenue, William W., Dinah Neal, and Selina Crowton Phillips, c. 1891

122 North C Street, Heber John, Kate Ada Miller, and Lena Bergstrom Romney, by 1884

123 North C Street, George and Mary Gibson Wareing, c. 1883

237 North C Street, A. J. and Rosine Arfsten, c. 1889

80 North D Street, Charles R., Annie Adkins, Mary Fowler, Ellen Fenn, and Annie Clowes Savage, c. 1862

286 North D Street, David P. Anderson, 1887

67 North E Street, Alfales and Ada Cottle Young, 1883

78 North E Street, John P., Catherine Fell, Johanna Jensen, Eleanor Cox, and Emily Swain Squires, c. 1856

303 North E Street, Jacques and Maria Ruban Held, c. 1886

176–182 North G Street, ?Henry Lewis, c. 1860

Twenty-First Ward

637 East Second Avenue, Amos J. and Caroline Maiben Lucas, 1881

585 East Third Avenue, Arthur J. Durnford, by 1883

673 East Seventh Avenue, George P. and Lucie C. Clark, c. 1891

Sugar House Ward

1075 East Harvard Avenue, Lorenzo Dow and Ellen Jones Young, 1888

984 South 1100 East, John and Jane Roxbrugh, c. 1870

1263 East 1700 South, William Henry Sutcliffe Hodgson, 1872

Liberty Park
Isaac Chase home (1854) and Mill (1852)

Fort Douglas
Post Commander's House (part), 1863
Post Surgeon's Quarters (part), 1864

Other Areas
1303 West 400 South, builder unknown, 1900?
1335 West Indiana Avenue, builder and date unknown
339 East Hampton Avenue, Christian Steffensen, 5 Acre Plat A, c. 1881

Notes

Introduction and Background

1. Leonard J. Arrington, *Great Basin Kingdom: Economic History of the Latter-day Saints, 1830–1900* (Cambridge: Harvard University Press, 1958), 28.
2. S. Augustus Mitchell, *A New Map of Texas, Oregon, and California with the Regions Adjoining* (Philadelphia: S. A. Mitchell, 1846).
3. For an in-depth discussion of the history of the LDS Church, see James B. Allen and Glen M. Leonard, *Story of the Latter-day Saints*, 2nd ed. (Salt Lake City: Deseret Book Company, 1992).
4. Will Bagley, ed., *The Pioneer Camp of the Saints: The 1846 and 1847 Mormon Trail Journals of Thomas Bullock* (Spokane: Arthur H. Clark, 2001), 130.
5. William Clayton, *William Clayton's Journal: A Daily Record of the Journey of the Original Company of "Mormon" Pioneers from Nauvoo, Illinois, to the Valley of the Great Salt Lake* (Dallas: S. K. Taylor, c. 1973), entry for July 27, 1847.
6. Richard E. Bennett, *We'll Find the Place: The Mormon Exodus, 1846–1848* (Norman: University of Oklahoma Press, 1997), 231–33.
7. David H. Burr, "Map of Salt Lake City," Utah State Historical Society, c. 1856.
8. James G. Lund, "The Prophet Joseph Smith's Plat of the City of Zion, June 25, 1833," [map] prepared from the original by James G. Lund, 1979 (?), LDS Church History Library, Salt Lake City, Utah.
9. LDS Church, General Minutes, September 3–4, 1847, LDS Church History Library, Salt Lake City, Utah.
10. Bagley, *The Pioneer Camp of the Saints*, 263.
11. Rudyard Kipling, "The Galley Slave," in Kipling, *Departmental Ditties and Other Verses*, 4th ed. (London: Thacker, Spink & Co., 1890).
12. Clayton, *William Clayton's Journal*, 326.
13. Thomas Carter, *Building Zion: The Material World of Mormon Settlement* (Minneapolis: University of Minnesota Press, 2015), 29.
14. W. Randall Dixon, personal communication, December 5, 2013.
15. Andrew Jenson, *Encyclopedic History of the Church of Jesus Christ of Latter-day Saints* (Salt Lake City: Deseret News Publishing Co., 1941), 741.

16. Ronald W. Walker, "'Going to Meeting' in Salt Lake City's Thirteenth Ward, 1849–1881: A Microanalysis," in *New Views of Mormon History: A Collection of Essays in Honor of Leonard J. Arrington*, ed. Davis Bitton and Maureen Ursenbach Beecher (Salt Lake City: University of Utah Press, 1987), 139–61.

17. LDS Church, Minutes of Bishops' Meetings, January 17, 1861, cited in John K. Hulmston, "Mormon Immigration in the 1860s: The Church Trains," *Utah Historical Quarterly* 58, no. 1 (1990): 32–48.

18. Daniel H. Ludlow, ed., *Encyclopedia of Mormonism* (New York: Macmillan, 1992), 1075.

19. Arrington, *Great Basin Kingdom*, 67–71.

20. "Railroad Meeting," *Deseret News*, February 2, 1854.

21. Carter, *Building Zion*, 16.

22. John McCormick, *The Gathering Place* (Salt Lake City: Signature Books, 2000), 60–64.

23. *Salt Lake City Directory for 1889* (Salt Lake City: Kelly & Co., 1889).

24. Edward L. Sloan, *Gazeteer of Utah and Salt Lake City Directory* (Salt Lake City: Salt Lake Herald Publ. Co., 1874).

25. Salt Lake City key map, 1889 (New York: Sanborn Map Co., 1889).

26. Hannah S. Newman, "History of Hannah Selley Newman," (n.d.) Pioneer Memorial Museum, History Department, Salt Lake City.

27. U.S. Federal Census, Utah Territory, 1870, Sixteenth Ward, near John Perkins's residence.

28. U.S. Federal Census, Utah Territory, 1880, Sixteenth Ward.

29. U.S. Federal Census, Utah Territory, 1870.

30. U.S. Federal Census, Utah Territory, 1880.

31. See map on page ix.

32. A list of the current street names in Salt Lake City, with their earlier equivalents, can be found at the end of on pages xiii and xv in this volume.

33. LDS Church Journal History, October 11, 1848, 1; Orson F. Whitney, *History of Utah in Four Volumes* (Salt Lake: George Q. Cannon & Sons, 1904), 4:202.

34. Donna T. Smart, ed., *Mormon Midwife: The 1846–1888 Diaries of Patty Bartlett Sessions* (Logan: Utah State University Press, 1997), 153.

35. Thomas Carter and Peter Goss, *Utah's Historic Architecture, 1847–1940* (Salt Lake City: Utah State Historical Society, 1988), 2

36. Thomas Carter, "Folk Design in Utah Architecture, 1849–1890," in *Images of an American Land: Vernacular Architecture in the Western United States*, ed. Thomas Carter (Albuquerque: University of New Mexico Press, 1997), 41–60.

37. Carter and Goss, *Utah's Historic Architecture, 1847–1940*.

38. An association of Mormon women.

39. Members of the LDS Church donate one-tenth of their increase or profit to the church each year. Tithing helps support the work of the church and benefits members in need of assistance.

40. Smart, *Mormon Midwife*, 108.

41. John F. Squires, "Autobiographical Sketch," n.d., LDS Church History Library, folder 1.

42. LDS Church, FamilySearch https://familysearch.org/ ark:/61903/2:1:M7FC-JVP

43. Malvern Tipping, "Identifying Clay Construction Buildings in a Norfolk Market Town," Federacion Internationale des Geometres Congress, Proceedings, Sydney, Australia, 2010.

44. Clayton, *William Clayton's Journal,* entry for July 23, 1847.

45. C. Mark Hamilton, *Nineteenth Century Mormon Architecture and City Planning* (New York: Oxford University Press, 1995), 57–58, n. 17.

46. "The History of Joseph Buckley," n.d., Pioneer Memorial Museum, History Department.

47. LDS Church Historian's Office Journal, June 24, 1852.

48. Lorenzo Brown, "Journal of Lorenzo Brown 1823–1890," (Moccasin, AZ: Lorenzo John Brown Family Organization, 1974), entry for June 23, 1852.

49. Richard F. Burton, *City of the Saints and Across the Rocky Mountains to California.* (New York: Harper and Brothers, 1862), 197.

50. Church of Jesus Christ of Latter-day Saints, Journal of Discourses, 1854, 1–2:218.

51. Aroet L. Hale, "Diary of Aroet Lucious Hale, 1828–1849," LDS Church History Library.

52. Donette S. Kesler, *Reminiscenses* (Salt Lake City: Elbert C. Kirkham Co., 1952), 104. Letter from Alfred Lambson written in 1897.

53. "An Ordinance," *Deseret News,* May 11, 1854.

54. "Local and Other Matters," *Deseret News,* March 19, 1879.

55. Robert L. Sloan, *Utah Gazetteer and Directory for Logan, Ogden, Provo, and Salt Lake Cities, for 1884* (Salt Lake City: Herald Printing Co., 1884).

56. LDS Church Historian's Office Journal, May 6, 1861.

57. James Leach, "James Leach Reminiscences and Diary, 1852 November–1859 June," LDS Church History Library, fd. 1.

58. Jeffrey Carlstrom and Cynthia Furse, *The History of Emigration Canyon* (Logan: Utah State University Press, 2003), 56.

59. "A Superb Residence," *Salt Lake Herald,* October 7, 1883.

60. "Cremated Alive," *Salt Lake Herald,* July 9, 1893.

61. "Our Buildings," *Salt Lake Tribune,* April 20, 1881; "Our Business Affairs," *Salt Lake Tribune,* May 15, 1889; "In the Line of Progress," *Salt Lake Tribune,* April 23, 1893; "Another Old Landmark Gives Way to Business," *Salt Lake Herald,* November 30, 1909; "Bungalow Vogue Reaches Salt Lake in Force," *Deseret News,* April 18, 1908.

62. "An Ordinance," *Salt Lake Herald,* June 18, 1904.

63. Often praised for his successful orchard, it is clear from Elizabeth Wood Kane's *Twelve Mormon Homes* (Salt Lake City: University of Utah Tanner Trust Fund, 1974), 86, that Lorenzo Dow Young's wives had cared for the fruit trees, both in the wagons that carried them west and after they were planted around his homes in the Eighteenth Ward and in Sugar House.

64. Elizabeth Fovargue Smith, "Elizabeth F. Smith journal, 1884–1891," LDS Church History Library, reel 1.

65. The U.S. Library of Congress has more than 10 million newspaper pages online at chroniclingamerica.loc.gov.

66. "1867 Mormon Tabernacle Pews Are Casualties of a Face-Lift," *New York Times*, October 6, 2006.

First Ward

1. U.S. Federal Census, Utah Territory, 1860.

2. Salt Lake City, sheet 189, 1889 (New York: Sanborn Map Co., 1889).

3. Brigham Young University, Mormon Migration Index, http://mormonmigration.lib.byu.edu/Search/showDetails/db:MM_MII/t:passenger/id:15039/keywords:August+Dittman; *Salt Lake City Directory for 1889*, Kelly & Co.; T. B. H. Stenhouse & Co., *Utah Gazetteer 1892–93* (Salt Lake City: Stenhouse & Co., 1892).

4. In 1888, the *Salt Lake Tribune* began publishing an annual list of building projects in the city for the prior year. Neither Dittman's name nor this location appears in the lists for 1887–1889. See *Salt Lake Tribune*, January 1, 1891.

5. Salt Lake County Recorder, title abstracts and Great Salt Lake City Plat B, c. 1856.

6. Salt Lake County Recorder, title abstracts.

7. R. L. Polk & Co., *Polk's Salt Lake City Directory for 1896* (Salt Lake City: R. L. Polk & Co., 1896), 346; Upton Sinclair, *The Profits of Religion: An Essay in Economic Interpretation* vol. 6, *Mazdaznan* (Pasadena, CA: self-published, 1917). Hanisch called himself "prophet of the Sun God, Prince of Peace, Manthra Magi of Temple El Katman, Kalantar of Zoroastrian Breathing and Envoy of Mazdaznan living, Viceroy-Elect and International Head of Master-Thot"; *Polk's Salt Lake City Directory*, 1898; "Echo Heard of Old and Notorious Case," *Salt Lake Tribune*, October 14, 1908.

8. Department of Agriculture and Food, Division of Animal Industry, Brand books, Utah State Archives and Records Service, series 540; U.S. Federal Census, Utah, 1900 and 1910

9. "Deaths," *Salt Lake Telegram*, July 9, 1926; "Mrs. Dittman Dies," *Salt Lake Herald*, October 10, 1912; Death certificate, Utah State Archives and Records Service, series 81448.

10. "Emigrants for Utah," *Deseret* News, August 6, 1856; Edmund Ellsworth, "Autobiography, 1819–1885," n.d., Utah Division of State History, Utah State Historical Society Collections; U.S. Federal Census, Utah Territory, 1860; Public Works account books, 1848–1887, LDS Church History Library; George Owens, *Salt Lake City Directory, Including a Business Directory of Provo, Springville, and Ogden, Utah Territory* (Salt Lake City: George Owens, 1867).

11. Salt Lake County Recorder, title abstracts. The pioneer land distribution system did not comply with federal laws. Land title certificates provided federally recognized title to land the settlers had received under the earlier system.

12. Robert L. Sloan, *Utah Gazetteer and Directory for Logan, Ogden, Provo, and Salt Lake Cities, for 1884* (Salt Lake City: Herald Printing Co., 1884).

13. Stephen L. Carr and Robert W. Edwards, *Utah Ghost Rails* (Salt Lake City: Western Epics, 1989), 90–94.

14. Personal observation, April 15, 2011.

15. U.S. Federal Census, Utah Territory, 1880.

16. R. L. Polk, *Utah State Gazetteer and Business Directory, 1903–1904* (R. L. Polk & Co.: Salt Lake City, 1903); Utah Division of State History, Cemeteries and Burials database.

17. Salt Lake County Recorder, title abstracts; U.S. Federal Census, Utah, 1900; Polk, *Utah State Gazetteer and Business Directory, 1903–1904*; "Gallant Sergeant Is Laid to Rest," *Salt Lake Telegram*, May 21, 1914; "Sergeant Spears Is Buried," *Salt Lake Telegram*, May 22, 1914.

18. Polk, *Polk's Salt Lake City Directory*, 1935; Death Certificate, Utah State Archives and Records Service, Series 81448.

Second Ward

1. British Mission Emigration Register, Book #1048, 48, LDS Church History Library; "List of Passengers," *Deseret News*, August 17, 1864; Utah Division of State History, Cemeteries and Burials database.

2. Brigham Young University, Mormon Migration Index: http://mormonmigra-tion.lib.byu.edu/Search/showDetails/db:MM_MII/t:passenger/id:18187/key-words:jane+kipling; British Mission Emigration Register, Book #1047, 138; U.S. Federal Census, Nebraska Territory, 1860; "Names of Immigrants," *The Mountaineer*, August 18, 1860.

3. George Owens, *Salt Lake City Directory, Including a Business Directory of Provo, Springville, and Ogden, Utah Territory* (Salt Lake City: George Owens, 1867); Ruby B. Corley, "Sketch of the Life of Jane Ann Kipling Buckley, Pioneer of 1860," 1939, Pioneer Memorial Museum, History Department; "Latter Day Saints' Immigration," *Deseret* News, August 24, 1859.

4. Edward L. Sloan, *The Salt Lake Directory and Business Guide, for 1869* (E. L. Sloan & Co.: Salt Lake City, 1869); U.S. Federal Census, Utah Territory, 1870; Eli S. Glover, *Bird's-Eye View of Salt Lake City from the North looking South-east, Utah* (Cincinnati: Strobridge & Co., 1875).

5. Salt Lake County Recorder, title abstracts.

6. Salt Lake City Assessor, Tax Assessment rolls, Utah State Archives and Records Service, Series 4922.

7. "Mangled by Wheels," *Salt Lake Herald*, December 5, 1895; Death Certificate, Utah State Archives and Records Service, Series 81448.

8. Brigham Young University, Mormon Migration database, http://

mormonmigration.lib.byu.edu/Search/showDetails/db:MM_MII/t:passenger/id:82077/keywords:Westmoreland; James Jensen, "Reminiscences," in Joseph M. Tanner, *A Biographical Sketch of James Jensen* (Salt Lake City: Deseret News, 1911), 23–40.

9. LDS Church History Library, Mormon Pioneer Overland Travel database, http://history.lds.org/overlandtravels/pioneerDetail?lang=eng&pioneerId=42192; Matilda Jensen, "The Life of Mrs. Matilda Cathryn Andreson Jensen," n.d., Pioneer Memorial Museum, History Department; Salt Lake County Recorder, title abstracts.

10. Henry L. A. Culmer, *Utah Directory and Gazetteer for 1879–80* (Salt Lake City: J. C. Graham & Co., 1879); Kelly & Co., *Salt Lake City Directory for 1889, and Business Directory and Guide to Public Streets and Avenues* (Salt Lake City: Kelly & Co., 1889).

11. R. L. Polk & Co., *Polk's Salt Lake City Directory* (Salt Lake City: R. L. Polk & Co., 1890); U.S. Federal Census, Utah, 1900. The family included nine children; U.S. Federal Census, Utah, 1910.

12. Salt Lake City, 1898, sheet 169, and Salt Lake City, 1911, sheet 176 (New York: Sanborn Map Co., 1898 and 1911).

13. Salt Lake County Recorder, title abstracts.

14. LDS Church, Mormon Pioneer Overland Travel database, https://history.lds.org/overlandtravels/pioneerDetail?lang=eng&pioneerId=3439.

15. "Home Items," *Deseret News*, August 5, 1868; Salt Lake County Civil and Criminal case files, box 13, folder 31, Utah State Archives and Records Service, Series 373; "Items," *Deseret News*, December 30, 1868; "Lamentable Occurrence," *Deseret News*, August 10, 1864; "Local and Other Matters," *Deseret News*, April 26, 1876.

16. Glover, *Bird's-Eye View of Salt Lake City*, 1875; Utah Division of State History, Cemeteries and Burials database; LDS Church, FamilySearch, https://familysearch.org/ark:/61903/2:1:MWQX-RQC.

17. James H. Hawley, *History of Idaho, the Gem of the Mountains*, (S. J. Clarke: Chicago, 1920), 2:567; Salt Lake County Recorder, title abstracts.

18. Sanborn Map Co., Salt Lake City, 1898, sheet 169; Salt Lake County Recorder, title abstracts.

19. Richard L. Jensen and Maurine C. Ward, "Names of Persons and Sureties Indebted to the Perpetual Emigrating Fund Company, 1850–1877," *Mormon Historical Studies* (Fall 2000): 231; "Names of Immigrants," *Deseret News*, September 24, 1862; Owens, *Salt Lake City Directory*, 1867.

20. U.S. Federal Censuses, Utah Territory and Utah, 1860–1900; "Aged Resident Dies," *Deseret News*, June 6, 1901; *Polk's Salt Lake City Directory*, 1917; Death Certificate, Utah State Archives and Records Service, Series 81448.

Third and Fourth Wards

1. George Owens, *Salt Lake City Directory, Including a Business Directory of Provo, Springville, and Ogden, Utah Territory* (Salt Lake City: George Owens, 1867).

Fifth Ward

1. Death Certificate, Utah State Archives and Records Service, Series 81448; LDS Church, FamilySearch, https://familysearch.org/ark:/61903/2:1:M726-SF3.
2. British Mission Emigration Record, Book 1041, 270.
3. Edward L. Sloan, *The Salt Lake City Directory and Business Guide, for 1869* (Salt Lake City: E. L. Sloan & Co., 1869); Edward L. Sloan, *Gazeteer of Utah and Salt Lake City Directory* (Salt Lake City: Salt Lake Herald Publ. Co., 1874).
4. Salt Lake County Recorder, title abstracts; Salt Lake County Assessor Tax Assessment rolls, 1884, Utah State Archives and Records Service, Series 18188; Sloan, *Gazeteer*, 1874.
5. Salt Lake County Recorder, title abstracts.
6. "Third District Court," *Ogden Junction*, February 12, 1879; "Deaths," *Deseret News*, February 3, 1886; untitled, *Deseret News*, January 30, 1890, 3; Utah Division of State History, Cemeteries and Burials database; Death Certificate, Utah State Archives and Records Service, Series 81448.

Sixth Ward

1. Salt Lake County Recorder, title abstracts.
2. British Mission Emigration Record, Book 1042, 263.
3. Robert L. Sloan, *Utah Gazetteer and Directory for Logan, Ogden Provo, and Salt Lake Cities, for 1884* (Salt Lake City: Herald Printing Co., 1884); Salt Lake County Recorder, title abstracts; Death Certificate, Utah State Archives and Records Service, Series 81448.
4. Untitled, *Salt Lake Herald*, September 4, 1891, 2; U.S. Federal Census, Utah, 1900; Death Certificate, Utah State Archives and Records Service, Series 81448.

Seventh Ward

1. Augustus Koch, *Bird's Eye View of Salt Lake City, Utah Territory* (Chicago: Chicago Lithographing Co., 1870); Salt Lake City Assessor, Tax Assessment rolls, 1872, Utah State Archives and Records Service, Series 4922.
2. LDS Church, FamilySearch, https://familysearch.org/ark:/61903/2:1:M72C-21W; British Mission Emigration Record, Book 1044, 162; "Obituary," *Deseret News [Weekly]*, July 20, 1883.
3. U.S. Federal Census, Utah Territory, 1870. Kelly's neighbors in 1870 lived at the same relative locations as in 1867, as indicated in George Owens's city directory for that year.
4. "Local and Other Matters," *Deseret News*, February 22, 1871; "Local and Other Matters," *Deseret News*, September 18, 1878.
5. "Was a Pioneer Bookbinder," *Deseret News*, October 28, 1899; LDS Church, FamilySearch, https://familysearch.org/ark:/61903/2:1:M72C-21W.
6. Now known as edema, with symptoms of fluid retention that may be caused by heart or liver failure; "Died," *Deseret News*, April 18, 1877; U.S. Federal Census, Utah Territory, 1880.

7. "Local and Other Matters," *Deseret News*, July 25, 1883; U.S. Directory
   Publishing Co. of California, *Salt Lake City Directory* (San Francisco: U.S.
   Directory Publishing Co. of Cal., 1885).

Ninth Ward

1. Newton Tuttle, "Newton Tuttle Journal, 1854 April–July," LDS Church
   History Library, Folder 1, entry for June 26, 1854; U.S. Federal Census, Utah
   Territory, 1860; Salt Lake City Assessor, Tax Assessment rolls, Utah State
   Archives and Records Service, Series 4922.
2. LDS Church, FamilySearch, https://familysearch.org/
   ark:/61903/2:1:M7NW-K54; Salt Lake County Recorder, title abstracts;
   Augustus Koch, *Bird's Eye View of Salt Lake City, Utah Territory* (Chicago:
   Chicago Lithographing Co., 1870).
3. Salt Lake City, 1898, sheet 165 (New York: Sanborn Map Co., 1898);
   personal observation, February 6, 2011.
4. George Owens, *Salt Lake City Directory, Including a Business Directory
   of Provo, Springville, and Ogden, Utah Territory* (Salt Lake City: George
   Owens, 1867); Salt Lake City Assessor, Tax Assessment rolls, Utah State
   Archives and Records Service, Series 4922; Utah Division of State History,
   Cemeteries and Burials database.
5. "Local and Other Matters," *Deseret News*, May 5, 1880; Robert L. Sloan,
   *Utah Gazetteer and Directory for Logan, Ogden, Provo, and Salt Lake Cities,
   for 1884* (Salt Lake City: Herald Printing Co., 1884); U.S. Federal Census,
   Idaho, 1910; LDS Church, FamilySearch, https://familysearch.org/
   ark:/61903/2:1:M7NW-K54.
6. Daniel Rolph, *Mormonism in Early Philadelphia*, Historical Society of
   Pennsylvania, 2011, http://hsp.org/blogs/hidden-histories/mormonism-
   in-early-philadelphia; Pennsylvania and New Jersey, Church and Town
   Records, 1708–1985, Historical Society of Philadelphia.
7. Edward C. and John Biddle, *MacElroy's Philadelphia Directory* (Philadelphia:
   Edward C. and John Biddle, 1856); "A Conference," *Deseret News*, October
   20, 1858, 2; U.S. Federal Census, Utah Territory, 1860; Death Certificate,
   Utah State Archives and Records Service, Series 81448; U.S. Federal Census,
   Utah Territory, 1870.
8. Salt Lake County Recorder, title abstracts; Salt Lake City Assessor, Tax
   Assessment rolls, Utah State Archives and Records Service, Series 4922;
   U.S. Federal Census, Utah Territory, 1870 (spelled "Renshaw").
9. Salt Lake City, 1898, sheet 120 (New York: Sanborn Map Co., 1898).
10. "Joseph Smith, Jr.," *Salt Lake Tribune*, November 24, 1876; Joseph Smith
    and Heman C. Smith, *History of the Reorganized Church of Jesus Christ of
    Latter Day Saints* (Independence, MO: Herald Publishing House, 1903),
    4:161–63.
11. U.S. Federal Census, Utah Territory, 1880; Salt Lake City Assessor, Tax
    Assessment rolls, Utah State Archives and Records Service, Series 4922;
    Sloan, *Utah Gazetteer and Directory, 1884*.

12. "Fashion and Gossip," *Salt Lake Herald*, October 18, 1885; Smith and Smith, *History of the Reorganized Church* (1888), 4: 595. "The Fourth Quorum of Elders reported losses as follows... P. H. Reinsimer... by death." No mention was made of place or date.

13. "Died," *Salt Lake Tribune*, October 19, 1894; Salt Lake City: City Recorder death and burial register, Utah State Archives and Records Service, Series 21866, p. 104, line 4226. Her gravestone gives an incorrect death date of October 19, 1895.

Tenth Ward

1. Alfred Cordon Emigrating Company journal, 1851, June–September, LDS Church History Library; LDS Church, FamilySearch, https://familysearch. org/ark:/61903/2:1:M166-H62; Salt Lake County Recorder's Office, Plat B, Great Salt Lake City, n.d., c. 1856.

2. Salt Lake City Assessor, Tax Assessment rolls, 1856, Utah State Archives and Records Service, Series 4922; personal observation, May 2014.

3. "Died," *Deseret News*, April 21, 1875; George Owens, *Salt Lake City Directory, Including a Business Directory of Provo, Springville, and Ogden, Utah Territory* (Salt Lake City: George Owens, 1867).

4. U.S. Federal Census, Utah Territory, 1870. The surname is spelled "Manley."

5. http://gladdenfamilyhistories.blogspot.com/2008/07/george-baddley-1825-1875.html; "Died," *Deseret News*, April 21, 1875; Utah Division of State History, Cemeteries and Burials database; Salt Lake County Recorder, title abstracts.

6. LDS Church, FamilySearch, https://familysearch.org/ ark:/61903/2:1:99PJ-5DP.

7. "Died," *Deseret News [Weekly]* May 3, 1876; "E. J. Swaner Dead," *Deseret News*, July 23, 1907.

8. Henry L. Culmer, *Utah Directory and Gazetteer for 1879–80* (Salt Lake City: H. L. A. Culmer & Co., 1879); U.S. Federal Census, Utah Territory, 1880; Salt Lake County Recorder, title abstracts; "Deaths," *Deseret News*, February 13, 1892.

9. Salt Lake City, 1898, sheet 176, and 1911, sheet 260 (New York, Sanborn Map Co., 1898 and 1911); Korral Brochinsky, Historic Site Form, Utah State Historic Preservation Office, 2009.

10. Salt Lake City, 1898, sheet 178 (New York: Sanborn Map Co., 1898); Eli S. Glover, *Bird's-Eye View of Salt Lake City from the North looking South-east, Utah* (Cincinnati: Strobridge & Co., 1875).

11. U.S. Federal Census, Utah Territory, 1870; Anton H. Lund, *Scandinavian Jubilee Album: Issued in Commemoration of the Fiftieth Anniversary of the Introduction of the Gospel to the Three Scandinavian Countries by Elder Erastus Snow, an Apostle of Jesus Christ; and Fellow Laborers* (Salt Lake City: Deseret News, 1900), 111.

12. LDS Church, Mormon Pioneer Overland Travel database, https://history.lds.

org/overlandtravels/pioneerDetail?lang=eng&pioneerId=56220.

13. LDS Church, FamilySearch, https://familysearch.org/
    ark:/61903/2:1:M1ST-WN1; U.S. Federal Census, Utah Territory, 1870; Utah
    Division of State History, Cemeteries and Burials database.

14. Jean B. White, *Church, State and Politics: The Diaries of John Henry Smith*
    (Salt Lake City: Signature Books, 1990), 110; British Mission Emigration
    Register, Book 1042, 300.

15. Salt Lake County Recorder, title abstracts; U.S. Federal Census, Utah
    Territory, 1880; U.S. Federal Census, Utah, 1910.

16. "Before Judge Zane," *Deseret News*, December 6, 1890; Death
    Certificate, Utah State Archives and Records Service, Series
    81448; FindAGrave database, http://www.findagrave.com/cgi-bin/
    fg.cgi?page=gr&GRid=73853624.

17. "Before Judge Zane"; Death certificates, Utah State Archives and Records
    Service, Series 81448; [no article title], *Salt Lake Tribune*, April 12, 1916; Utah
    Division of State History, Cemeteries and Burials database.

18. Salt Lake City, 1911, sheet 262 (New York: Sanborn Map Co. 1911); Korral
    Broschinsky, Historic Site Form, Utah State Historic Preservation Office,
    2009; Salt Lake City, 1898, sheet 187 (New York: Sanborn Map Co., 1898).

19. LDS Church, Mormon Pioneer Overland Travel database, https://history.lds.
    org/overlandtravels/pioneerDetail?lang=eng&pioneerId=16466; "Pioneer
    of 1852 Is Dead," *Salt Lake Herald*, May 10, 1913; Noble Warrum, ed., *Utah
    Since Statehood: Historical and Biographical* (Chicago: S. J. Clarke, 1919),
    2:612–13; Death Certificate, Utah State Archives and Records Service, Series
    81448 (Emma Swaner).

20. Kate B. Carter, *Heart Throbs of the West* (Salt Lake City: Daughters of Utah
    Pioneers, 1944), 5:96; Laurie J. Bryant, "American Original: William Fuller
    and Fuller's Hill Pleasure Gardens," 2011, in The Laurie J. Bryant Papers,
    Utah State Historical Society.

Eleventh Ward

1. U.S. Federal Census, Utah Territory, 1860 and 1870.

2. LDS Church History Library, Mormon Pioneer Overland Travel database,
   https://history.lds.org/overlandtravels/pioneers/23360/francis-sproul;
   Richard L. Jensen and Maurine Ward, "Names of Persons and Sureties
   indebted to the Perpetual Emigrating Fund Company 1850–1877," *Mormon
   Historical Studies* (Fall 2000): 224; Edward L. Sloan, *The Salt Lake City
   Directory and Business Guide, for 1869* (Salt Lake City: E. L. Sloan & Co.,
   1869); Indian War service affidavits, 1909, Utah State Archives and Records
   Service, Series 2217.

3. Salt Lake County Recorder, title abstracts; Salt Lake City, 1898, sheet 172
   (New York: Sanborn Map Co., 1898).

4. R. L. Polk & Co., *Polk's Salt Lake City Directory* (Salt Lake City: R. L. Polk &
   Co., 1893).

5. "Aged Resident Killed by Car," *Salt Lake Herald*, October 2, 1918.

6. "Accident Kills Woman, 95, in Ambulance," *Salt Lake Telegram*, November 6, 1944.

7. Augustus Koch, *Bird's Eye View of Salt Lake City, Utah Territory* (Chicago: Chicago Lithographing Co., 1870); LDS Church History Library, Mormon Pioneer Overland Travel database, https://history.lds.org/overlandtravels/pioneers/9860524848718125303o/nicholas-rumel; Samuel Burgess, ed., *Reorganized Church of Jesus Christ of Latter Day Saints, Journal of History* (Independence, MO: Herald Publishing House, 1925), 18:18; U.S. Federal Census, Nebraska Territory, 1870.

8. Salt Lake County Recorder, title abstracts; Edward L. Sloan, *Gazeteer of Utah and Salt Lake City Directory* (Salt Lake City: Salt Lake Herald Publ. Co.,, 1874); LDS Church FamilySearch, https://familysearch.org/ark:/61903/2:1:M7VB-YK9.

9. Salt Lake County Recorder, title abstracts.

10. "Marriage of Miss Beattie and Mr. Joy Johnson," *Salt Lake Herald*, January 25, 1900; U.S. Federal Census, Hawaii, 1910; Death Certificate, Utah State Archives and Records Service, Series 81448; Utah State Historic Preservation Office, National Register of Historic Places nomination form.

11. Utah Division of State History, Cemeteries and Burials database.

12. Salt Lake County Recorder, title abstracts.

13. Sloan, *Gazeteer of Utah and Salt Lake City Directory*, 1874; Henry L. A. Culmer, *Utah Directory and Gazetteer for 1879–80* (Salt Lake City: H. L. A. Culmer & Co., 1879).

14. Robert L. Sloan, *Utah Gazetteer and Directory for Logan, Ogden, Provo, and Salt Lake Cities, for 1884* (Salt Lake City: Herald Printing Co., 1884); "Handcart Pioneer Dies of Old Age At His Home Here," *Salt Lake Evening Telegram*, October 24, 1908; LDS Church History Library, Mormon Pioneer Overland Travel database, https://history.lds.org/overlandtravels/pioneerDetail?lang=eng&pioneerId=36134; Death Certificate, Utah State Archives and Records Service, Series 81448.

15. Salt Lake County (Utah), Probate Court Civil and Criminal case files, case 472, 1875, Utah State Archives and Records Service, Series 1621; LDS Church, Church History Library, Record of Members collection.

16. Salt Lake County (Utah), Probate Court Civil and Criminal case files, case 472, 1875, Utah State Archives and Records Service, Series 1621; Salt Lake County Recorder, title abstracts; Salt Lake City Assessor Tax Assessment rolls, 1872, 1877, Utah State Archives and Records Service, Series 4922.

17. U.S. Federal Census, Utah Territory, 1870 and 1880; Salt Lake County (Utah), Probate Court Civil and Criminal case files, case 472, 1875, Utah State Archives and Records Service, Series 1621; Salt Lake County Recorder, title abstracts.

18. John Hampton Doan, *Hampton History: An Account of the Pennsylvania Hamptons in America, in the Line of John Hampton, Jr. of Wrightstown* (Milton,

KY: Solomon E. Hampton, 1911); U.S. Federal Census, Washington, 1900; Book C, Missionary Department, (1953?–), LDS Church History Library; U.S. Federal Census, San Francisco County, California, 1910.

19. Salt Lake County Recorder, title abstracts; U.S. Federal Census, Great Salt Lake County, Utah Territory, 1860; U.S. Federal Census, Utah Territory, 1880; "Died," *Deseret News*, March 7, 1883; U.S. Federal Census, Utah Territory, 1880; Death Certificate, June 8, 1916, Utah State Archives and Records Services, Series 81448; "Funeral Notices," *Salt Lake Herald*, June 8, 1906.

20. Salt Lake County Recorder, title abstracts; U.S. Federal Census, Salt Lake County, Utah, 1910; Laurie J. Bryant, "American Original: William Fuller and Fuller's Hill Pleasure Gardens," in The Laurie J. Bryant papers, Utah State Historical Society, 2011.

21. Salt Lake County Recorder, title abstracts, Book A, indicates Brain "built a house" in 1853; Salt Lake City, 1898, sheet 153, (New York: Sanborn Map Co., 1898); LDS Church, FamilySearch, https://familysearch.org/ark:/61903/2:1:M7LY-XL7; untitled, *Deseret News*, September 18, 1852, 2; Salt Lake City Assessor, Tax Assessment rolls, 1856, Utah State Archives and Records Service, Series 4922.

22. "City Property," *Deseret News*, February 16, 1859; Salt Lake County Recorder, title abstracts; "Mahala Briggs (1809–1869)," Family History of Richard Crookston and Rebecca Clark, http://www.rcrookston.com/More%20 Gardner%20Histories/mahala_briggs.htm; LDS Church, Mormon Pioneer Overland Travel database, https://history.lds.org/overlandtravels/ pioneerDetail?lang=eng&pioneerId=60566; Salt Lake City Assessor, Tax Assessment rolls, 1861, Utah State Archives and Records Service, Series 4922; Owens, *Salt Lake City Directory*, 1867; "Snow Slide at South Mill Creek," *Deseret News*, April 14, 1869.

23. Salt Lake County Recorder, title abstracts; LDS Church, FamilySearch, https://familysearch.org/ark:/61903/2:1:MB23-MTB

24. Edward L. Sloan, *Gazeteer*, 1869; Salt Lake County Recorder, title abstracts; FindAGrave, http://www.findagrave.com/cgi-bin/fg.cgi?page=gr&GRid= 71562629.

25. "The Life Work of S. W. Sears," *Deseret News*, April 11, 1903; "Local News," *Deseret News*, July 1, 1885; Kate B. Carter, *Heart Throbs of the West* (Salt Lake City: Daughters of Utah Pioneers, 1949), 10:398.

26. Utah State Historical Society, digital photograph collection, Shipler #09321. This image of the house at 49 South 800 East also captures a corner of 51 South 800 East as it looked in 1909, before the original west facade had been obscured.

27. Salt Lake City, 1898, sheet 171, and 1950, sheet 245 (New York: Sanborn Map Co., 1898 and 1950).

28. British Mission Emigration Register, Book 1048, 253; "Captain Daniel Thompson, memorandum book 1, 1866," in Perpetual Emigrating Fund Company church trains accounts 1861–1868, Captains' accounts 1862–1868, LDS Church History Library.

29. George Owens, *Salt Lake City Directory, Including a Business Directory of Provo, Springville, and Ogden, Utah Territory* (Salt Lake City: George Owens, 1867); Salt Lake County Recorder, title abstracts; LDS Church, FamilySearch, https://familysearch.org/ark:/61903/2:1:MW49-SY4; Salt Lake City Tax Assessment rolls, 1875, Utah State Archives and Records Service, Series 4922.

30. British Mission Emigration Register, Book 1041, 353; "Useful Career Is Closed in Sleep," *Deseret Evening News*, June 25, 1912; "Funeral of Mrs. Cushing," *Deseret News*, June 17, 1908; Death Certificate, Utah State Archives and Records Service, Series 81448.

Twelfth Ward

1. E. L. Holladay in U.S. Federal Census, Utah Territory, 1860.

2. Salt Lake City, 1889, sheet 37 (New York: Sanborn Map Co., 1889); "2nd Company," *Deseret News*, September 18, 1852; Salt Lake County Recorder, title abstracts.

3. LDS Church, FamilySearch, https://familysearch.org/ark:/61903/2:1:M7XK-ZDT; Salt Lake County Recorder, title abstracts; Kelly & Co., *Salt Lake City Directory for 1889, and Business Directory and Guide to Public Streets and Avenues* (Salt Lake City: Kelly & Co., 1889).

4. *Salt Lake City Directory for 1889.*

5. LDS Church, Mormon Pioneer Overland Travel database, https://history.lds.org/overlandtravels/pioneerDetail?lang=eng&pioneerId=38269; "Arrival," *Deseret News*, December 3, 1856.

6. LDS Church, Mormon Pioneer Overland Travel database, https://history.lds.org/overlandtravels/pioneerDetail?lang=eng&pioneerId=12554; Richard L. Jensen and Maurine C. Ward, "Names of Persons and Sureties Indebted to the Perpetual Emigrating Fund Company, 1850–1877," *Mormon Historical Studies* (Fall 2000): 154, 155.

7. U.S. Federal Census, Utah Territory, 1860; Salt Lake County Recorder, title abstracts; George Owens, *Salt Lake City Directory, Including a Business Directory of Provo, Springville, and Ogden, Utah Territory* (Salt Lake City: George Owens, 1867). The notation "n e c" [northeast corner] is probably an error.

8. Robert L. Sloan, *Utah Gazetteer and Directory for Logan, Ogden, Provo, and Salt Lake Cities, for 1884* (Salt Lake City: Herald Printing Co., 1884); R. L. Polk & Co., *Salt Lake City Directory* (Salt Lake City: R. L. Polk & Co., 1911); Death Certificate, Utah State Archives and Records Service, Series 81448.

Thirteenth and Fourteenth Wards

1. Ronald W. Walker, "'Going to Meeting' in Salt Lake City's Thirteenth Ward, 1849–1881: A Microanalysis," in *New Views of Mormon History: A Collection of Essays in Honor of Leonard J. Arrington,* ed. Davis Bitton and Maureen Ursenbach Beecher (Salt Lake City: University of Utah Press, 1987).

Fifteenth Ward

1. LDS Church, Mormon Pioneer Overland Travel database,https://history.lds. org/overlandtravels/companyPioneers?lang=eng&companyId=256; British Mission Emigration Register, Book 1047, 141.
2. Edward L. Sloan, *The Salt Lake Directory and Business Guide, for 1869* (Salt Lake City: E. L. Sloan & Co., 1869); Salt Lake County Recorder, title abstracts.
3. U.S. Federal Census, Utah Territory, 1870; Salt Lake County Recorder, title abstracts.
4. "Uncle Josh Billings Is Postoffice Veteran," *Salt Lake Tribune*, August 25, 1912; U.S. Federal Census, Utah Territory, 1860; "List of Volunteers with Connor in Utah," *Sacramento Daily Union*, November 4, 1862.
5. Edward W. Tullidge, *History of Salt Lake City* (Salt Lake City: Star Printing Co., 1886), 1:180; U.S. Federal Census, Utah, 1920; "Uncle Josh Billings is Postoffice Veteran."

Sixteenth Ward

1. LDS Church, Mormon Pioneer Overland Travel database, https://history. lds.org/overlandtravels/pioneerDetail?lang=eng&pioneerId=10743; George Kirkman Bowering, "Journal, 1842–1875," 79–118, LDS Church History Library.
2. Wedding photograph of Peter Olsen and Sarah Julia Hepworth, http:// honorancestors.blogspot.com/2013/08/peter-olsen-and-sarah-julia- hepworth.html; U.S. Federal Census, Utah Territory, 1880; Robert L. Sloan, *Utah Gazetteer and Directory for Logan, Ogden, Provo, and Salt Lake Cities, for 1884* (Salt Lake City: Herald Printing Co., 1884).
3. Salt Lake County Recorder, title abstracts; Sloan, *Utah Gazatteer and Directory*, 1884; R. L. Polk & Co., *Polk's Salt Lake City Directory for 1890* (Salt Lake City: R. L. Polk & Co., 1890).
4. Salt Lake City, sheet 49, 1911 (New York: Sanborn Map Co., 1911).
5. "Deaths," *Los Angeles Herald*, May 2, 1908; "Local Briefs," *Salt Lake Herald*, May 5, 1908.
6. U.S. Federal Census, Utah, 1910 and 1920; Death Certificate, Utah State Archives and Records Service, Series 81448.
7. Church of Jesus Christ of Latter-day Saints, Journal of Discourses, 1861, 9:32; Daniel H. Ludlow, ed., *Encyclopedia of Mormonism* (New York: Macmillan, 1992), 1312–14.
8. "Correspondence," *Deseret News*, February 3, 1869.
9. Ardis Parshall, "Josephine de la Harpe Ludert Ursenbach: From the Tsar's Court to the Kingdom of God," http://www.keepapitchinin. org/2009/06/03/josephine-marie-augustine-de-la-harpe-ludert-ursenbach- from-the-tsars-court-to-the-kingdom-of-god/, 2009. Also, "Died," *Deseret News*, February 27, 1878.
10. "From Switzerland," *Deseret News*, September 18, 1867; Richard E. Egan, "Journal," LDS Church History Library, MS 8795, reel 13, no. 5; LDS Church,

FamilySearch, https://familysearch.org/ark:/61903/2:1:MWMN-LRP.

11. Salt Lake County Assessor, Tax Assessment rolls, 1865, Utah State Archives and Records Service, Series 18188; George Owens, *Salt Lake City Directory, Including a Business Directory of Provo, Springville, and Ogden, Utah Territory* (Salt Lake City: George Owens, 1867).

12. Third District Court (Salt Lake County): Probate Case Files, folder 15, case 587, 1878, Utah State Archives and Records Service, Series 1621.

13. Edward L. Sloan, *Gazeteer of Utah and Salt Lake City Directory* (Salt Lake City: Salt Lake Herald Publ. Co., 1874); Salt Lake City Recorder, Death and Burial Register, Utah State Archives and Records Service, Series 21866; Henry L. A. Culmer, *Utah Directory and Gazetteer for 1879–80* (Salt Lake City: H. L. A. Culmer & Co., 1879). See also Comton [*sic*], George, in this volume; U.S. Federal Census, Los Angeles County, California, 1940; Utah Division of State History, Cemeteries and Burials database.

14. Personal observation, August 15, 2013, during demolition.

15. http://griffinsofessex.blogspot.com/2012/03/albert-bailey-griffins-salt-lake-city.html.

16. Salt Lake County Recorder, title abstracts; Council Point Emigrating Company, Journal, 1851 November–1852 September, entry for November 29, 1852, LDS Church History Library; Salt Lake County Recorder, title abstracts.

17. Owens, *Salt Lake City Directory*, 1867.

18. Salt Lake City Recorder, Death and Burial Register, Utah State Archives and Records Service, Series 21866; "Accidentally Killed," *Deseret News*, April 3, 1897.

19. Salt Lake County Recorder, title abstracts; "A Father in Israel Is Dead," *Deseret News*, March 9, 1864; "Correspondence," *Latter-day Saints Millennial Star* 28, no. 13, 206; British Mission Emigration Register, Book 1048, 117; "Voyage of the Ship Hudson," *Deseret News*, March 23, 1895; LDS Church, Mormon Pioneer Overland Travel database, https://history.lds.org/overlandtravels/pioneerDetail?lang=eng&pioneerId=55130.

20. Frank Esshom, *Pioneers & Prominent Men of Utah, 1847–1868* (Salt Lake City: Utah Pioneer Book Publishing Co., 1913); Edward L. Sloan, *The Salt Lake City Directory and Business Guide, for 1869* (Salt Lake City: E. L. Sloan & Co., 1869); U.S. Federal Census, Utah Territory, Salt Lake County, 1870.

21. U.S. Federal Census, Utah Territory, Salt Lake County, 1870; Salt Lake City Assessor, Tax Assessment rolls, 1869–1871, Utah State Archives and Records Service, Series 4922; Sloan, *Gazeteer of Utah and Salt Lake City Directory*, 1874.

22. U.S. Federal Census, Utah Territory, Cache County, 1880; U.S. Federal Census, Utah, Juab County, 1900; U.S. Federal Census, Salt Lake County, Utah, 1900; LDS Church, FamilySearch https://familysearch.org/ark:/61903/2:1:M7LR-SG3.

23. Sloan, *Gazeteer of Utah and Salt Lake City Directory*, 1874.

24. Salt Lake City Assessor, Tax Assessment rolls, 1872, Utah State Archives and Records Service, Series 4922; Salt Lake County Recorder, title abstracts.

25. Culmer, *Utah Directory and Gazetteer for 1879–80.*
26. U.S. Federal Census, Utah Territory, Salt Lake and Cache Counties, 1880.
27. Salt Lake County Recorder, title abstracts; Korral Broschinsky, Historic Site Form, 2014, Utah State Historic Preservation Office, Salt Lake City.
28. Personal observation, August 2013; Thomas Carter, personal communication, August 2013.
29. Brigham Young University, Mormon Migration Index, Samuel Hanna [*sic*], Jane, and seven children, http://mormonmigration. lib.byu.edu/Search/showDetails/db:MM_MII/t:voyage/id:166/ keywords:Hamer; *Nauvoo Neighbor,* August 16, 1843; U.S. Federal Census, Pottawattamie County, Iowa, 1850; LDS Church, Mormon Pioneer Overland Travel database, https://history.lds.org/overlandtravels/ search?first-name=&last-name=Hamer&birth-year=&death-year=.
30. John Hamer received his property sometime between 1854 and 1859; Salt Lake County Recorder, Deed Book A and Transfer Book B, n.d.; "Local and Other Matters," *Deseret News,* November 12, 1873; Salt Lake County Recorder, title abstracts; Salt Lake City Assessor, Tax Assessment rolls, 1858, Utah State Archives and Records Service, Series 4922.
31. "Death of a Pioneer," *Salt Lake Herald,* February 9, 1895; U.S. Federal Census, Utah Territory, 1880.
32. Sloan, *Utah Gazatteer and Directory,* 1884; "Bound Over," *Deseret News,* June 15, 1887.
33. "The Dead," *Deseret News [Weekly],* February 16, 1895; Death Certificate, Utah State Archives and Records Service, Series 81448; "Shining Marks Among Salt Lake's Old Citizens Sought out by Death," *Salt Lake Telegram,* December 20, 1902.
34. British Mission Emigration Register, Book 5, 1042; U.S. Federal Census, Utah Territory, Salt Lake County, 1880.
35. Sloan, *Utah Gazatteer and Directory,* 1884; "Secret Societies," *Salt Lake Herald,* October 30, 1899; R. L. Polk, *Polk's Salt Lake City Directory* (Salt Lake City: R. L. Polk & Co.), 1892.
36. "Died," *Salt Lake Herald,* October 13, 1899; Death Certificate, Utah State Archives and Records Service, Series 81448.
37. LDS Church, Mormon Pioneer Overland Travel database, https://history.lds. org/overlandtravels/pioneerDetail?lang=eng&pioneerId=2029740930 4971814080; U.S. Federal Census, Utah Territory, Davis County, 1850.
38. LDS Church, Journal History, January 8, February 12, and October 8, 1866; Eli S. Glover, *Bird's-Eye View of Salt Lake City from the North looking South- east, Utah* (Cincinnati: Strobridge & Co., 1875).
39. Salt Lake County Recorder, title abstracts; U.S. Federal Census, Utah Territory, Salt Lake County, 1880; U.S. Federal Census, Utah Territory, Salt Lake County, 1870 (spelled "Connell").
40. "Chips," *Salt Lake Herald,* February 26, 1881; Third District Court, Salt Lake County, Probate case files, case 727 and 742, Utah State Archives and Records Service, Series 1621.

41. Salt Lake City Recorder, Death and Burial Register, April 30, 1881, Utah State Archives and Records Service, Series 21866; LDS Church, "Journal History," April 30, 1881, 3; Salt Lake County Recorder, title abstracts.

42. Third District Court, Salt Lake County, Probate case files, case 742, Utah State Archives and Records Service, Series 1621; Brigham Young University, Mormon Migration database, http://mormonmigration.lib.byu.edu/Search/showDetails/db:MM_MII/t:passenger/id:71628/keywords:John+Clinton. If their ages as given were correct, John would have been born about 1813, Isabella about 1820, making them too young to be this John Clinton's parents. They may have been related in some other way. The Kaghin family did not reach Utah.

43. Clinton and the Llewellyn Daniels family were recorded in Utah in the 1880 U.S. Federal Census; "Utah Western Railway," *Salt Lake Herald*, December 15, 1874.

Seventeenth Ward

1. LDS Church, Mormon Pioneer Overland Travel database, https://history.lds.org/overlandtravels/pioneerDetail?lang=eng&pioneerId=3122.

2. Alfred Randall, *Alfred Randall Autobiographical Sketch*, n.d., LDS Church History Library, MS 9947.

3. Salt Lake County Recorder, title abstracts; Salt Lake City Assessor, Tax Assessment rolls, Utah State Archives and Records Service, Series 4922; "Report of the 15th Quorum," *Deseret News*, April 13, 1854; "Bathsheba W. Bigler Smith photograph collection," PH 8004, box 2, fd. 29, item 8, LDS Church History Library; Utah State Historical Society, digital photograph 7516, with thanks to W. Randall Dixon for supplying evidence needed to locate the earlier Randall house.

4. U.S. Federal Census, Great Salt Lake City, Utah Territory, July 17, 1860; FamilySearch https://familysearch.org/ark:/61903/2:1:M7FZ-K7K, May 30, 1860; LDS Church, Mormon Pioneer Overland Travel database, https://history.lds.org/overlandtravels/pioneerDetail?lang=eng&pioneerId=3122; Mildred M. Boyce, *Biographical Sketch of Mildred Eliza Johnson Randall*, 1979, LDS Church History Library, MS 10528.

5. U.S. Federal Census, Utah Territory, 1870. "Nichelson Groosebeck" lived near T. H. W. Stenhouse, whose address in the 1869 city directory was "cor. Vine and 1 N.," one block east of this house and probably the nearest residence.

6. U.S. Federal Census, Utah Territory, 1870; Robert L. Sloan, *Utah Gazetteer and Directory for Logan, Ogden, Provo, and Salt Lake Cities, for 1884* (Salt Lake City: Herald Printing Co., 1884).

7. Salt Lake City, 1889, sheet 2, and 1898, sheet 64 (New York: Sanborn Map Co., 1889 and 1898).

8. Utah State Historical Society, digital photograph collection, no. 7475; Salt Lake County Recorder, title abstracts.

9. George Owens, *Salt Lake City Directory, Including a Business Directory of*

Provo, Springville, and Ogden, Utah Territory (Salt Lake City: George Owens, 1867); Salt Lake City Recorder, Death and Burial Register, Utah State Archives and Records Service, Series 21866; Salt Lake County Assessor, Tax Assessment rolls, 1868, Utah State Archives and Records Service, Series 4922; Edward L. Sloan, *Salt Lake City Directory and Business Guide for 1869* (Salt Lake City: E. L. Sloan & Co., 1869).

Eighteenth Ward

1. U.S. Federal Census, Utah Territory, Salt Lake County, 1860.
2. U.S. Federal Census, Utah Territory, Salt Lake County, 1870; David Buice, "'All Alone and None to Cheer Me': The Southern States Mission Diaries of J. Golden Kimball," *Dialogue: A Journal of Mormon Thought* 24, no. 1 (1991): 35–53; U.S. Federal Census, Utah Territory, Rich County, 1880.
3. J. C. Graham, *The Utah Directory for 1883–84* (Salt Lake City: J. C. Graham & Co., 1883); James N. Kimball, "J. Golden Kimball: Private Life of a Public Figure," *Journal of Mormon History* 24, no. 2 (1998): 55–84; Death Certificate, Utah State Archives and Records Service, Series 81448.
4. Utah State Historical Society, photograph 19056, C. R. Savage, 1873, and photograph 19060, Carleton D. Watkins, c. 1875 (not digitized).
5. Salt Lake County Recorder, title abstracts.
6. R. L. Polk & Co., *Polk's Salt Lake City Directory* (Salt Lake City: R. L. Polk & Co., 1890); Robert L. Sloan, *Utah Gazetteer and Directory for Logan, Ogden, Provo, and Salt Lake Cities, for 1884* (Salt Lake City: Herald Printing Co., 1884); LDS Church Journal History, November 11, 1886, 4; Salt Lake County Recorder, title abstracts.
7. Death Certificate, Utah State Archives and Records Service, Series 81448; "PanAm Flight Victim's Family in Utah Enlist Politicos in Fight for Settlement," *Salt Lake Tribune*, July 16, 2011.

Nineteenth Ward

1. Russell Burrows, "The Mormon Samson: Porter Rockwell," *Weber: The Contemporary West* 21, no. 3 (2004): 72–94.
2. Salt Lake County Recorder, title abstracts.
3. Andrew Jenson, *Latter-day Saint Biographical Encyclopedia* (Salt Lake City: Deseret News Press, 1901), 1, 672; Carolyn C. King, "Biography of Julia Curtis Raleigh," n.d., Pioneer Memorial Museum, History Department.
4. U.S. Federal Census, Utah Territory, Salt Lake County, 1870. The last name was spelled Raleigh, Raley, and Ilriah; U.S. Directory Publishing Co. of California, *Salt Lake City Directory for the Year Commencing August 1, 1885.* (San Francisco: U.S. Directory Publishing Co. of California, 1885); Kelly & Co., *Salt Lake City Directory for 1889, and Business Directory and Guide to Public Streets and Avenues* (Salt Lake City: Kelly & Co., 1889); R. L. Polk, *Polk's Salt Lake City Directory* (Salt Lake City: R. L. Polk & Co., 1890); U.S. Federal Census, Utah, Salt Lake County, 1900; Salt Lake City Recorder, Death and Burial Register, Utah State Archives and Records Service, Series 21866.

5. "Final Act in Church Outrage," *Salt Lake Tribune*, October 29, 1905; Salt Lake City Recorder, Death and Burial Register, Utah State Archives and Records Service, Series 21866.

6. "First Precinct," *Salt Lake Tribune*, January 1, 1890.

7. Rootsweb, http://wc.rootsweb.ancestry.com/cgi-bin/igm.cgi?op=GET&db=ryder10&id=I31628.

8. Salt Lake County Recorder, Plat A, n.d., c. 1856; Joseph G. Hovey, "*Joseph G. Hovey Papers, 1845–1856*," c. 1933, LDS Church History Library, Salt Lake City. Includes family history arranged by grandson Merlin R. Hovey; LDS Church, FamilySearch, https://familysearch.org/ark:/61903/2:1:M7FP-MLK; U.S. Federal Census, Utah Territory, Cache County, 1860.

9. Personal observation, April 2012.

10. Salt Lake City, 1898, Sheet 80, and 1950, sheet 9 (New York: Sanborn Map Co., 1898 and 1950).

11. U.S. Federal Census, Salt Lake County, Utah Territory, 1870. Spelled "Haway"; Salt Lake County Recorder, title abstracts; Utah Division of State History, Cemeteries and Burials database.

12. Anders W. Winberg, "Anders W. Winberg reminiscences," n.d., LDS Church History Library; Eve W. Creagh, "*History of Andrine Winberg*," c. 1915, LDS Church History Library; Salt Lake City, 1898, sheet 80 (New York: Sanborn Map Co., 1898); Salt Lake County Recorder, title abstracts; A. J. Russell, "Photographic Views of Salt Lake City and Vicinity," 1869, LDS Church History Library, PH 3821, fd. 9.

13. Eli S. Glover, *Bird's-eye View of Salt Lake City from the North Looking Southeast, Utah* (Cincinnati: Strobridge & Co., 1875); W. Randall Dixon, personal communication, September 9, 2013.

14. George Owens, *Salt Lake City Directory, Including a Business Directory of Provo, Springville, and Ogden, Utah Territory* (Salt Lake City: George Owens, 1867); Sloan, *Gazeteer of Utah and Salt Lake City Directory* (Salt Lake City: Salt Lake Herald Publ. Co., 1874); *Latter-day Saints Millennial Star* 38, no. 276 (1876).

15. U.S. Federal Census, Utah Territory and Utah, 1880, 1900; "Elder Editor Winberg," *Salt Lake Tribune*, November 25, 1886; Death Certificate, Utah State Archives and Records Service, Series 81448.

16. U.S. Federal Census, Jefferson County, Missouri, 1860; LDS Church, FamilySearch, https://familysearch.org/ark:/61903/2:1:M7FJ-YJH; Immigrant ships Transcribers' Guild, *American Eagle*, 1855, http://www.immigrantships.net/v7/1800v7/americaneagle18550720.html.

17. "List of Passengers," *Deseret Evening News*, August 17, 1868.

18. Salt Lake County Recorder, title abstracts; Heber J. Grant, *Heber J. Grant Collection, 1852–1945* (bulk 1880–1945), LDS Church History Library; Henry L. A. Culmer, *Utah Directory and Gazetteer for 1879–80* (Salt Lake City: H. L. A. Culmer & Co., 1879); Utah Division of State History, Cemeteries and Burials database, Mary Lambourne; "Deaths," *Deseret News*, August 27, 1884.

19. Annie was the granddaughter of William Hawk, whose log cabin, built between 1848 and 1852, stands at 458 North 300 West; Death Certificate, Utah State Archives and Records Service, Series 81448; "G. L. Lambourne Dies: Takes Chloroform," *Salt Lake Telegram*, February 14, 1916.
20. Utah Division of State History, Cemeteries and Burials database.
21. U.S. Federal Census, Utah Territory, 1870 and 1880. Both records suggest birth dates c. 1823; LDS Church, Mormon Pioneer Overland Travel database, https://history.lds.org/overlandtravels/ pioneerDetail?lang=eng&pioneerId=59490.
22. Utah Division of State History, Cemeteries and Burials database, Charles Fred Slater.
23. Owens, *Salt Lake City Directory*, 1867; Salt Lake City Assessor, Tax Assessment rolls, 1867, Utah State Archives and Records Service, Series 4922; Edward L. Sloan, *Salt Lake City Directory and Business Guide, for 1869* (Salt Lake City: E. L. Sloan & Co., 1869); "19th Wd, bet Quince & Central"; Salt Lake County Recorder, title abstracts.
24. E.g., U.S. Federal Census, Utah Territory, 1870; U.S. Directory Publishing Co., *Salt Lake City Directory*, 1885; "Fifty-four More Citizens," *Salt Lake Herald*, June 8, 1889.
25. Salt Lake City Recorder, Death and Burial Register, Utah State Archives and Records Service, Series 21866; "Funeral Notice," *Salt Lake Herald*, September 1, 1899; "School for Undertakers," *Salt Lake Tribune*, August 30, 1899; Salt Lake County Recorder, title abstracts.
26. British Mission Emigration Register, Book 1046, 105; "Latter Day Saints' Immigration," *Deseret News*, August 24, 1859.
27. U.S. Federal Census, Utah Territory, Tooele County, 1860; Salt Lake City Assessor, Tax Assessment rolls, 1868–1875, Utah State Archives and Records Service, Series 4922; Augustus Koch, *Bird's Eye View of Salt Lake City, Utah Territory* (Chicago: Chicago Lithographing Co., 1870); Glover, *Bird's-eye View of Salt Lake City*, 1875.
28. Sterling E. Beesley, *Kind Words: The Beginnings of Mormon Melody: A Historical Biography and Anthology of the Life and Works of Ebenezer Beesley, Utah Pioneer Musician, Containing an Account from the Emigration of 1859 and the Evolution of Latter-day Saint Psalmody* (Salt Lake City: Ebenezer Beesley Genealogical Research Foundation, 1980).
29. U.S. Federal Census, Utah Territory, 1880; Death Certificates, Utah State Archives and Records Service, Series 81448; Utah State Historical Society, photo #18185, Beesley, Ebenezer, residence.
30. "Mr. Beesley Is Buried," *Salt Lake Herald*, March 26, 1906; Utah Division of State History, Cemeteries and Burials database.
31. Dan Irie, previous owner, personal communication, March 12, 2013.
32. Brigham Young University, Mormon Migration Index, http:// mormonmigration.lib.byu.edu/Search/showDetails/db:MM_MII/ t:passenger/id:69905/keywords:Charles+Player; http://mormonmigration. lib.byu.edu/Search/showDetails/db:MM_MII/t:passenger/id:71038/

keywords:Betsey+Ode; St. Louis Marriage Index, 1804–1876 (St. Louis, MO: St. Louis Genealogical Society, 2000); U.S. Federal Census, Pottawattamie County, Iowa, 1850.

33. James Chauncey Snow Emigrating Company, "Journal, 1852 July–October," LDS Church History Library, MS 1756, fd. 1.

34. Salt Lake County Recorder, title abstracts, and Plat C, n.d., c. 1856; Department of Agriculture and Food, Division of Animal Industry, Brand Books, page 16, Utah State Archives and Records Service, Series 540, December 1849–December 1884; Salt Lake City Assessor, Tax Assessment rolls, 1856, Utah State Archives and Records Service, Series 4922; International Society Daughters of Utah Pioneers, *Pioneer Women of Faith and Fortitude* (Salt Lake City: Publisher's Press, 1998), 3:241.

35. "Deaths," *Deseret News*, September 3, 1884.

36. Gwen Haywood, Mary Lou Walker, and Madelyn Player, "Elizabeth 'Betsey' Oades Robins Player," n.d., Pioneer Memorial Library, History Department; Death Certificate, Utah State Archives and Records Service, Series 81448.

37. Salt Lake County Recorder, title abstracts.

38. Richard L. Jensen and Maurine C. Ward, "Names of Persons and Sureties Indebted to the Perpetual Emigrating Fund Company, 1850–1877," *Mormon Historical Studies* (Fall 2000): 141–241; LDS Church, Mormon Pioneer Overland Travel database, https://history.lds.org/overlandtravels/pioneers/58496/john-flower; U.S. Federal Census, Utah Territory, 1860; LDS Church, Mormon Pioneer Overland Travel database, https://history.lds.org/overlandtravels/pioneerDetail?lang=eng&pioneerId=50594.

39. Personal observation, June 2014; Russell, "Photographic views of Salt Lake City and vicinity," LDS Church History Library, Salt Lake City, catalog no. PH 3821, fd 9.

40. Scott Christensen, personal communication, May 2014.

41. Heber J. Grant collection, 1852–1945, LDS Church History Library.

42. Salt Lake County, Probate Court, Civil and Criminal Case Files, Utah State Archives and Records Service, Series 373, reel 24, box 18, fd. 66; U.S. Federal Census, Utah Territory, 1880; Kate B. Carter, *Treasures of Pioneer History* (Salt Lake City: Daughters of Utah Pioneers, 1954), 4:389–90.

43. "Obituary," *Deseret News*, August 2, 1876; LDS Church, Mormon Pioneer Overland Travel database, https://history.lds.org/overlandtravels/companyPioneers?lang=eng&companyId=298.

44. "Old Salt Lakers," *Deseret News*, August 17, 1901.

45. Salt Lake County Recorder, title abstracts; U.S. Federal Censuses, Utah Territory, 1860, 1870.

46. Sloan, *Gazeteer of Utah and Salt Lake City Directory*, 1874; Culmer, *Utah Directory and Gazetteer for 1879–80*; Salt Lake County Recorder, title abstracts.

47. Salt Lake County Recorder, title abstracts.

48. "Merritt's Divorce Grind," *Salt Lake Tribune*, November 11, 1894; "Tax Payers Protest," *Salt Lake Herald*, June 30, 1896; "Died," *Salt Lake Herald*, February 14, 1901.

49. Salt Lake County Recorder, title abstracts; Kelly & Co., *Salt Lake City Directory for 1889.*

50. Elizabeth F. Smith, "Diary of Elizabeth F. Smith," *1884–1891*, LDS Church History Library, MS 20438, fd. 1.

51. Ibid.

52. Salt Lake City Assessor, Tax Assessment rolls, 1856, Utah State Archives and Records Service, Series 4922.

53. Salt Lake County Clerk Death Registers, Utah State Archives and Records Service, Series 3864, 1902.

54. Lila L. Dahlstrom, "William Frederick John Albrand," 1976, Pioneer Memorial Museum, History Department; "Death of Thomas Steed, *Deseret News*, June 27, 1910.

55. Salt Lake County Recorder, title abstracts; Thomas Steed, "The Life of Thomas Steed," LDS Church History Library, MS 270.1, fd. 1.

56. Jane Ann Richardson Albrand, "Autobiographical Sketch," in Biographical Sketches, 1891–2013, LDS Church History Library, CR 100 18; "Married," *Deseret News*, May 11, 1859; U.S. Federal Census, Utah Territory, 1860. "Common laborer" was a term used for men who were only sporadically employed.

57. Salt Lake City Assessor Tax Assessment rolls, 1860, Utah State Archives and Records Service, Series 4922; Salt Lake City, 1898, sheet 72 (New York: Sanborn Map Co., 1898); U.S. Federal Census, Utah Territory, 1870 (spelled "Albbind").

58. Utah Division of State History, Cemeteries and Burials database; Salt Lake County, Probate Court, Civil and Criminal Case Files, Utah State Archives and Records Service, Series 373, Box 23, fd. 145, 1879.

59. Korral Brochinsky, historic site form, Utah State Historic Preservation Office, 2000; "Died," *Salt Lake Tribune*, May 27, 1901.

60. "Old Resident Dead," *Deseret News*, January 19, 1903.

61. Maria Richards's brother was LDS Church apostle Franklin D. Richards; LDS Church, Mormon Pioneer Overland Travel database, https://history. lds.org/overlandtravels/pioneerDetail?lang=eng&pioneerId=40983; Utah Territorial Census, 1856; U.S. Federal Census, Utah Territory, 1860.

62. Matilda W. Bliss, "Matilda W. Bliss History of Walter Eli Wilcox," c. 1939, LDS Church History Library, MS 7794, fd. 1; U.S. Federal Census, Utah Territory, 1880.

63. LDS Church, Mormon Pioneer Overland Travel database, https://history.lds. org/overlandtravels/pioneerDetail?lang=eng&pioneerId=42453.

64. U.S. Federal Census, Utah Territory, 1870; Bette Williams, "Cynthia Maria Wilcox Arnold," 2008, Pioneer Memorial Museum, History Department.

65. Darrell E. Jones and W. Randall Dixon, "'It Was Very Warm and Smelt Very Bad': Warm Springs and the First Bath House in Salt Lake City," *Utah Historical Quarterly* 76, no. 4 (2008): 225; Salt Lake County Recorder, title abstracts, Lot 5, Block 139, Plat A.

66. "General Items," *Deseret News*, October 6, 1886; "Death of Henry Arnold," *Deseret News*, September 26, 1888; Kelly & Co., *Salt Lake City Directory for 1889*.

67. "Cynthia Maria Wilcox Arnold," *Deseret News*, May 10, 1917.

68. Salt Lake City, sheet 4, 1911 and 1950 (New York: Sanborn Map Co., 1911 and 1950).

69. British Mission Emigration Register, Book 1047, 133; "Names of Immigrants," *Deseret News*, September 24, 1862.

70. Salt Lake County Recorder, title abstracts.

71. "Edwin Rawling's Term," *Deseret News*, September 26, 1888.

72. Nelson Knight, "The Edwin, Annie & Marie Rawlings House," Capitol Hill (Salt Lake City, Utah) Newsletter, August 2004; Salt Lake County Assessor, http://slco.org/assessor/new/valuationInfoExpanded. cfm?parcel_id=0836428002000&nbhd=150&PA=1.

73. Salt Lake County Recorder, title abstracts; British Mission Emigration Register, Book 1047, 294; Jensen and Ward, "Perpetual Emigrating Fund," 161; LDS Church, FamilySearch, https://familysearch.org/ ark:/61903/2:1:M7FH-8NM; Sloan, *Salt Lake City Directory and Business Guide*, 1869; "Cricket," *Salt Lake Herald*, April 11, 1877.

74. Sloan, *Gazeteer of Utah and Salt Lake City Directory*, 1874; Salt Lake City Assessor, Tax Assessment rolls, 1874, Utah State Archives and Records Service, Series 4922; *Latter-day Saints Millennial Star* 38, no. 276 (1876).

75. LDS Church, FamilySearch, https://familysearch.org/pal:/MM9.2.1/M7FH-8NM; U.S. Federal Census, Utah Territory, 1880.

76. "Two Out of a Possible Three," *Salt Lake Herald*, January 26, 1887; "Before Judge Zane," *Salt Lake Herald*, May 1, 1887.

77. Utah Division of State History, Cemeteries and Burials database.

78. "Permits for Building," *Salt Lake Tribune*, June 16, 1895.

79. Richard Van Waggoner, "Sarah M. Pratt: The Shaping of an Apostate," *Dialogue: A Journal of Mormon Thought* 19, no. 2 (1986): 71–82.

80. Ibid., 88.

81. Ibid., 93.

82. LDS Church, Journal History, November 26, 1875; Sloan, *Gazeteer of Utah and Salt Lake City Directory*, 1874.

83. Job Smith, "Autobiography," c. 1902, LDS Church History Library, MS 4809, fd. 1; untitled, *Deseret News*, October 23, 1861, 7; LDS Church, Mormon Pioneer Overland Travel database, https://history.lds.org/ overlandtravels/pioneerDetail?lang=eng&pioneerId=45890; LDS Church, FamilySearch, https://familysearch.org/ark:/61903/2:1:MC8B-GFD.

84. U.S. Federal Census, Utah Territory, 1870.

85. Salt Lake County Recorder, title abstracts.

86. LDS Church, Journal History, October 1, 1878, 3; *Latter-day Saints' Millennial Star* 41, no. 608 (1879); U.S. Federal Census, Utah Territory, 1880; Robert L. Sloan, *Utah Gazetteer and Directory for Logan, Ogden, Provo, and Salt Lake Cities, for 1884* (Salt Lake City: Herald Printing Co., 1884).

87. Ola Larson, "My Journal," n.d., http://jerryjan.com/olalarsonjournal.pdf, original in possession of Jerry Larson, Tualatin, Oregon; Orson Smith, "Orson Smith Papers," Utah State University Library, Special Collections and Archives, MS 357, box 1, folder 5, February 2, 1894; U.S. Federal Census, Utah, 1900–1920; Salt Lake City Recorder, Death and Burial Registers, Utah State Archives and Records Service, Series 21866, p. 98.

88. Salt Lake County Recorder, title abstracts.

89. Utah State Historic Preservation Office, National Register nomination form; "Salt Lake's Queer Streets," *Salt Lake Tribune*, April 13, 1902; Salt Lake City, 1898, sheet 64 (New York: Sanborn Map Co., 1898).

90. Florence C. Youngberg, ed., *Conquerors of the West: Stalwart Mormon Pioneers* (Salt Lake City: Sons of Utah Pioneers, 1999). 1:1292; "Passenger List," *Deseret News*, September 26, 1866; Salt Lake City Cemetery, gravestone, plot G-6-4-4E shows marriage date; U.S. Federal Census, Utah Territory, Salt Lake County, 1870.

91. Salt Lake County, Probate Court Civil and Criminal Case Files, 1871, Box 13, Fd. 115, Utah State Archives and Records Service, Series 373; Salt Lake County Recorder, title abstracts; Salt Lake City Recorder, Death and Burial Register, Utah State Archives and Records Service, Series 21866; Salt Lake City Cemetery, gravestone, plot G-6-4-4E.

92. Salt Lake County Recorder, title abstracts; U.S. Directory Publishing Co., *Salt Lake City Directory*, 1885; U.S. Federal Census, Salt Lake and Tooele Counties, Utah Territory, 1880, 1900; U.S. Federal Census, Salt Lake County, Utah, 1920; Death Certificate, Utah State Archives and Records Service, Series 81448.

93. LDS Church, Mormon Pioneer Overland Travel database, https://history.lds.org/overlandtravels/pioneerDetail?lang=eng&pioneerId=59581.

94. Sloan, *Salt Lake City Directory and Business Guide*, 1869; U.S. Federal Census, Utah Territory, 1870; "Died," *Deseret News*, March 18, 1874; "Died," *Deseret News*, August 5, 1874.

95. "Salt Lake's Queer Streets," *Salt Lake Tribune*, April 13, 1902; Sloan, *Utah Gazatteer and Directory*, 1884; untitled, *Salt Lake Tribune*, January 1, 1891.

96. "City and Neighborhood," *Deseret News*, July 16, 1901; Index to Compiled Service Records of Volunteer Union Soldiers Who Served in Organizations from the State of Missouri, 1862, U.S. National Archives, Record Group 94, microfilm number M 390, 4 pages.

97. "Report of the Immigration," *Deseret News*, September 17, 1862; Sloan, *Salt Lake City Directory and Business Guide*, 1869.

98. LDS Church, FamilySearch, https://familysearch.org/ark:/61903/2:1:M7T1-TZK; *The Latter-day Saints' Millennial Star* 32, no. 523 (1870).

99. U.S. Federal Census, Utah Territory, 1870 and 1880.

100. Salt Lake City Recorder, Death and Burial Register, Utah State Archives and Records Service, Series 21866; Utah Division of State History, Cemeteries and Burials database.

101. Koch, *Bird's Eye View of Salt Lake City*, 1870; Salt Lake City, 1898, sheet 61 (New York: Sanborn Map Co., 1898).

102. Salt Lake County Recorder, title abstracts; LDS Church, FamilySearch, https://familysearch.org/ark:/61903/2:1:M1R2-2G3; British Mission Emigration Register, Book 0145, 84; "Immigration to Utah," *Deseret News*, October 15, 1856.

103. U.S. Federal Census, Utah Territory, 1870 (spelled "Ilriah"); FindAGrave website, http://www.findagrave.com/cgi-bin/fg.cgi?page=gr&GRid=57714882.

104. Salt Lake County Recorder, title abstracts; U.S. Federal Census, Utah, 1910; "Deaths," *Salt Lake Telegram*, January 26, 1924; Capitol Hill Neighborhood Council Bulletin, August 2007, http://chnc-slc.org/bulletin/2007/AUG-07.pdf.

105. Salt Lake City, 1911, sheet 12 (New York: Sanborn Map Co., 1911).

106. Sloan, *Gazeteer of Utah and Salt Lake City Directory*, 1874; "Died," *Deseret News*, October 2, 1878; U.S. Federal Census, San Francisco County, CA, 1900, 1910.

107. "Local News," *Salt Lake Democrat*, April 2, 1885; "Mining Notices," *Salt Lake Tribune*, September 4, 1875; Salt Lake City, 1911, sheet 11 (New York: Sanborn Map Co., 1911) at 136–146 West 600 North; Salt Lake County Recorder, title abstracts.

108. "Police Court," *Salt Lake Herald*, June 11, 1878; "James Wyatt and the 'News,'" *Salt Lake Tribune*, August 23, 1885; "Wyatt's Wickedness," *Salt Lake Herald*, January 31, 1886; LDS Church, Journal History, January 19, 1886, 5.

109. U.S. Federal Census, California, 1900, 1910; Salt Lake County Recorder, title abstracts; untitled, *Marin* (California) *Journal*, November 25, 1920, 1.

110. Andrew Jenson, *Latter-day Saint Biographical Encyclopedia*, (Salt Lake City: Andrew Jenson History Co., 1920), 3:277; "Latter Day Saints' Immigration," *Deseret News*, August 24, 1859; U.S. Federal Census, Utah Territory, 1860.

111. "Died," *Deseret News*, May 18, 1864.

112. Owens, *Salt Lake City Directory*, 1867.

113. LDS Church, Mormon Pioneer Overland Travel database, https://history.lds.org/overlandtravels/pioneers/52231/james-watson; Jenson, *Latter-day Saint Biographical Encyclopedia*, 1920, 3:277.

114. U.S. Directory Publishing Co., *Salt Lake City Directory*, 1885; Kelly & Co., *Salt Lake City Directory for 1889*.

115. "Probate Court Business," *Salt Lake Tribune*, February 12, 1896.

116. "Mrs. Annie Watson Dies at Her Home," *Salt Lake Telegram*, May 13, 1926.

117. Maud Bliss Allen, Ruth Huhl Glissmeyer, and Darro H. Glissmeyer, "History of William Watmough, 1808–1879," 2007, Pioneer Memorial Museum, History Department; British Mission Emigration Register, Horizon, 1856, 176; "Captain Miller's Company," *Deseret News*, September 17, 1862; U.S. Federal Census, Massachusetts, 1860.

118. LDS Church, FamilySearch, https://familysearch.org/ark:/61903/2:1:M761-TT8; Frank Esshom, *Pioneers and Prominent Men of Utah, 1847–1868* (Salt Lake City: Utah Pioneer Book Publishing Co., 1913), 1246; Matilda W. Bliss, "Matilda W. Bliss History of Walter Eli Wilcox," c. 1939, LDS Church History Library, MS 7794.

119. U.S. Federal Census, Utah Territory, 1870 (spelled "Wetough"); Sloan, *Salt Lake City Directory and Business Guide*, 1869; Allen, Glissmeyer, and Glissmeyer, "History of William Watmough"; "Salt Lake County Schools," *Salt Lake Tribune*, December 30, 1900.

120. Salt Lake City, 1898, sheet 63 (New York: Sanborn Map Co.), 1898; photograph in possession of Rosemarie Glissmeyer, Salt Lake City, UT, showing west elevation and family members.

121. Kate B. Carter, *Treasures of Pioneer History* (Salt Lake City: Daughters of Utah Pioneers, 1957) 6:199.

122. U.S. Federal Census, Utah Territory, 1870.

123. Allen, Glissmeyer, and Glissmeyer, "History of William Watmough."

124. U.S. Federal Census, Utah Territory, 1880; "Taxes Abated," *Salt Lake Herald*, August 8, 1891; "County Taxes," *Salt Lake Herald*, August 13, 1892; "County Equalizers," *Salt Lake Herald*, July 28, 1894; "Real Estate Transfers," *Salt Lake Herald*, March 1, 1895; Polk, *Polk's Salt Lake City Directory*, 1893.

125. LDS Church, FamilySearch, https://familysearch.org/ark:/61903/2:1:MWCK-NDR; Coleorton Parish population census, 1851, http://www.coleorton.org.uk/1851.html.

126. Emily Price Smith, "Sketch of the Life of Emily Price Platts and her Husband John Platts, Pioneers of 1854," n.d., Pioneer Memorial Museum, History Department; British Mission Emigration Register, Book 1040, 4; LDS Church, Mormon Pioneer Overland Travel database, https://history.lds.org/overlandtravels/pioneerDetail?lang=eng&pioneerId=50176.

127. Personal observation, June 2014.

128. Utah State Historic Preservation Office, National Register nomination form.

129. U.S. Federal Census, Utah Territory, 1860; Platts's cricket bat can be seen in the Pioneer Memorial Museum in Salt Lake City.

130. Smith, "Sketch of the Life of Emily Price Platts."

131. Nelson W. Whipple, "Nelson W. Whipple Autobiography and Journal, 1859–1887," LDS Church History Library, MS 9995.

132. British Mission Emigration Register, Book 1042, 109.

133. "By Telegraph," *Deseret News*, November 7, 1877; LDS Church, FamilySearch, https://familysearch.org/ark:/61903/2:1:M7YK-PH1; U.S. Directory Publishing Co., *Salt Lake City Directory*, 1885.

134. Culmer, *Utah Directory and Gazetteer for 1879–80*; U.S. Federal Census, Utah Territory, 1880; "Town Talk," *Salt Lake Herald*, April 10, 1896; "Local and Other Briefs," *Salt Lake Herald*, May 15, 1890.

135. Salt Lake County Recorder, title abstracts.

136. LDS Church, FamilySearch, https://familysearch.org/ark:/61903/2:1:M7RQ-CBZ; British Mission Emigration Record, Book 1041, 276; *Lethbridge* (Alberta) *Herald*, September 16, 1937; "Deaths," *Deseret News*, January 11, 1888.

137. Salt Lake County Recorder, title abstracts.

138. U.S. Directory Publishing Co., *Salt Lake City Directory*, 1885; address was

then 90 North; Salt Lake City, 1898, sheet 63 (New York: Sanborn Map Co., 1898); Polk, *Polk's Salt Lake City Directory*, 1899; Judith Nilsson, *Stirling, Its Story and People: 1899–1980 (*Stirling, Alberta: Sunset Society, 1981), 365–66.

139. Village of Stirling, National Historic Site, http://stirling.ca/visit/history/.

140. LDS Church, FamilySearch, https://familysearch.org/ ark:/61903/2:2:SRX3-RZ2; British Mission Emigration Register, Book 1041, 268; Salt Lake County Recorder, title abstracts; Salt Lake City Recorder, Death and Burial Register, Utah State Archives, Ser. 21866; "Deaths," *Deseret News*, March 5, 1895; Salt Lake City Cemetery, plot K-22-3-6W.

141. Salt Lake County Recorder, title abstracts; "Utah," *Salt Lake Tribune*, January 1, 1888.

142. Brigham Young University, Mormon Migration database, http:// mormonmigration.lib.byu.edu/Search/showDetails/db:MM_MII/ t:passenger/id:67158/keywords:Matthias+Cowley; LDS Church, Mormon Pioneer Overland Travel database, https://history.lds.org/overlandtravels/ companyDetail?companyId=116.

143. LDS Church, FamilySearch, https://familysearch.org/ark:/61903/2:1:M72L-WPN; "Old Resident Passes Away," *Salt Lake Tribune*, December 26, 1899.

144. Polk, *Polk's Salt Lake City Directory*, 1893; Polk, *Polk's Salt Lake City Directory*, 1898.

145. "The Services," *Deseret News*, January 2, 1892.

146. Salt Lake County Recorder, title abstracts; U.S. Federal Census, Utah, 1900.

147. LDS Church, FamilySearch, https://familysearch.org/photos/ stories/1069856; U.S. Federal Census, Philadelphia, Pennsylvania, 1850; Emma Jane Hamson, https://familysearch.org/photos/stories/1069719.

148. *Salt Lake City Directory*, 1885; Polk, *Polk's Salt Lake City Directory*, 1893.

149. Salt Lake City Recorder, Death and Burial Register, Utah State Archives and Records Service, Series 21866.

150. "Utah," *Salt Lake Tribune*, January 1, 1888.

151. Salt Lake County Recorder, title abstracts.

152. Korral Brochinsky, Historic Site Form, Utah State Historic Preservation Office, 2001.

153. "George W. Hill," *Deseret News*, February 26, 1894.

154. U.S. Federal Census, Utah Territory, 1850, 1860, 1870; Scott Christensen, 2011, personal communication to Alan Barnett (Utah State Archives and Records Service).

155. J. C. Graham, *The Utah Directory for 1883–84* (Salt Lake City: J. C. Graham & Co., 1883); Theresa Snow Hill, *The Life and Times of George Washington Hill: A Historical Novel by Theresa Snow Hill* (St. George, UT: CFP Books, c. 1996).

156. Korral Brochinsky, Historic Site Form, Utah State Historic Preservation Office, 2001; "County to Sell Its Only Brothel," *Salt Lake Tribune*, June 19, 1985.

157. LDS Church, Mormon Pioneer Overland Travel database, https://history.

lds.org/overlandtravels/pioneerDetail?lang=eng&pioneerId=35787; Ronald
G. Watt, comp., *Perpetual Emigrating Fund Ledger Index* (Salt Lake City: LDS
Church Historical Department, 1992).

158. U.S. Federal Census, Utah Territory, 1870; untitled, *Salt Lake Tribune*,
January 1, 1892, 34; Salt Lake County Recorder, title abstracts; Salt Lake
City Assessor, Tax Assessment rolls, 1876, Utah State Archives and Records
Service, Series 4922.

159. U.S. Federal Census, Utah Territory, 1880; "Directors' Report," *Deseret News*,
March 7, 1888; "The Mullett Case," *Deseret News*, March 21, 1888; "He Has
Skipped," *Deseret News*, March 28, 1888; "Executive Pardon Asked," *Salt Lake
Tribune*, December 7, 1892.

160. District Court (Third District: Salt Lake County) Criminal case files, case
2976, 1912, Utah State Archives and Records Service, Series 1471; Death
Certificate, Utah State Archives and Records Service, Series 81448.

161. R. L. Polk & Co., *Utah State Gazetteer and Business Directory* (Salt Lake City:
R. L. Polk & Co., 1900).

162. Albert Merrill, "Albert Merrill family record, circa 1845–1917," LDS Church
History Library, MS 1990, fd. 1; U.S. Federal Census, Utah Territory, 1860.

163. U.S. Federal Census, Utah Territory, 1870; LDS Church, FamilySearch,
https://familysearch.org/ark:/61903/2:1:M7XW-6ZS.

164. Sloan, *Gazeteer of Utah and Salt Lake City Directory*, 1874; Salt Lake County
Recorder, title abstracts.

165. "List of Immigrants," *Deseret News*, October 19, 1864; Esshom, *Pioneers and
Prominent Men of Utah*, 766; Salt Lake County Recorder, title abstracts.

166. British Mission Emigration Record, Book 1040, 90; Anonymous,
"Elizabeth Hollis Roe," n.d., Pioneer Memorial Museum, History
Department; LDS Church, Mormon Pioneer Overland Travel database,
Charles Harper Co., 1855, https://history.lds.org/overlandtravels/
companyPioneers?lang=eng&companyId=143.

167. Owens, *Salt Lake City Directory*, 1867; Salt Lake City Assessor, Tax
Assessment rolls, 1868 and 1872, Utah State Archives and Records
Service, Series 4922; Salt Lake City, 1898, sheet 61 (New York: Sanborn
Map Co., 1898); LDS Church, FamilySearch, https://familysearch.org/
ark:/61903/2:1:M7FF-R4T; U.S. Federal Census, Utah, 1900.

168. Salt Lake County Recorder, title abstracts; U.S. Federal Census, Utah
Territory, 1870.

169. Sloan, *Gazeteer of Utah and Salt Lake City Directory*, 1874; U.S. Federal
Census, Utah Territory, 1880; "Man Falls Forty Feet," *Salt Lake Tribune*,
September 11, 1898; U.S. Federal Census, Utah, 1920.

170. Priscilla's death certificate incorrectly gives her father's name as George Alfred
Boyd; Utah Division of State History, Cemeteries and Burials database.

171. Salt Lake County Recorder, title abstracts; Alexander E. Carr, "The First One
Hundred Years of the Nineteenth Ward of the Salt Lake Stake of Zion,"
1949, 26, LDS Church Family History Library, Salt Lake City.

172. British Mission Emigration Record, Book 1042, 368.

173. Sloan, *Utah Gazatteer and Directory*, 1884; Kelly & Co., *Salt Lake City Directory for 1889* (the house address then was 68 Back Street); U.S. Federal Census, Utah, 1900, 1910, 1920; U.S. Directory Publishing Co., *Salt Lake City Directory*, 1885.

174. Salt Lake County Recorder, title abstracts.

175. W. Randall Dixon, personal communication, October 2012.

Twentieth Ward

1. Salt Lake City Assessor, Tax Assessment rolls, 1856, Utah State Archives and Records Service, Series 4922.

2. Linda H. Smith, "Ellen Birchall Barton," Pioneer Memorial Museum, History Department, 2006; British Mission Emigration Record, Book 1047, 155; "The Immigration," *Deseret News* [Weekly] August 15, 1860; U.S. Federal Census, Utah Territory, 1870.

3. Francis Kirkham, ed., *Tales of a Triumphant People: A History of Salt Lake County, Utah, 1847–1900* (Salt Lake City: Daughters of Utah Pioneers, 1995), 66; Salt Lake County Recorder, title abstracts; Brigham Young University, Mormon Migration index, http://mormonmigration.lib.byu.edu/Search/showDetails/db:MM_MII/t:voyage/id:156/keywords:caste.

4. LDS Church, Mormon Pioneer Overland Travel database, https://history.lds.org/overlandtravels/pioneerDetail?lang=eng&pioneerId=51914; LDS Church, FamilySearch, https://familysearch.org/ark:/61903/2:1:MW9P-T6S.

5. Nora B. Sparks, "History of Sarah Foster Barton," 1945, Pioneer Memorial Museum, History Department; R. L. Polk, *Polk's Salt Lake City Directory for 1890* (Salt Lake City: R. L. Polk & Co., 1890); Sarah later lived with her children and their families in a larger house at 280 North I Street. She died of uterine cancer at age seventy.

6. U.S. Federal Census, Utah Territory, 1870; Kate B. Carter, *Heart Throbs of the West* (Salt Lake City: Daughters of Utah Pioneers, 1948), 9:161.

7. John Daniel Thompson McAllister, "John D. T. McAllister Journals," LDS Church History Library, MS 1257, box 1 for July 16, 1862: Minnie's name is variously given as Amelia M., Minerva M., or Minnie on the *Manchester*'s roster, manifest, and pioneer company list; "Names of Immigrants," *Deseret News*, September 24, 1862.

8. LDS Church, FamilySearch, https://familysearch.org/ark:/61903/2:1:M7KS-8RT; Edward L. Sloan, *Salt Lake City Directory and Business Guide, for 1869* (Salt Lake City: E. L. Sloan & Co., 1869); Edward L. Sloan, *Gazeteer of Utah and Salt Lake City Directory* (Salt Lake City: Salt Lake Herald Publ. Co., 1874).

9. Salt Lake County Recorder, title abstracts; "Resources of Utah," *Salt Lake Tribune*, January 10, 1873; Lloyd Shaw, *The City of Salt Lake!: Her Relations as a Centre of Trade: Manufacturing Establishments and Business Houses: Historical, Descriptive and Statistical* (Salt Lake City: Sylvanus, Stone & Shaw, 1890), 15;

Eli S. Glover, *Birds-Eye View of Salt Lake City from the North Looking South-east, Utah* (Cincinnati: Strobridge & Co., 1875).

10. Betty F. Evans, *Elizabeth Alldredge Evans*, 1962, Pioneer Memorial Museum, History Department; "A Good Man Departed," *Deseret News*, March 12, 1876; J. C. Graham, *The Utah Directory for 1883–84* (Salt Lake City: J. C. Graham & Co., 1883).

11. "John A. Evans Is in Perilous Condition," *Deseret News*, June 2, 1906; "Death of a Good Woman," *Deseret* News, July 31, 1906; Utah State Historic Preservation Office, Site Information Form.

12. British Mission Emigration Register, Book 1043, 61; Index to Death Records in the City of St. Louis, 1850–1902, St. Louis Genealogical Society, 1999; LDS Church, FamilySearch, https://familysearch.org/ark:/61903/2:2:3S2B-9C8; Salt Lake County Recorder, title abstracts; U.S. Federal Census, Utah Territory, 1860.

13. LDS Church, FamilySearch, https://familysearch.org/ark:/61903/2:1:M7R8-3V3; Charles Sansom, *Autobiography and Journals, 1873–1907*, LDS Church History Library, MS 8372.

14. Sloan, *Gazeteer of Utah and Salt Lake City Directory*, 1874; Henry L. A. Culmer, *Utah Directory and Gazeteer for 1879–80* (Salt Lake City: H. L. A. Culmer & Co., 1879).

15. LDS Church, Journal History, November 18, 1873, 3; Salt Lake County Recorder, title abstracts.

16. Gertrude D. Osterloh, "Samuel and Eunice Neslen Biography," Brigham Young University, Harold B. Lee Library, Tom Perry Special Collections, Provo, Utah, 1971; British Mission Emigration Record, Book 1044, 66; Hannah Tapfield King, *The Journals of Hannah Tapfield King* (S.l. (F. T. Watkins, n.d.), LDS Family History Library, Salt Lake City.

17. Salt Lake County Recorder, title abstracts. Part of the chain of title seems to be missing, as Lynch had not been recorded as owning any part of the lot prior to selling it; 1856 Utah Census Index (Salt Lake City: Index Publishing, 1983); George Owens, *Salt Lake City Directory, Including a Business Directory of Provo, Springville, and Ogden, Utah Territory* (Salt Lake City: George Owens, 1867); Salt Lake City Assessor, Tax Assessment rolls, 1867, Utah State Archives and Records Service, Series 4922.

18. "Local and Other Briefs," *Salt Lake Herald*, February 24, 1891.

19. Owens, *Salt Lake City Directory*, 1867; LDS Church, Mormon Pioneer Overland Travel database, https://history.lds.org/overlandtravels/pioneerDetail?lang=eng&pioneerId=13640; Christopher Arthur Emigrating Company Journal, 1853, February–October, LDS Church History Library, MS 1429, fd. 1, April 29; U.S. Federal Census, Utah Territory, 1860.

20. U.S. Federal Census, Utah Territory, 1870; Sloan, *Gazeteer of Utah and Salt Lake City Directory*, 1874; Salt Lake County Recorder, title abstracts; "The Stockton Blaze," *Salt Lake Herald*, October 17, 1886.

21. "Utah," *Salt Lake Tribune*, January 1, 1888; "Died," *Salt Lake Herald*, May 22, 1897; Death Certificate, Utah State Archives and Records Service, Series 81448.

22. British Mission Emigration Register, Book 1044, 145. Mercy's name was given as Mary; "Deaths," *Deseret Evening News*, November 26, 1888, 3; Brigham Young University, Mormon Migration index, http://mormonmigration.lib.byu.edu/Search/showDetails/db:MM_MII/t:passenger/id:51581/keywords:george+robinson; "Immigration to Utah," *Deseret News*, October 15, 1856.

23. Salt Lake County Recorder, title abstracts; Owens, *Salt Lake City Directory*, 1867; U.S. Federal Census, Utah Territory, 1860; LDS Church, Trustee-in-Trust, Public Works account books, 1848–1887, LDS Church History Library. Robinson made adobe molds and a coffin; LDS Church, FamilySearch, https://familysearch.org/ark:/61903/2:1:M7XC-GJB.

24. Our Family Genealogy Pages, wayneandbonniegenealogy.net/genealogy/showmedia.php?&mediaID=523&medialinkID=661&page=1, William H. Robinson Jr., "The Story of the Old Mud Wall and Life in City Creek Canyon, 1942."

25. "Local and Other Matters—Suffocated and Burned to Death," *Deseret News*, December 18, 1878; "The Inquest," *Salt Lake Herald*, December 11, 1878. The city asylum probably was in the southeast quarter of Section 10, Township 1 N, Range 1 E, on what is now the Bonneville Golf Course.

26. LDS Church, FamilySearch, https://familysearch.org/ark:/61903/2:1:M7XC-GJB; Salt Lake City Recorder, Death and Burial Register, Utah State Archives and Records Service, Series 21866; R. L. Polk, *Polk's Salt Lake City Directory for 1899* (Salt Lake City: R. L. Polk & Co., 1899).

27. Salt Lake County Recorder, title abstracts.

28. LDS Church, Mormon Pioneer Overland Travel database, https://history.lds.org/overlandtravels/companyPioneers?lang=eng&companyId=284; Brigham Young University (Idaho), Western States Marriage Records Index, http://abish.byui.edu/specialCollections/westernStates/westernStatesRecordDetail.cfm?recordID=270199; Death Certificate, Utah State Archives and Records Service, Series 81448; U.S. Federal Census, Utah Territory, 1860.

29. Vincy R. Stone Barker, "Samuel Dean Biographical Sketch," *Genealogical Charts and Biographical Sketches of Members of the L.D.S. Church, Ogden Stake* (Ogden, UT: LDS Church Relief Society, 1915–1920), 24:178; U.S. Federal Census, Utah Territory, Green River County, 1860.

30. William A. Carter notice of appointment for Samuel Dean, "William A. Carter papers," L. Tom Perry Special Collections, MSS SC 490, Brigham Young University; "Letter from Salt Lake," *Sacramento Daily Union*, August 17, 1863.

31. U.S. Federal Census, Davis County, Kansas, 1870; "Local and Other Matters," *Deseret News*, January 8, 1873; U.S. Federal Census, Utah Territory, 1880.

32. U.S. Federal Census, Utah, 1900; Death Certificate, Utah State Archives and Records Service, Series 44881; Salt Lake County Recorder, title abstracts; "First Precinct," *Salt Lake Tribune*, January 1, 1890 (the article includes all precincts).

33. Brigham Young University, Mormon Migration Index, https://

mormonmigration.lib.byu.edu; LDS Church History Library, Mormon Pioneer Overland Travel database; U.S. Federal Census, Utah Territory, 1870; Salt Lake County Recorder, title abstracts; Robert L. Sloan, *Utah Gazetteer and Directory for Logan, Ogden, Provo, and Salt Lake Cities, for 1884* (Salt Lake City: Herald Printing Co., 1884); R. L. Polk, *Polk's Salt Lake City Directory for 1900* (Salt Lake City: R. L. Polk & Co., 1900); Salt Lake County Recorder, title abstracts.

34. Salt Lake City, 1898, sheet 131 (New York: Sanborn Map Co., 1898).

35. Except as noted, the information source is Bruce A. Van Orden, *Prisoner for Conscience' Sake* (Salt Lake City: Deseret Book, 1992).

36. British Mission Emigration Register, Book 1048, 91.

37. Salt Lake County Recorder, title abstracts; LDS Church, FamilySearch, https://familysearch.org/ark:/61903/2:1:99JN-KRP.

38. U.S. Federal Census, Utah Territory, 1880.

39. Salt Lake County Recorder, title abstracts.

40. Salt Lake City, 1898, sheet 132, and 1911, sheet 42 (New York: Sanborn Map Co., 1898 and 1911).

41. U.S. Federal Census, Utah, 1900.

42. "Funeral of George Reynolds," *Deseret News*, August 12, 1909.

43. Alice Louise Reynolds, "Alice Louise Reynolds Autobiography," 1937, LDS Church History Library, MS 5850, fd. 1.

44. LDS Church, FamilySearch, https://familysearch.org/ark:/61903/2:1:M7LV-64K; "List of Names in Incoming Passenger Trains," *Deseret News*, August 16, 1866; LDS Church, FamilySearch, https://familysearch.org/ark:/61903/2:1:M7LV-64KUS; U.S. Federal Census, Utah Territory, 1870.

45. British Mission Emigration Register, Book 1048, 108; LDS Church, Mormon Pioneer Overland Travel database, https://history.lds.org/overlandtravels/companyPioneers?lang=eng&companyId=87; Frank Esshom, *Pioneers and Prominent Men of Utah, 1847–1868* (Salt Lake City: Utah Pioneer Book Publishing Co., 1913), 1118.

46. Salt Lake County Recorder, title abstracts; Salt Lake City, 1898, sheet 132 (New York: Sanborn Map Co., 1898); U.S. Federal Census, Utah Territory, 1880; Utah Division of State History, Cemeteries and Burials database.

47. Sloan, *Gazeteer of Utah and Salt Lake City Directory, 1874*.

48. "Local and Other Matters," *Deseret News*, August 12, 1874; C. R. Savage, photograph, "Board of Directors, 20th Ward Institute, 1872," Brigham Young University, Harold B. Lee Library, C. R. Savage collection; "Local and Other Matters," *Deseret News*, April 7, 1875.

49. "Proved to Be Henry Puzey," *Salt Lake Tribune*, May 9, 1896; Utah State Historic Preservation Office, Site Information Forms.

50. Salt Lake County Recorder, title abstracts; Sloan, *Salt Lake Directory and Business Guide, 1869*; U.S. Federal Census, St. Louis, Missouri, 1860 (spelled "Lambourn"); "Passenger List," *Deseret News*, September 19, 1866 (spelled "Sambourn").

51. Salt Lake City, 1898, sheet 133 (New York: Sanborn Map Co., 1898).

52. LDS Church, FamilySearch, https://familysearch.org/ark:/61903/2:1:M7J6-QGB, and https://familysearch.org/ark:/61903/2:2:9CWV-3G1; U.S. Federal Census, Utah Territory, 1880 (none of the family appears in 1870 census records); Martha Wernham Lambourne, "Biography," n.d., Pioneer Memorial Museum, History Department.

53. U.S. Federal Census, Utah Territory, 1880.

54. U.S. Directory Publishing Co. of California, *Salt Lake City Directory for the Year Commencing August 1, 1885* (San Francisco: U.S. Directory Publishing Co. of California, 1885); Kelly & Co., *Salt Lake City Directory for 1889, and Business Directory and Guide to Public Streets and Avenues* (Salt Lake City: Kelly & Co., 1889).

55. Death Certificate, Utah State Archives and Records Service, Series 81448; LDS Church, FamilySearch, https://familysearch.org/ark:/61903/2:1:M4C5-LVM; Salt Lake County Recorder, title abstracts.

56. Davis County (Utah) County Clerk marriage license record books, Utah State Archives and Records Service, Series 23384; "Husband Knocks Her Senseless," *Salt Lake Herald*, February 1, 1908; U.S. Federal Census, Utah, 1910; "Estate Worth $67,000," *Salt Lake Herald*, September 2, 1904; Death Certificate, Utah State Archives and Records Service, Series 81448.

57. Death Certificate, Utah State Archives and Records Service, Series 81448; "William Lambourne, Teacher of Violin, Answers Last Call," *Salt Lake Herald*, September 12, 1915; "Funerals," *Salt Lake Telegram*, September 11, 1930.

58. William Joseph Castleton, "Autobiographical Sketch," LDS Church History Library, 1939, MS 18829, fd. 1, 1; Sloan, *Salt Lake City Directory and Business Guide*, 1869; Salt Lake County Recorder, title abstracts; Sloan, *Utah Gazatteer and Directory*, 1884.

59. U.S. Federal Census, Utah Territory, 1880; "Local and Other Matters: Relieved by Death," *Deseret News*, November 29, 1882; Polk, *Polk's Salt Lake City Directory for 1893*.

60. LDS Church, FamilySearch, https://familysearch.org/ark:/61903/2:1:M7NF-P39; Death Certificate, Utah State Archives and Records Service, Series 81448; U.S. Federal Census, Utah Territory and Utah, 1880–1920; Salt Lake County Recorder, title abstracts; "Mrs. Kate Castleton Dead," *Deseret News*, March 20, 1902.

61. Anglicized spelling of Hans's surname was Young or Yonge; Salt Lake County Recorder, title abstracts; LDS Church, FamilySearch, https://familysearch.org/ark:/61903/2:1:9S63-C4C; "Mrs. Amelia Pike Young Answers Death's Call," *Deseret News*, April 7, 1919; Salt Lake County Recorder, title abstracts.

62. Will Bagley, ed., *The Pioneer Camp of the Saints: The 1846 and 1847 Mormon Trail Journals of Thomas Bullock* (Spokane: Arthur H. Clark, 2001), 131; U.S. Federal Census, Utah Territory, 1860; LDS Church, FamilySearch, https://familysearch.org/ark:/61903/2:1:M7FM-4F5.

63. Commissioner of Indian War Records, Indian War service affidavits, 1909, Utah State Archives and Records Service, Series 2217; U.S. Federal Census, Utah Territory, 1870; A. W. Bowen & Co., *Progressive Men of the State of Wyoming* (Chicago: A. W. Bowen & Co., 1901), 961; Swaner Preserve and Nature Center, Utah State University, http://www.swanerecocenter.org/about_us/history.html.

64. U.S. Directory Publishing Co., *Salt Lake City Directory*, 1885; U.S. Federal Census, Utah Territory, 1880; Kelly & Co., *Salt Lake City Directory for 1889*; R. L. Polk, *Salt Lake City Directory*, 1904; Utah Division of State History, Cemeteries and Burials database; Death Certificate, Utah State Archives and Records Service, Series 81448.

65. "Mrs. Lippman Killed in Yellowstone Park," *Salt Lake Herald*, August 27, 1899; Death Certificate, Utah State Archives and Records Service, Series 81448; "Mrs. Amelia Pike Young Answers Death's Call," *Washington County (Utah) News*, April 17, 1919.

66. British Mission Emigration Register, Book 1047, 147; "Names of Immigrants," *Deseret News*, September 24, 1862.

67. Sloan, *Salt Lake City Directory and Business Guide*, 1869; LDS Church, Journal History, February 9, 1884, 3. Ebenezer Beesley's band furnished the music for a bishop's party and Goodman acted as the "prompter"; "Local and Other Matters," *Deseret News*, February 6, 1878.

68. British Mission Emigration Register, Book 1041, 73; U.S. Federal Census, Utah Territory, 1880.

69. Salt Lake City Assessor, Tax Assessment rolls, 1872, Utah State Archives and Records Service, Series 4922; Sloan, *Gazeteer of Utah and Salt Lake City Directory*, 1874; Salt Lake County Recorder, title abstracts (Executor's deed, paid $2).

70. Salt Lake City, Division of Building Services and Licensing: Building permit registers, #180, Utah State Archives and Records Service, Series 8690.

71. Salt Lake County Recorder, title abstracts; "St. Johns," *Deseret News*, September 17, 1884; U.S. Directory Publishing Co., *Salt Lake City Directory*, 1885; Kelly & Co., *Salt Lake City Directory for 1889*.

72. "Obituary Notes," *Deseret News* [Weekly], September 1, 1894. Defined as locomotor ataxia or multiple sclerosis; "Died," *Salt Lake Tribune*, March 12, 1912.

73. "Good Potatoe Land," *Deseret News*, July 21, 1875.

74. U.S. Federal Census, Utah Territory, 1870; British Mission Emigration Register, Book 1048, 300; ibid., 343; LDS Church, FamilySearch, https://familysearch.org/ark:/61903/2:1:M7K5-GY4.

75. Sloan, *Gazeteer of Utah and Salt Lake City Directory*, 1874; Culmer, *Utah Directory and Gazetteer for 1879–80*; Salt Lake City Recorder, Death and Burial Register, Utah State Archives and Records Service, Series 21866; Death Certificate, Utah State Archives and Records Service, Series 81448; U.S. Federal Census, Utah, 1900, 1910.

76. Sloan, *Salt Lake City Directory and Business Guide*, 1869; John W. VanCott, *Utah Place Names* (Salt Lake City: University of Utah Press, 1990).

77. British Mission Emigration Register, Book 1040, 175, voyage of the *Clara Wheeler*. Notation: "John H. Picknell, being arrested and detained . . . did not go"; LDS Church, FamilySearch, https://familysearch.org/ark:/61903/2:1:M7PJ-GYJ.

78. British Mission Emigration Register, Book 1040, 223; "Immigration List," *Deseret News*, September 12, 1855.

79. U.S. Federal Census, Utah Territory, 1860; "Sarah Reid papers," n.d., Chester Fritz Library, University of North Dakota, Grand Forks; U.S. Federal Census, Nebraska, 1870.

80. LDS Church, FamilySearch, https://familysearch.org/ark:/61903/2:1:M7PJ-GYJ; U.S. Federal Census, Utah Territory, 1870.

81. *Latter-day Saints Millennial Star* 38, no. 294 (1876); "Died," *Deseret News*, July 10, 1878.

82. Salt Lake City, 1911, sheet 60 (New York: Sanborn Map Co.), 1911; Salt Lake County Recorder, title abstracts.

83. LDS Church, FamilySearch, https://familysearch.org/ark:/61903/2:1:9SNM-GTZ; spelling variants include Elenore; Commissioner of Indian War Records, Indian War Records, box 2, folder 21, 1909, Utah State Archives and Records Service, Series 2217; Sloan, *Gazeteer of Utah and Salt Lake City Directory*, 1874.

84. JuneAnn Bailey, "Elenore Ann Mitchell Neslen," from a taped interview with Elenore Meyer White Sahlberg, 2000, Pioneer Memorial Museum, History Department; Salt Lake County Probate Court, Civil and Criminal case files, box 25, folder 87, Utah State Archives and Records Service, Series 373; Death Certificate, Utah State Archives and Records Service, Series 81448.

85. LDS Church, FamilySearch, https://familysearch.org/ark:/61903/2:1:9SNM-GTZ; Salt Lake City Recorder, Death and Burial Register, Utah State Archives, Series 21866.

86. U.S. Federal Census, Utah, 1900; LDS Church, FamilySearch, https://familysearch.org/ark:/61903/2:1:9SNM-GTZ; "William F. Neslen, Pioneer of 1853, Dies," *Salt Lake Herald*, January 23, 1918; Bailey, "Elenore Ann Mitchell Neslen," 2000.

87. Death Certificate, Utah State Archives and Records Service, Series 81448.

88. Andrew Jenson, *Latter-day Saint Biographical Encyclopedia* (Salt Lake City: Deseret News Press, 1920), 2:257; Owens, *Salt Lake City Directory*, 1867; Salt Lake City Assessor, Tax Assessment rolls, 1868, Utah State Archives and Records Service, Series 4922; U.S. Federal Census, Utah Territory, 1870. John and Mary ultimately had eleven children, one of whom lived to be one hundred years old; U.S. Federal Census, Utah Territory, 1870, 1880; "Randolph Woman Dies of Heart Failure," *Deseret Evening News*, April 23, 1920.

89. Salt Lake County Recorder, title abstracts; Michael Hicks, *Mormonism and Music: A History* (Champaign: University of Illinois Press, 2003), 95; Sloan, *Gazeteer of Utah and Salt Lake City Directory*, 1874.

90. LDS Church, Mormon Pioneer Overland Travel database, https://history.lds.org/overlandtravels/pioneerDetail?lang=eng&pioneerId=51593; Sloan,

Gazeteer of Utah and Salt Lake City Directory, 1874; *Latter-day Saints' Millennial Star* 41, no. 459 (1879); Salt Lake City Recorder, Death and Burial Register, Utah State Archives and Records Service, Series 21866; "Sad and Sudden Death," *Salt Lake Herald,* July 17, 1885.

91. Salt Lake County Recorder, title abstracts.

92. Salt Lake City, sheet 132, 1898 (New York: Sanborn Map Co., 1898).

93. Oliver Hodgson, "Family History: Memoirs of Oliver Hodgson," n.d., Pioneer Memorial Museum, History Department; Salt Lake City Recorder, Death and Burial Register, Utah State Archives and Records Service, Series 21866; LDS Church, FamilySearch, https://familysearch.org/ark:/61903/2:1:M7N4-81F.

94. Owens, *Salt Lake City Directory,* 1867; Salt Lake City, sheet 139, 1898 (New York: Sanborn Map Co., 1898); Polk, *Polk's Salt Lake City Directory,* 1898.

95. "Hodgson Rites to Be Held Sunday," *Salt Lake Telegram,* February 20, 1932.

96. British Mission Emigration Register, Book 1040, 187. He gave his age as twenty; "Names of Passengers," *Deseret News,* October 17, 1855.

97. British Mission Emigration Register, Book 1040, 113; LDS Church, Journal History, September 7, 1885, 1.

98. LDS Church, FamilySearch, https://familysearch.org/ark:/61903/2:1:M4SD-P53 and https://familysearch.org/ark:/61903/2:1:9H-PY-L6B; Osmyn Merrit Deuel, "Diary," LDS Church History Library, MS 9985, fd. 1, 24–44, 47–49.

99. LDS Church, FamilySearch, https://familysearch.org/ark:/61903/2:1:M-7RC-PZ1; U.S. Federal Census, Utah Territory, 1860; Salt Lake County Recorder, title abstracts; Owens, *Salt Lake City Directory,* 1867; "Death of George Anderson," *Inter-Mountain Republican,* April 11, 1906; U.S. Federal Census, Utah Territory, 1870.

100. "George Anderson," n.d., Pioneer Memorial Museum, History Department; Salt Lake County Probate Court, Civil and Criminal case files, box 12, folder 83, and box 23, folder 138, Utah State Archives and Records Service, Series 373; "Local and Other Matters," *Deseret News,* November 12, 1873.

101. U.S. Federal Census, Utah Territory, 1880; Culmer, *Utah Directory and Gazetteer for 1879–80.*

102. George Edward Anderson Photograph Collection, photo #47, Brigham Young University, Harold B. Lee Library, Tom Perry Special Collections.

103. Nelson B. Wadsworth, *Set in Stone, Fixed in Glass: The Great Mormon Temple and Its Photographers* (Salt Lake City: Signature Books, 1992), 221; George Edward Anderson, "George Edward Anderson diaries," Nov. 12, 1895, Harold B. Lee Library, Brigham Young University; Death Certificate, Utah State Archives and Records Service, Series 81448.

104. Graham, *The Utah Directory for 1883–84,* 1883; U.S. Federal Census, Utah, 1900; "Equalizers at Work," *Salt Lake Herald,* July 1, 1896; Death Certificate, Utah State Archives and Records Service, Series 81448, November 1, 1926.

105. Salt Lake County Recorder, title abstracts.

106. "William Everill Not Expected to Live," *Salt Lake Herald,* January 25, 1895;

"Local and Other Matters," *Deseret News*, April 27, 1895; Polk, *Polk's Salt Lake City Directory*, 1898; Salt Lake County Recorder, title abstracts; Death Certificate, Utah State Archives and Records Service, Series 81448.

107. Sloan, *Utah Gazatteer and Directory*, 1884.

108. Salt Lake City Assessor, Tax Assessment rolls, 1869, 1871, Utah State Archives and Records Service, Series 4922; Thomas Carter, personal observation, 2013.

109. Salt Lake County Assessor, Tax Assessment rolls, 1865, Utah State Archives and Records Service, Series 18188; Owens, *Salt Lake City Directory*, 1867.

110. Jenson, *Latter-day Saint Biographical Encyclopedia*, 1920, 2:532, in the entry for Betsy Tempest Glover; LDS Church, FamilySearch, https://familysearch. org/ark:/61903/2:2:SRDK-V67.

111. U.S. Federal Census, Nebraska Territory, 1860; "Names of Emigrants," *The Mountaineer*, August 18, 1860.

112. Owens, *Salt Lake City Directory*, 1867; Sloan, *Salt Lake City Directory and Business Guide*, 1869; Salt Lake County Probate Court, Civil and Criminal case files, Reel 18, Box 13, Case 113, 1869, Utah State Archives and Records Service, Series 373; Salt Lake County Recorder, title abstracts.

113. LDS Church, FamilySearch, https://familysearch.org/ark:/61903/2:1:M7JJ-XVT and https://familysearch.org/ark:/61903/2:1:9MBB-GR3; Salt Lake County Recorder, title abstracts; "Obsequies," *Deseret News*, October 6, 1875; "Before Judge Bartsch," *Salt Lake Herald*, June 28, 1892; U.S. Federal Census, Utah, 1910; Death Certificate, Utah State Archives and Records Service, Series 81448.

114. British Mission Emigration Record, Book 1047, 109; LDS Church, Mormon Pioneer Overland Travel database, https://history.lds.org/overlandtravels/ pioneerDetail?lang=eng&pioneerId=22961.

115. Edward E. Steele, "Millard Bell and Harriet Husbands," freepages.genealogy. rootsweb.ancestry.com/~steeles/Bell-Husbands.html; Owens, *Salt Lake City Directory*, 1867; Utah Division of State History, Cemeteries and Burials database; Salt Lake County Recorder, title abstracts.

116. FindAGrave database, forums.findagrave.com/cgi-bin/fg.cgi?page=gr&GSv cid=231646&GRid=96340043&; Sloan, *Gazeteer of Utah and Salt Lake City Directory*, 1874; U.S. Federal Census, 1880, as Harriet Bell; Salt Lake County Recorder, title abstracts.

117. Salt Lake City Recorder, Death and Burial Register, Utah State Archives and Records Service, Series 21866; Salt Lake County Recorder, title abstracts.

118. "Against the Admission of Utah as a State," The Miscellaneous Documents: The U.S. House of Representatives, Second Session of the Forty-Second Congress, 1871–1872, 65; Utah Division of State History, Cemeteries and Burials database.

Twenty-First Ward

1. Brigham Young University, Mormon Migration Index, http://

mormonmigration.lib.byu.edu/Search/showDetails/db:MM_MII/ t:passenger/id:45583/keywords:Robert+pringle; LDS Church, FamilySearch, https://familysearch.org/ark:/61903/2:1:M4DF-8PS.

2. Edward L. Sloan, *Gazeteer of Utah and Salt Lake City Directory* (Salt Lake City: Salt Lake Herald Publ. Co., 1874); Henry L. A. Culmer, *Utah Directory and Gazetteer for 1879–80* (Salt Lake City: H. L. A. Culmer & Co., 1879); "Legal Notices," *Salt Lake Tribune*, December 9, 1875; "A Machinest [*sic*]," *Utah Journal*, October 15, 1880; "Random References," *Ogden Standard*, October 26, 1883; "Local News," *Deseret News*, April 16, 1884.

3. "In Probate Court," *Salt Lake Tribune*, November 23, 1893; "Complaints from Taxpayers," *Salt Lake Tribune*, July 28, 1894; U.S. Federal Census, Utah, 1900, 1910, 1920.

4. Salt Lake County Recorder, title abstracts; "Lived Nearly a Century," *Salt Lake Tribune*, March 20, 1897.

5. Andrew Jenson, *Latter-day Saint Biographical Encyclopedia*, (Salt Lake City: Andrew Jenson History Co., 1920), 3:73; U.S. Directory Publishing Co. of California, *Salt Lake City Directory for the Year Commencing August 1, 1885* (San Francisco: U.S. Directory Publishing Co. of California, 1885); Salt Lake City Recorder, Death and Burial Register, Utah State Archives and Records Service, Series 21866. James's birthdate is usually given as July 1863, although his mother died in June; LDS Church, FamilySearch, https://familysearch.org/ark:/61903/2:1:M464-L6F gives the most likely date, July 11, 1862.

6. Salt Lake County Recorder, title abstracts; "Local and Other Matters," *Deseret News*, March 27, 1897.

7. U.S. Directory Publishing Co., *Salt Lake City Directory*, 1885; U.S. Federal Census, Utah, 1900, 1910; "J. O. Ellerbeck, Sportsman, to Be Buried Thursday," *Salt Lake Telegram*, March 8, 1927; Robert L. Sloan, *Utah Gazetteer and Directory for Logan, Ogden, Provo, and Salt Lake Cities, for 1884* (Salt Lake City: Herald Printing Co., 1884); Death Certificate, Utah State Archives and Records Service, Series 81448, also for James Leon and Clarence Brown Ellerbeck.

Conclusion

1. Thomas Carter, *Building Zion: The Material World of Mormon Settlement* (Minneapolis: University of Minnesota Press, 2015), 17; Elizabeth Fovargue Smith, "Elizabeth F. Smith Journal, 1884–1891," LDS Church History Library, Salt Lake City.

Bibliography

Archives and Library Collections

Brigham Young University, Harold B. Lee Library, L. Tom Perry Special Collections, Provo, Utah.

Brigham Young University, Mormon Migration database.

Church of Jesus Christ of Latter-day Saints, Church History Library and Archives, Salt Lake City, including Mormon Pioneer Overland Travel database.

Church of Jesus Christ of Latter-day Saints, Family History Library, Salt Lake City, including British Mission Emigration Registers and FamilySearch database.

University of Utah, J. Willard Marriott Library Special Collections, Salt Lake City.

Utah Division of State History, Utah State Historical Society Collections, Salt Lake City.

Utah Division of State History, Cemeteries and Burials database.

Utah State Archives and Records Service, Salt Lake City.

Directories and Printed Data Sources

Culmer, Henry L. A. *Utah Directory and Gazetteer for 1879–80.* Salt Lake City: H. L. A. Culmer & Co., 1879.

Graham, J. C. *The Utah Directory for 1883–84.* Salt Lake City: J. C. Graham & Co., 1883.

Kelly & Co. *Salt Lake City Directory for 1889, and Business Directory and Guide to Public Streets and Avenues.* Salt Lake City: Kelly & Co., 1889.

Owens, George. *Salt Lake City Directory, Including a Business Directory of Provo, Springville, and Ogden, Utah Territory.* Salt Lake City: George Owens, 1867.

Polk, R. L., & Co. *Polk's Salt Lake City Directory.* Salt Lake City: R. L. Polk & Co., 1890, 1893, 1896, 1898, 1899, 1900, 1903, 1911, 1917, 1935.

Polk, R. L., & Co. *Utah State Gazetteer and Business Directory.* Salt Lake City: R. L. Polk & Co., 1900.

Sanborn Fire Insurance Maps, Salt Lake City, Utah. New York: Sanborn Map Co., 1884 through 1969.

Sloan, Edward L. *Salt Lake Directory and Business Guide, for 1869.* Salt Lake City: E. L. Sloan & Co., 1869.

Bibliography

Sloan, Edward L. *Gazeteer of Utah and Salt Lake City Directory.* Salt Lake City: Salt Lake Herald Publ. Co., 1874.

Sloan, Robert L. *Utah Gazetteer and Directory for Logan, Ogden, Provo, and Salt Lake Cities, for 1884.* Salt Lake City: Herald Printing Co., 1884.

Stenhouse, T. B. H., & Co. *Utah Gazetteer 1892–93.* Salt Lake City: Stenhouse & Co., 1892.

U.S. Directory Publishing Co. of California. *Salt Lake City Directory for the Year Commencing August 1, 1885.* San Francisco: U.S. Directory Publishing Co. of California, 1885.

Books, Manuscripts, and Articles

Allen, James B., and Glen M. Leonard. *Story of the Latter-day Saints.* 2nd ed. Salt Lake City: Deseret Book Company, 1992.

Ancestry.com. Pennsylvania and New Jersey, Church and Town Records, 1708–1985.

Arrington, Leonard J. *Great Basin Kingdom: Economic History of the Latter-day Saints, 1830–1900.* Cambridge: Harvard University Press, 1958.

Bagley, Will, ed. *The Pioneer Camp of the Saints: The 1846 and 1847 Mormon Trail Journals of Thomas Bullock.* Spokane: Arthur H. Clark, 2001.

Barker, Vincy R. Stone. "Samuel Dean Biographical Sketch." In *Genealogical Charts and Biographical Sketches of Members of the L.D.S. Church, Ogden Stake.* Ogden, UT: LDS Church Relief Society, 1915–1920.

Beesley, Sterling E. *Kind Words, The Beginnings of Mormon Melody: A Historical Biography and Anthology of the Life and Works of Ebenezer Beesley, Utah Pioneer Musician, Containing an Account from the Emigration of 1859 and the Evolution of Latter-day Saint Psalmody.* Salt Lake City: Ebenezer Beesley Genealogical Research Foundation, 1980.

Bennett, Richard E. *We'll Find the Place: The Mormon Exodus, 1846–1848.* Norman: University of Oklahoma Press, 1997.

Biddle, Edward C., and John Biddle. *MacElroy's Philadelphia Directory.* Philadelphia: Edward C. and John Biddle, 1856.

Bowen, A. W. & Co. *Progressive Men of the State of Wyoming.* Chicago: A. W. Bowen & Co., 1901.

Brown, Lorenzo. "Journal of Lorenzo Brown 1823–1890." Moccasin, AZ: Lorenzo John Brown Family Organization, 1974.

Bryant, Laurie J. The Laurie J. Bryant Papers. Utah State Historical Society, 2011.

Buice, David. "'All Alone and None to Cheer Me': The Southern States Mission Diaries of J. Golden Kimball." *Dialogue: A Journal of Mormon Thought* 24, no. 1 (1991): 35–53.

Burgess, Samuel, ed. *Reorganized Church of Jesus Christ of Latter Day Saints, Journal of History.* 18 volumes. Independence, MO: Herald Publishing House, 1925.

Burr, David H. "Map of Salt Lake City." Utah State Historical Society, c. 1856.

Burrows, Russell. "The Mormon Sampson: Porter Rockwell." *Weber: The Contemporary West* 21, no. 3 (2004): 72–94.

Burton, Richard F. *City of the Saints and Across the Rocky Mountains to California.* New York: Harper and Brothers, 1862.

Carlstrom, Jeffrey, and Cynthia Furse. *The History of Emigration Canyon.* Logan: Utah State University Press, 2003.

Carr, Stephen L., and Robert W. Edwards. *Utah Ghost Rails.* Salt Lake City: Western Epics, 1989.

Carter, Kate B. *Heart Throbs of the West.* Vol. 5. Salt Lake City: Daughters of Utah Pioneers, 1944.

———. *Heart Throbs of the West.* Vol. 9. Salt Lake City: Daughters of Utah Pioneers, 1948.

———. *Heart Throbs of the West.* Vol. 10. Salt Lake City: Daughters of Utah Pioneers, 1949.

———. *Treasures of Pioneer History.* Vol. 4. Salt Lake City: Daughters of Utah Pioneers, 1954.

———. *Treasures of Pioneer History.* Vol. 6. Salt Lake City: Daughters of Utah Pioneers, 1957.

Carter, Thomas. *Building Zion: The Material World of Mormon Settlement.* Minneapolis: University of Minnesota Press, 2015.

———. "Folk Design in Utah Architecture, 1849–1890." In Thomas Carter, ed., *Images of an American Land: Vernacular Architecture in the Western United States,* 41–60. Albuquerque: University of New Mexico Press, 1997.

Carter, Thomas, and Peter Goss. *Utah's Historic Architecture, 1847–1940.* Salt Lake City: Utah State Historical Society, 1988.

Church of Jesus Christ of Latter-day Saints. Journal of Discourses. Volume 1 and 2. 1854. Volume 9. 1861.

Clayton, William. *William Clayton's Journal: A Daily Record of the Journey of the Original Company of "Mormon" Pioneers from Nauvoo, Illinois, to the Valley of the Great Salt Lake.* Dallas: S. K. Taylor, c. 1973.

Daughters of Utah Pioneers. *Pioneer Women of Faith and Fortitude.* 4 volumes. Salt Lake City: International Society Daughters of Utah Pioneers, 1998.

Doan, John Hampton. *Hampton History: An Account of the Pennsylvania Hamptons in America, in the Line of John Hampton, Jr. of Wrightstown.* Milton, KY: Solomon E. Hampton, 1911.

Esshom, Frank. *Pioneers and Prominent Men of Utah, 1847–1868.* Salt Lake City: Utah Pioneer Book Publishing Co., 1913.

Glover, Eli S. *Bird's-Eye View of Salt Lake City from the North Looking South-east, Utah.* Cincinnati: Strobridge & Co., 1875. Map.

Hamilton, C. Mark. *Nineteenth Century Mormon Architecture and City Planning.* New York: Oxford University Press, 1995.

Hawley, James H. *History of Idaho, the Gem of the Mountains.* 3 volumes. Chicago: S. J. Clarke, 1920.

Hicks, Michael. *Mormonism and Music: A History.* Champaign: University of Illinois Press, 2003.

Hill, Theresa Snow. *The Life and Times of George Washington Hill: A Historical Novel by Theresa Snow Hill.* St. George, UT: CFP Books, c. 1996.

Hulmston, John K. "Mormon Immigration in the 1860s: The Church Trains." *Utah Historical Quarterly* 58, no. 1 (1990): 32–48.

Jensen, Richard L., and Maurine C. Ward. "Names of Persons and Sureties Indebted to the Perpetual Emigrating Fund Company, 1850–1877." *Mormon Historical Studies* (Fall 2000): 141–241.

Jenson, Andrew. *Latter-day Saint Biographical Encyclopedia.* Salt Lake City: Deseret News Press, 1901.

———. *Latter-day Saint Biographical Encyclopedia.* 4 volumes. Salt Lake City: Andrew Jenson History Co., 1920.

———. *Encyclopedic History of the Church of Jesus Christ of Latter-day Saints.* Salt Lake City: Deseret News Publishing Co., 1941.

Jones, Darrell E., and W. Randall Dixon. "'It Was Very Warm and Smelt Very Bad': Warm Springs and the First Bath House in Salt Lake City." *Utah Historical Quarterly* 76, no. 4 (2008): 212–26.

Kane, Elizabeth Wood. *Twelve Mormon Homes.* Salt Lake City: University of Utah Tanner Trust Fund, 1974.

Kesler, Donette S. *Reminiscenses.* Salt Lake City: Elbert C. Kirkham Co., 1952.

Kimball, James N. "J. Golden Kimball: Private Life of a Public Figure." *Journal of Mormon History* 24, no. 2 (1998): 55–84.

King, Hannah T. *The Journals of Hanna Tapfield King.* S.I.: F. T. Watkins, nd. LDS Family History Library, Salt Lake City.

Kipling, Rudyard. "The Galley Slave." In Kipling, *Departmental Ditties and Other Verses.* 4th ed. London: Thacker, Spink & Co., 1890.

Kirkham, Francis, ed. *Tales of a Triumphant People: A History of Salt Lake County, Utah 1847–1900.* Salt Lake City: Daughters of Utah Pioneers, 1995.

Koch, Augustus. *Bird's Eye View of Salt Lake City, Utah Territory.* Chicago: Chicago Lithographing Co., 1870. Map.

LDS Church Journal History, 1830–1972, card index, printed copy, microfilm. LDS Church History Library, Salt Lake City.

Ludlow, Daniel H., ed. *Encyclopedia of Mormonism.* 4 vols. New York: Macmillan, 1992.

Lund, Anton H. *Scandinavian Jubilee Album: Issued in Commemoration of the Fiftieth Anniversary of the Introduction of the Gospel to the Three Scandinavian Countries by Elder Erastus Snow, an Apostle of Jesus Christ; and Fellow Laborers.* Salt Lake City: Deseret News, 1900.

McCormick, John. *The Gathering Place.* Salt Lake City: Signature Books, 2000.

Mitchell, S. Augustus. *A New Map of Texas, Oregon, and California with the Regions Adjoining.* Philadelphia: S. A. Mitchell, 1846.

Nilsson, Judith. *Stirling, Its Story and People: 1899–1980.* Stirling, Alberta: Sunset Society, 1981.

Shaw, Lloyd. *The City of Salt Lake! Her Relations as a Centre of Trade: Manufacturing Establishments and Business Houses: Historical, Descriptive and Statistical.* Salt Lake City: Sylvanus, Stone & Shaw, 1890.

Sinclair, Upton. *The Profits of Religion: An Essay in Economic Interpretation.* Vol. 6, *Mazdaznan.* Pasadena, CA: self-published, 1917.

Smart, Donna T., ed. *Mormon Midwife: The 1846–1888 Diaries of Patty Bartlett Sessions.* Logan: Utah State University Press, 1997.

Smith, Elizabeth Fovargue. "Elizabeth F. Smith Journal, 1884–1891." Microfilm, LDS Church History Library, Salt Lake City.

Smith, Joseph, and Heman C. Smith. *History of the Reorganized Church of Jesus Christ of Latter Day Saints.* 4 volumes. Independence, MO: Herald Publishing House, 1888 and 1903.

Tipping, Malvern. "Identifying Clay Construction Buildings in a Norfolk Market Town." Sydney, Australia: Federacion Internationale des Geometres Congress, Proceedings, 2010.

Tanner, Joseph M. *A Biographical Sketch of James Jensen.* Salt Lake City: Deseret News, 1911.

Tullidge, Edward W. *History of Salt Lake City.* Salt Lake City: Star Printing Co., 1886.

VanCott, John W. *Utah Place Names.* Salt Lake City: University of Utah Press, 1990.

Van Orden, Bruce A. *Prisoner for Conscience' Sake.* Salt Lake City: Deseret Book, 1992.

Van Waggoner, Richard. "Sarah M. Pratt: The Shaping of an Apostate." *Dialogue: A Journal of Mormon Thought* 19, no. 2 (1986): 69–99.

Wadsworth, Nelson B. *Set in Stone, Fixed in Glass: The Great Mormon Temple and Its Photographers.* Salt Lake City: Signature Books, 1992.

Walker, Ronald W. "'Going to Meeting' in Salt Lake City's Thirteenth Ward, 1849–1881: A Microanalysis." In *New Views of Mormon History: A Collection of Essays in Honor of Leonard J. Arrington,* edited by Davis Bitton and Maureen Ursenbach Beecher, 138–61. Salt Lake City: University of Utah Press, 1987.

Warrum, Noble, ed. *Utah since Statehood: Historical and Biographical.* 4 volumes. Chicago: S. J. Clarke, 1919.

Watt, Ronald G., comp. *Perpetual Emigrating Fund Ledger Index.* 2 volumes. Salt Lake City: LDS Church Historical Department, 1992.

White, Jean B. *Church, State and Politics: The Diaries of John Henry Smith.* Salt Lake City: Signature Books, 1990.

Whitney, Orson F. *History of Utah in Four Volumes.* Salt Lake: George Q. Cannon & Sons, 1904.

Youngberg, Florence C., ed. *Conquerors of the West: Stalwart Mormon Pioneers.* Salt Lake City: Sons of Utah Pioneers, 1999.

Index

Page numbers in *italics* indicate figures or photographs.

Subject Index